Woodturning

A GUIDE TO ADVANCED TECHNIQUES

Hugh O'Neill

The Crowood Press

First published in 1994 by
The Crowood Press Ltd
Ramsbury, Marlborough
Wiltshire SN8 2HR

British Library Cataloguing-in-Publication Data

A catalogue record for this book is available from the British Library.

ISBN 1 85223 836 4

Picture Credits
All photographs by the author except for those on pages 103 and 120 which are
reproduced by courtesy of Craft Supplies.
Line-drawings by Bob Constant

Throughout this book, 'he', 'him' and 'his' have been used as neutral pronouns
and as such refer to both males and females.

Typeset by Hope Services (Abingdon) Ltd.
Printed and bound in Great Britain by BPC Hazell Books Ltd.
A member of The British Printing Company Ltd.

Contents

Acknowledgements

First, my biggest vote of thanks must go to the Association of Woodturners of Great Britain. Throughout the book I have mentioned tricks of the trade of a number of masters. Each of these I have met through the Association – many demonstrating at AWGB international seminars. They have talked freely, offered the hand of friendship, shared their expertise, stimulated me and others to try new approaches, and inspired me to constantly try to develop. Many have invited me back to their workshops; and thank you all for that. There is no doubt that the Association must take a lot of the credit for the enormous development of woodturning that there has been in the UK in recent years.

I would also like to thank the editors of all the woodworking publications – they too have given me a lot of support, and their interest has been encouraging. It has been their requests for reviews of developments and test reports on new equipment that has prompted me to try out many things that I might not otherwise have thought about. Sometimes this has opened up valuable new avenues.

And all along there has been the support and encouragement of my own family. They even ask me to make things for them, and that must be the ultimate accolade. They have brought in income when times were not so good; manned the stall at craft fairs; humped boxes and dragged trees; delivered commissions; proofed articles; and brought regular meals out when I disappeared for days into the workshop. Thank you Eve, Kirsty, Kevin, Siobhan and Fiona.

Introduction

Just what is advanced woodturning?

Friends and professional turners were not much help when asked. Their answers to the question were along the lines of: 'Well, it is what you do after you have been turning for a few years.' Some identified specific types of turning, such as thin-walled hollow vessels; others said, 'It is making art pieces'; and a few suggested special techniques. Many said, and these gave the clearest direction, 'once you have built up a range of basic techniques, then it is applying these with ever-increasing skill, in more and more difficult situations.' One thing that did also emerge quite strongly was that the advanced turners got involved in a lot more peripheral activities, from the making of furniture to the felling and logging of their own trees. In answer to the question of what should go into a book on advanced turning the message was quite clear – more information on these peripheral activities.

From established experts there was an additional answer to the research questions – often expressed with some force: 'Focus upon design'. So this is the line that I have taken.

Advanced turning is using the same techniques of cutting wood that all turners use, but each is done better and with greater skill. Hence someone who has already acquired the basics really needs practice, a few wrinkles, and the incentive to push the boundaries for themselves. In order to advance even further, some, already quite skilled, need to understand what it is they are doing – the theory behind the basic techniques. Advanced turning also takes you into the realms of using special tools and even of making your own equipment.

It is, then, concerned with using a range of techniques on much bigger work or on tiny miniatures; and in difficult situations, on tricky design features and with some very testing timbers. It is done with greater skill and accuracy, to a consistently high finish, and often much more quickly.

One thing that does differentiate the more advanced from the less, is the design work. Once the turner is wholly in control of the processes, the better craftsmen give much more thought to shape and balance. One person questioned said: 'The competent turner is a craftsman, the advanced turner is an artist!'

Increasingly the better turners are experimenting with mixed materials and media. Sometimes it is with inlays of fine silver; with others, bits of iron, nails, ceramics and leather. Many turners are also working with colour and surface decoration. Carving is taking on an increased importance.

One thing is certain, very few advanced turners stick to one avenue of turning. There are some who only ever make bowls, and some of the best who focus entirely upon bowls, platters, and boxes. Many do, however, mix between centres work and face plate turning. There are others who only ever make lace bobbins – but what lace bobbins!

Many advanced turners do something of everything. They still make their art bowls, and they make ornaments and utilitarian pieces with between centres elements. They also make furniture.

So the full spectrum of advanced turning is very wide even before you enter into the special techniques of segmented work, ornamental turning and the like.

What the research has shown quite clearly is that advanced turners do not just go to the local craft suppliers and buy precut blanks. Many spend as much (or more) time finding, preparing and conditioning their timber as they do with it actually on the lathe. This is not just for reasons of economy, but because it is the only way of totally taking control of what you are making. As we will see, most bowl blanks bought precut mitigate against good design and proportion.

So it began to emerge that a book on advanced woodturning ought to be more about what the turner does before he gets the piece of wood on the lathe, and then on special things he does in the turning process, rather than on how he holds and presents a particular tool. This book therefore focuses more upon design, and on finish and decoration.

Before the turner has even reached the advanced stage, he will probably have made one or two changes of lathe. It is likely that he is still not satisfied with what he has now got; so, although there is not much to add to the basics of workshop layout covered in *Woodturning – A Manual of Techniques*, there are issues about the choice of the next lathe (or lathes) and its positioning in the workshop, that are important.

And, some words of warning! Turning does have its dangers and health hazards, and advanced turning even more so. When we start turning we approach things with caution. The size and nature of the work we do is not particularly demanding when we start out and is therefore basically safer. We have a few minor accidents, and learn to take even more care.

Then, as we become proficient, we try more testing things, and push boundaries. We also become blasé and take risks. Never underestimate the hazards. Already I know that my turning life is limited – it is going to be ten years or so shorter than I had hoped it would be. Why? Because of taking risks that failed. The fingers and knuckles of my left hand have been banged and twisted a few times too often, and there is now permanent pain in some knuckles from developing osteo-arthritis. There are only a few years of tool-holding ability left to me.

Some dusts are extremely hazardous. Blocks of wood becoming detached from a lathe turning at high speed can be lethal. The vase shown on page 148 has left a permanent lesion on my left arm.

There are times when breathing apparatus is essential (and not just a cloth face mask); metal toe-cap boots are required; hard hats and goggles are a must; gloves are needed; chain-saw protective overalls should be worn; the moment you think it is about time that you put on some item of protective gear, it is probably five minutes too late. Take precautions before you start, not when the dangers become apparent.

There is increasing concern over RSI (repetitive strain injury) and two pieces of equipment that I use worry me greatly in this respect.

There is not a chapter on health and safety, but wherever there is a particular hazard, I have included a note on it. Equally there are some places where you might expect a caution but there is nothing. This is because some turners fear things where there really is no need – I know some who even now will not use a skew chisel!

The overall message must be: whatever turning you do, have fun, but *please take care*.

1 As the Workshop Grows

GETTING THE LATHE RIGHT

By now you will probably be on your third lathe. Very, very few turners get the choice of lathe absolutely right the first time, and of those that do, many change direction after three or four years. It is likely that you will now have two or more lathes to cope with the many different types of turning that you are doing.

As the lathe or lathes are the corner-stone of the turner's workshop we must look at this aspect first. I know that the lathe has to fit into the workshop and that this will impose constraints that absolutely condition choice of machines; but it is interesting how many turners start with the lathe, then modify their workshop arrangements around the machine!

I currently have three lathes: a Multico 1000 I bought as a special introductory offer, a Wadkin for large work, and a variable-speed Poole Wood PW28/40. In the last couple of years, however, I have become more drawn towards furniture making and restoration – here the emphasis is upon spindle or between centres turning. Quite often too there may be small filials or feet to turn, and it seems 'unnatural' to turn tiny items on large to massive lathes such as the PW28/40 or the Wadkin. Increasingly I would like to do more fine work, even turn some of my scraps into fancy lace bobbins. There is no doubt that before long I will assemble a small lathe that will give speeds of up to 12,000rpm.

So you see that unless, even as an advanced turner, you intend to concentrate almost exclusively upon one type of turning, you will have more than one lathe. There will be more differences between each of yours than there are between the three I currently

The first workshop: a garden shed with a pile of decaying logs.

have. The ability to move lathes around a bit is worthwhile if, like me, you may have a requirement for one transportable lathe for demonstration purposes. I still fancy a Graduate bowl turner or short bed sited in a large clear space in the middle of the workshop. There is no reason why the dead side of one long bed lathe should not lie close to a wall – provided there is still room to swing a chisel across the lathe bed. However, this arrangement is just not suitable if you wish to turn large items off the outboard end; or do large hollow-form work over the bed itself.

It is essential to choose a main lathe for which there is a full range of accessories. Today, fortunately, there are fitment suppliers who offer most items for most lathes. We are no longer tied to the lathe makers' own bits and pieces. Hence every conceivable type of chuck is widely available for almost every lathe you can think of; index rings and carving devices, long-work steadies, pin chucks, plain and shaped tool rests can all be obtained; and what is not available off the shelf can usually be made. Axminster Power Tools have, within days, provided collars, face plates and adaptors for every weird device that I have ever worked on.

Life is a set of compromises! Even with half a dozen different lathes you will always find some jobs for which you do not have the ideal machine. No one can tell you what you should have. Other people have their own preferences and they may have the ideal machine for them. But they do not make what you make, and even if they did, they would be operating in a different environment and, possibly, using different techniques. So I can only talk about my preferences – and biases.

Size and Stability

Whatever the type of turning, you need to be 'on top of it' in terms of lathe capacity. With the possible exception of turning miniatures, always aim for a size of lathe one above that you think you will need.

Stability is essential for all turning. Lathes with solid, cast iron beds are infinitely better than any other form. They are, however, expensive and require solid foundations (not the wooden floor of a garden shed!).

Almost all the good headstocks, tailstocks and tool carriages that I have ever seen have been cast steel or cast iron. There are a few acceptable machines with heavy-gauge welded steel plate – but they are few! Cast iron certainly helps to dampen out vibration and flexing.

Today the twin-tube bed bars can be quite robust. There are, however, two drawbacks. First, it is more difficult to get a really rigid cramping between the tool carriage and the bed – often there is some movement under load and the corner of a moved tool rest makes a terrible mess of the square section on

a turned table leg! The second problem relates to turning large items, and this is that lathes with tube bed rails rarely come with an integral iron frame. Most are designed to bolt to some table or construction. Such arrangements can be extremely convenient and even essential if the lathe is moved regularly, but they are never solid enough when dealing with out-of-balance blanks.

Morse tapers on both headstock and tailstock are essential, as are hollow spindles for long-hole boring and taper ejection.

Motors

Modern motors are much lighter than they were on early machines, and the ratio of horsepower to weight is continually rising; this is no indication of the motor being inadequate. If a motor burns out on you then either you had a faulty motor or a questionable technique.

To an engineer, some modern motors do run hotter than is desirable. My PW28/40's motor quickly rises to a hot-to-the-touch condition but it then seems to reach a steady equilibrium. (The 1.5hp motor that I had supplied is a quarter of the size – and probably a tenth of the weight – of the identical power motor on the Wadkin.) The comments about being on top of the job do however apply, and for safety I always go for the largest capacity motor available.

Tailstock and Tool Rest

Two important tests concern the clamps of the tailstock and the tool rest. Clamp up a piece of moderately hard timber between the centres. Now wind the tailstock quill in as hard as you can. The tailstock block should not move on the bed rails. Next, mount a long tool rest and clamp this up tight. When you lean hard against the outermost tip of the carriage or tool rest, there must be no movement. This may seem an unnatural test as you never really lean on the tool rest – or do you? A little vibration, a little pressure, and the

Point to point alignment is a critical test of the accuracy of a lathe.

The Wadkin free-standing tool rest. This cannot be lifted by one man and provides great stability. Here it is being used for roughing a large bowl with a heavy-duty Marples gouge.

tool rest can move on to a near-finished work piece, which is highly annoying.

Later, when we look at special tools and techniques (Chapter 7), we will talk about shaped, 'bowl' tool rests. Probably the best buy that I have made in recent years has been the second-hand Wadkin floor-standing tool rest. This massive, cast-iron, three-footed column is wonderful. Originally intended for outboard-end turning, I am finding it very useful for working on the outside walls of large pieces turned over the step bed.

The Poole Wood comes with an interesting and very sturdy cantilevered tool rest for working off the front face. In fact, this device has now become redundant, as I prefer the flexibility achieved through using the free-standing rest.

Speed

I have found the infinitely variable speed control on the PW28/40 to be the greatest of boons. The external speed-change lever with a foot clutch as fitted to the Wadkin is a reasonable second best. Having to stop the lathe, open a lid, hand-shift a drive belt between pulleys, close, reclamp and restart is a pain and you often put off changing speeds when it is really appropriate to do so.

The infinite variability of speeds is also particularly good when working large pieces at slow revs. On any step pulley arrangement the difference between the slowest and the next speed is often more than double. The Wadkin goes from 200 to 500 revs and this is too wide a gap.

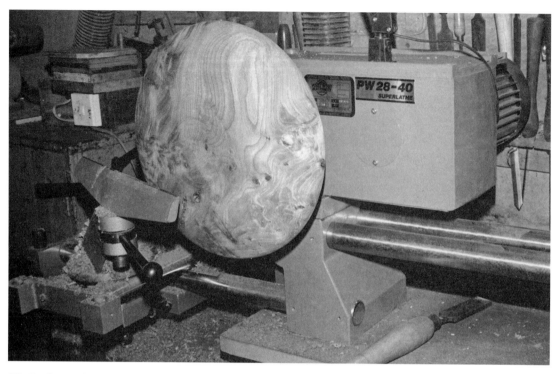

The Poole Wood outboard turning rest is a robust cantilever arrangement that is easily controlled.

However, infinitely variable speed drives are more prone to trouble. There were problems with the early Poole Wood (although mine has been trouble-free) and one continental-designed lathe was eventually withdrawn because it suffered from constant drive problems.

The speed range of the lathe is going to be very dependent upon the type of turning you do. Large bowls – particularly in natural top burrs – necessitate speeds at least down to 200rpm, and there are times when working out to the rim when 50rpm would be more appropriate. Spindles tend to whip or flex at high speed; however, turning detail is so much easier. Hence my frequent emphasis upon long-work steadies. Certainly for smaller spindles 5,000rpm is not unreasonable and for lace bobbins double or even treble this speed can be considered.

Remember it is not the speed of rotation that matters but the speed of wood past the cutting edge of the tool. There is an optimum range of between 20ft/sec (6m/sec) and 30ft/sec (9m/sec), and the closer you can keep to 25ft/sec (7.5m/sec) the better. The rim of a 20in (50cm) bowl spinning at 286rpm gives this surface speed. A lace bobbin would need to be rotated at 23,219rpm to give the same cutting speed.

The two formulae involved in calculating ideal lathe speeds are set out on page 11.

Other Attachments

To me it is absolutely essential that if I lock up the lathe (as when using a Stewart tool – *see* Chapters 7 and 9), then the drive should slip without stalling or burning out the motor (or damaging the drive system, or me).

1. $$\frac{\text{diam. of blank (in)} \times 3.142\ (\pi)}{12} \times \frac{\text{speed of lathe (RPM)}}{60} = \text{surface speed (ft/sec)}$$

or $$\frac{\text{diam. of blank (cm)} \times 3.142}{100} \times \frac{\text{speed of lathe (RPM)}}{60} = \text{surface speed (m/sec)}$$

2. $$\frac{\text{ideal surface speed (25ft/sec)}}{\left(\dfrac{\text{diam. of blank} \times 3.142}{12}\right)} \times 60 = \text{ideal lathe rotational speed (RPM)}$$

or $$\frac{\text{ideal surface speed (7.5m/sec)}}{\left(\dfrac{\text{diam. of blank} \times 3.142}{100}\right)} \times 60 = \text{ideal lathe rotational speed (RPM)}$$

The last essential item that is often built in to the better quality lathes is an indexing head. However, there are now index rings and pins that can be used on a range of chucks, and some of these are better than the standard arrangement supplied with some lathes. Many leave a lot to be desired and the arrangement fitted to the Poole Wood 28/40 is barely adequate.

POWER TOOLS

Although the lathe is the linchpin of the turner's work, it will not be his only piece of machinery. In fact most advanced turners find that they have at least as much capital tied up in other substantial machines, some as much as four times the amount of the value of their lathes.

Of course, it again depends upon the type of turning that you do as to precisely what ancillary equipment you have. Almost every turner requires a band saw and usually a large one – even a 12in (30cm) depth of cut and a 20in (50cm) gape does not meet all my requirements. I still do not have a table saw and planer, but with the increasing amount of furniture passing through my workshop, these are likely to be the next items of purchase. Incidentally, if you do need any heavy woodworking machines look to auction sales: if the item you want is not hobbyist equipment it is often virtually given away.

Just to give some idea of what can be involved, my bench and portable equipment includes:

Chain-saws, petrol, 2
Power planer
Router
Power drills, 3
Belt sander, hand
Portable 9in (23cm) saw

Orbital sander
Fordham carver
Pillar drill
Chain-saws, electric, 2
Angle grinders, 2
Die grinder
Power file
Belt sander, table
Jig saw
Power chisel
Scroll saw

Depending on what you make you could justify any or all of these. In my case this wide range has become necessary because of the varied nature of the projects that I have to illustrate for magazines.

DUST COLLECTORS

In my previous book I mentioned one professional who advised that even before you bought a lathe you should buy a dust collector. How right he was! Two years ago I ran into a chest problem in China. During treatment they found 'scar tissue' on the lungs. It was not there before I started turning. There may be no connection, but nobody has yet convinced me that the spores from spalted woods are safe to humans.

The problems with dust collection are many. First, dust collectors only take out a fraction of what is created. If sited in the workshop itself, they actually pass the finest and most dangerous dust back into the atmosphere. Even with a dust collector going all day long, the breathing pad on a respirator helmet dust mask will still pick up a tablespoonful of fine dust. Then there is the problem that the face masks get spotted and marked, and for a clear view of the finish we frequently raise the mask. Worst of all, when you finish the working and sanding you are no longer creating dust so you take off the mask, just at the moment when the concentration of dust in the air is at its highest! Don't forget to wear the respirator when you

A fan-driven Racal Airstream dust helmet – an essential item for the dusty environment generated when sanding.

are sweeping up the workshop either!

Many of the so-called dust collectors really only pick up large particles. Few have sufficient suction to really draw in all the dust from around a working zone. I am now convinced that a unit ducted directly to the working zone of a lathe, belt sander or band saw should have a minimum capacity of 1,500cu. M/HR, and this probably means a 2hp motor. If, as is highly likely, the collector is piped to a number of suction points, those not in use must be blanked off so that only one is open for business at any one time.

A face mask is also essential. The little metal face masks into which is clipped a rectangular pad do not appear to be good enough. All too often there are gaps allowing direct ingress of dust. The moulded fibre masks seem to be much better. Some of the rubber masks into which filter pads are fitted are better still.

I now believe that a dust collector and a face mask are not really enough, and so I am considering installing a high-volume, swept-air system to scour the workshop continually, discharging outside to the atmosphere. The dust collector motor and bag have long since been banished to an external housing; it is ducted in through the wall and around the workshop with black plastic soil piping.

The worry is not only about dust in the lungs and bronchial passages. My skin is reasonably robust. Working with quarry dusts, engine oil, diesel and paraffin oils over the years has never caused any trouble (these substances give dermatitis to some people). Dust from pernambuco and padauk have given a mild irritation; but recently I worked some iroko. The parts of my face outside the mask, the neck under the collar band, and the backs of my hands and wrists all came out in a nasty rash for over twenty-four hours.

Of course the more skilful the use of tools the less sanding will be needed, and sanding is the greatest creator of dusts; but with some rotten and spalted timbers some sanding is always required. On top of this, some surface-texturing methods create a lot of dust and particles. Band saws create a surprising amount of dust; add to this the power finishing of furniture elements, and problems are inevitable.

KEEPING CLEAN AND TIDY

Dust and shavings are a problem in another way in the workshop.

I always admire the friends whose workshops are immaculate by the time they lock up at night. Some achieve this by sweeping up at midday and then clearing up totally each evening. It was walking into the workshop of Bert Marsh that really gave me a buzz – and the plans for my new workshop. Bert has a work-bench which he clears up each day. His main machines – lathe and band saw

– are out in free space. Everything else is in cupboards and the doors are kept closed.

Most of my tools are clipped to boards on the open walls, and the finishes and so on are on open shelves. Each has a little cone of dust and chippings on top. This must be changed.

In future all walls will have shallowish cupboards and *everything* will be kept in them. Some will have shelves for boxes, finishes and bit and pieces. Tools will still be clipped against the wall, but within the tool sections there will be sliding panels in the middle of the units with swinging doors in front. Hence a 10in (25cm) deep cupboard will have large tools over the entire back wall with two layers of large sliding panels in front of these, which will slightly more than double the capacity – these will have the medium-sized turning tools on. The backs of the swinging doors will carry the small carving chisels and the like. The outsides will be painted white gloss to give maximum light reflection and no foothold for adhering dust. I am even considering housing the pillar drill and belt sander in a dust cabinet coupled to the dust collector venting.

The only thing that will then remain will be the discipline of keeping the work-bench top clear – my wife tells me that really is a pipe dream!

The cleaner you keep the atmosphere the more cold air you are likely to be drawing in. Working in a cold workshop is quite hazardous. You are more inclined to slip, and cold hands cut or abrade much more readily than do warm ones. A source of heating becomes necessary when working in the winter, and the natural answer is a small wood-burning stove.

One thing that has happened in my shop over the years is the breeding that has been going on. I can find no other explanation for the continuous growth in the number of power sockets and lights. I suppose it is just possible that dust and old age are dimming my sight! There are now separate (and separately controlled) light clusters for each working area and at least two double-outlet power points behind each machine. This became necessary because of the short flexes fitted by many power-tool manufacturers today. It has, however, proved to be a useful safety factor in that shorter flexes are far less likely to get caught up around things and the cable damage rate has dropped significantly. The whole workshop is driven off a 60-amp switched fuse and spur from the main junction box of the house. It is all single phase (which meant fitting a phase converter to the three-phase Wadkin).

I use fluorescent tubes for zonal lighting but find the use of reflector spots on to working surfaces helps considerably. I have also found that a small light placed to shine obliquely across the face of a piece of work is marvellous for picking up any fine blemishes or remaining sanding marks.

Space and Location

Almost every turner that I know is an absolute squirrel. We seem to hoard everything – particularly every tiny off-cut of exotic wood. How often have I said to myself 'Umm, that will make a nice lamp pull (or whatever)'. They never do get made into that lamp pull, until one day you cannot even get in through the workshop door. Some advanced turners are more disciplined, but even the best know that you cannot keep your timber supplies in the workshop. You will need quite a large outside area for log storage, a large drying area under cover, another shed for prepared blanks (and the infernal saved off-cuts). My current stocks are

inadequate (quite seriously); yet I have two large piles in the garden, a full garage, and stacks in the sheds of two friends out in the country. Even tidy Bert Marsh has a timber store and large quantities of logs around his garden.

When I was planning a new large workshop for myself, I was faced with the option of occupying units on a local industrial estate. This idea did not appeal. However well you have done during the day you often want to run on to finish off a job. Then some evenings you have a couple of hours to spare. If the workshop is within walking distance this is no problem. Once it becomes a drive away, however short, the tendency is to operate on a nine-to-five basis. I work much harder and longer when I am working from/at home. Most of the professionals that I know hold a similar view, and almost all have their workshops at home. Turning is now more of a cottage industry than it has ever been since before the industrial revolution.

It is only those who operate production shops with a number of employees who tend towards industrial premises. Others work near home. Maybe this is not so silly, as my own costings have shown. To build one new 800sq. ft workshop was going to cost about £15,000 with fittings, but excluding all equipment and machines. One of the timber stores I rent is in a sound building in an old farmyard. It is spacious, lit, clean and dry, and costs only £60 per month. At that price it would take me over twenty years to recover the outlay on building my own workshop – even if I could get planning permission.

2 Timber for Turning

BUYING THE TIMBER

The advanced turner has much stricter purchasing specifications for timber than the novice.

When we start turning we take any piece of wood we can get, or that takes our eye at the craft timber suppliers. We then look at it and decide what to make out of it and what shape will get the biggest item out of the block, and will best suit the figure. We have then to learn to live with the problems that follow – movement, checking, hidden faults and so on – and, at best, indifferent design.

The advanced turner, professional or amateur, is much more likely to start with an end result in mind and then seek out wood suitable for the job. Often they will be working to a specific commission, and certainly to a preconceived design. This takes time and costs money.

Sometimes we quickly find what we want, but I lost one very valuable commission when it took nineteen months to find a suitably sized and shaped jarrah burr. In the end I found what I wanted, as I often do, at John Boddy's in Borough Bridge.

While we are searching there is usually something else going on. When it becomes generally known that you are a turner, friends, relatives, and people you have never even met, phone you up and offer you the 'huge tree' that has just come down in their garden. When you get there you find it little more than a sapling. Sometimes the tree is not 'down', and the offer is conditional upon you felling the tree first. This time it turns out to be a 500-year-old, massive oak standing between the house, a greenhouse and a kindergarten school!

More and more I am finding that most offers of free timber are a waste of time. Even when the piece has promise, you have to bring it back and store it. Then you forget it, or more immediate work piles up. A few years later you decide you just have to do something with the log pile you have accumulated, and you then find that you have a heap of split logs, decayed sap wood, rotten and spalting, and most of it is only fit for the fire. I have wasted days and days of valuable turning time on bringing in free timber.

The only way is to process the timber as soon as you get it: plank it, cut it to blanks, wax it, put it to dry, kiln it or something. If you cannot do this *immediately*, just decline the offer graciously.

So you start with a job in mind. You now have to find timber that will do that job, not have too much waste, and not give any trouble. To most turners trouble comes in the way of unexpected movement. Properly dried timber and careful control over storage and moisture content is therefore essential. The first requisite is a moisture meter (*see* details in Chapter 3)

Obviously if you are making furniture you cannot tolerate *any* post-construction movement. Joints are very precisely made to a tight fit, and there can be no allowance for shrinkage. Timber for furniture has to be living-room dry before you start to work on it.

Not only is moisture content important, but so too is trueness of grain. You cannot tolerate slanting grain (diagonally cut timber) for the turned legs of a chair. Usually there is a need to match figure, texture and colour of two or three pieces. I recently turned a tall standard for a candelabra. The column was in three jointed pieces. Only when I tried to get the finish did I notice that the top section had a much more open pore structure than the lower two. Whatever I did with it I could not get it to provide a reasonable match with the two lower sections.

Often checks and splits are a positive feature of some of the largest bowls that I turn. At least I thought they were! However the market for work with 'cracks' in is quite limited. So, much as I like it, it is not really commercial. Therefore I have to look at the block and estimate what movement or splitting I can expect. Sometimes you do want a particular pattern of movement and you can fairly accurately predict what you will get. You can actually use the fact that timber moves more tangentially than it does lengthways and that outer growth rings contract more than inner. What starts out as a round hollow vessel can, with careful planning, end up a distinct oval. I have even been asked if one piece was 'off-centre turned?'

For many years elm burr was the salvation of poor turners. The figure was so dramatic that almost anything they turned out of it looked absolutely marvellous. As supplies of elm started to dry up we moved to the jarrahs and beautiful gums of Australia. Exotic figuring still compensated for indifferent design.

Price does get in the way with the Australian burrs. They are very dense and therefore heavy, and at £3 (and upwards) per kilo for the gum burrs, a larger bowl may cost £60 or so for the timber. Mark this up by the necessary four times and you start to get bowls which have to be sold for over £250. There are not many customers for such pieces unless you achieve something quite wonderful with the design, *and* can then place it in the right sales outlet.

Most professional turners have now gone away from the ultra-exotic figures and work with more demanding timbers where design has to be good to lift what would otherwise be an indifferent item to something of worth. The moment you enter this world, design and finish are all important; and checks and distortion are definitely out. So timber selection becomes the very top concern.

The third face of advanced turning is in the 'art end'. Again you often start with a design idea in mind and one which probably exhibits some particular features. A frequent example is a hollow-form vessel turned from a burr where the natural contours of the burr leave holes through the wall of the finished piece; what some call 'naturally-pierced turning'. So now the block does not just have to be of a nature that would provide appropriate colour and figure, but also has to have a form and features that are specifically required.

We all get commissions needing a piece of wood that we do not have in stock. The most important thing is to get the right wood in the right condition, and quickly.

For exotics and imported timbers, the craft timber suppliers are often the best bet for a one-off job, and we quickly find out who stocks what on a regular basis. It is worthwhile developing contact with three or four who are actual importers and evaluating the prices of each.

For furniture timbers and for regularly used quantity items, some of the crafts suppliers are too expensive – their price structure is really geared to the hobbyist turner. Even when they have offered you a 10 per cent professional discount their materials are still not viable to the professional. Ten per cent off a lot of money is still a lot of money!

Some importing yards will accept relatively small orders, particularly for one-off pieces of exotics; but there are some yards that only deal in truckloads, and many who only sell whole planks. With home-grown materials it is usually best to go to merchants who operate their own saw mill. Unfortunately, there are ever-fewer of these around the country.

There are specialist yards and timber merchants with whom a relationship may be built. They will look out for wood for you and contact you whenever they come across a particularly attractive plank or log. A great deal of the Fiddleback olive ash never gets into retail outlets: it has usually been found and offered to known users.

Disregard the labels describing the condition of wood. 'Part-seasoned' means anything. It can mean a few days in the air after felling and planking, right through to a few months. 'Air dried' usually means that it has had a period of time since it was planked, but it does not tell you how long, or under what conditions of storage. The air in some parts of the country appears to be at least three times as damp as does the air in other parts! Even 'kiln dried' has to be treated with caution. In one yard this means a few days standard cycle through the kiln tunnel; from other sources it covers whatever period of time is necessary to take the wood to a stated moisture content.

Some timbers do not dry readily – oak is a very slow drier. Some yards kiln dry everything for the same (sometimes very short) time. They then store the dried timber in the air and it picks up atmospheric moisture. Moisture content becomes increasingly important to the advanced turner as he makes multi-element turnings that have to fit together. We need to consider the whole question of drying in more detail, and this is the substance of the next chapter.

SEASONING THE WOOD

Wood will keep its condition better and for longer if, after felling, the trunk is left whole with the bark on until it can be planked. It should be put on bearers so that it is raised clear of the ground. A beech trunk left lying on the ground will probably spalt right through in about two years.

Removing a whole trunk from the site where it was felled is clearly a job for heavy, specialist equipment. Car trailers are not man enough!

The best solution, if you do find yourself in this situation, is to plank the log on the spot and here there are two possibilities. There are many depots around the country with portable band saws, the most common being the Wood-Mizer, the Forrester, and the Trekkasaw. These may be hired with an operator. Much of the cost is associated with delivery and setting up, so for three or four hours sawing you could be faced with a day or more hire and transportation charges – typically £250 plus VAT per day. If there are several logs to be planked it all becomes worthwhile. The tree officer from the local

A Wood-Mizer portable band saw squaring off a log.

An emergency job. A smaller saw unit slabbing a gale felled tree by the roadside.

council will probably be in touch with companies who provide hire services.

Typically the planking units consist of a saw table with ramps and/or a grapple for positioning and rotating the log. There is a rail along which the power-driven band saw carriage moves, and, of course, the saw head. Some units are self-powered while others are driven off the power take-off of the towing vehicle (a tractor or a four-wheel drive vehicle). The units most frequently available for hire have a capacity for logs up to 20ft (6m) in length and 30in (76cm) in diameter. They are capable of handling 175–500cu. ft (50–140cu. m) of timber a day with a two-man team and will reduce this down to board and slab with minimum kerf wastage. It is said that the production costs of these units is between 25p and 50p per cubic foot processed to plank. They cost between £10,000 and £20,000 to buy, depending upon the model, should you feel like splashing out!

The second alternative is again often available locally, but you may even consider buying one if there is a small group of turners working as a co-operative. This is a specially adapted chain-saw with a small supporting cage/carriage. A range of units is offered by Stihl, going from an 18in (45cm) bar single-header for a one-man operation, costing about £1,100, to massive double-handed, double-headed (a drive motor at each end of the bar) units with 48in (12cm) wide guide bars at nearer £2,000. At one time there were also the Cole Chainmills but I cannot now locate them.

The double-handed mills are quite effective, although somewhat 'mauling' to operate. The first run or two is on rails that consist of two wooden battens nailed to the trunk. Thereafter the cage and rollers work off the cut top of the log.

The log lies on the ground as felled. If of oversize girth it is squared off, rolling it through 90 degrees between cuts. Obviously this again requires the use of cant-hooks, tractor or mechanical lifting devices. Once the log is reduced to manageable size it is blocked up for later cuts.

Remarkably clean true cuts can be

The control possible with some portable saw units will produce near veneer-quality slices.

achieved, but with a chain-saw there is obviously a broader kerf and therefore much more wastage than there is with a band-saw mill.

Branch Wood

We still have the limbs that were lopped off the felled trunk to deal with – plus any 'trees', branches and blocks that well-meaning friends have given to us. These may also be used for turning – often as natural top and special pieces.

It is important that they be kept green. The moment they start drying they will split and quickly become useless. They are not easy to deal with and we just have to face up to the fact that if not used within a couple of years they will almost all go to waste.

There does appear to be an exception to the foregoing – namely, yew tree branches. These appear to dry well, move little and rarely check. I have also had some success in keeping smaller-diameter walnut branches.

The first essential with all branch (and other) woods is to keep the bark intact. The second is to seal the ends. The third is to limit the circulation of air, and the fourth is to keep them out of the sun and wind.

Three methods of end sealing have proved useful. First there is Mobil C End Sealer – an emulsified wax that is painted on. It requires five or six coats initially and then a top-up couple of coats every six months. The second is to have a heated bath of paraffin wax into which the ends are dipped. This coating lasts two or three years without a top-up. The third is a thick coating of tar or bitumen. Some people then build sealed logs into a pile and wrap them in an 'air-tight' cocoon of thick, black polythene sheet. The cocoon method does, however, trap the moisture within a damp envelope, and with some timbers this will quickly cause spalting and decay. Sealing the end grain on planked timber in stacks put 'in stick' (*see* Chapter 3) will also help to reduce end splitting, particularly on the larger thicknesses. ·

Turning Green Wood

Some advanced turners specialize in turning green wood. Their problem is keeping the wood green enough. They actually like to turn it when it is so green that sap flies out of it as it is being worked.

So what are the respective advantages of green and dry turning?

Fundamentally they are different and have substantially different objectives. Green turning can only be done where dimensional stability is unimportant. Hence it is particularly appropriate in art work where some movement may even add to the impact of the piece. It is, or at least was, very widely practised in country furniture making – as in the chairs produced in quantities by the bodgers of the Chilterns.

Micro-thin turning is really only possible with green timbers. When Dell Stubbs produces his show-piece goblets he not only starts with freshly felled green timber, but he also keeps sponging down the piece with cold water as he is working.

There are advantages to green turning. Wood slices more easily when green, and therefore turns much more cleanly straight off the tool. Cutting across end grain is particularly easy and there is less tendency to tear. It also avoids all the space requirements of long-term timber storage. On top of this, supplies of green timber are usually only a trip to the timber yard away from being on the lathe.

Of course green wood is difficult to sand, so you may have to resort to using wet or dry and frequent swabbings with water. The finished object then has to be dried before any type of finish can be applied.

One useful effect is that on drying you can get a very interesting 'textured' surface. Burr woods can be particularly attractive in that the blind branches are likely to contract more than the main timber matrix, giving flared lines across the surface – the effect can be of antique leather.

For dimensional stability there is no alternative to turning very dry.

CUTTING UP THE WOOD

Planks

Planks of timber to be used for turning are, at some stage, going to have to be sawn up. This may be into spindle lengths, or into disc blanks. It is best to delay this process until the timber is required for use. This enables the maximum amount of air drying to have occurred and with it, hopefully, the worst of the movement.

All turners will have a large-capacity band saw, and this, with careful use of a sawing 'gauge' can produce good spindle lengths. The more fortunate will have a table saw for ripping work. Immediately after sawing and unless the timber is to be used right away, it again requires end-sealing. The end grain must be coated. This means the two ends of any planks or spindle lengths, and the complete outside circumference of all discs and bowl blanks. Here melted wax is to be pre-ferred. It takes only a few minutes and costs only a few pence but it saves pounds in wasted, checked blanks. A bucket, or better a fish kettle of wax can be heated gently on an electric ring.

Planks may be inches thick. I would usually have a log planked into 3–8in (7–20cm) thicknesses for turning, 1–3in (2.5–7cm) for furniture, and into 4, 5 and 6in (10, 12, 15cm) thick slab blanks for carving blocks. Later we will be reconsidering the size to cut blanks into for turning, as 3–4in (7–10cm) does not encourage good bowl design.

Cutting Blocks

Not all my logs are going to be cut into planks. Some are going to be cut up into blocks for the turning of larger items and others are going to be cut to provide natural-top items.

Much natural top is worked green, or with a moisture content 'as found'. It is therefore kept in the log right up to the time it is

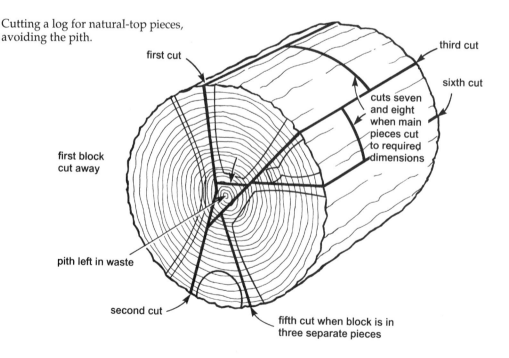

Cutting a log for natural-top pieces, avoiding the pith.

first cut

third cut

sixth cut

cuts seven and eight when main pieces cut to required dimensions

first block cut away

pith left in waste

second cut

fifth cut when block is in three separate pieces

required for turning. The considerations then are:

1 How much movement can we tolerate?
2 Would checks be acceptable/unacceptable?
3 What would be the best cutting pattern to reduce checking?
4 Are we going to rough turn then dry?
5 What is the size and shape of the larger items we wish to produce?
6 What is the best arrangement of sawing the log to give maximum usable pieces?

One basic rule is that we try to avoid including the very centre, the pith, of the log in any of the blanks, as checking always starts at the pith. Try to cut the log so that the pith falls in a waste zone. Similarly, large knots from major branches are prone to checking. However, the knots can make an interesting figure, so sometimes we choose to risk it and take extra care in the later drying.

Occasionally you find trees where several branches have formed around one zone of the trunk. Monkey-puzzle trees often have rings of branches, and the crowns of pollarded or pruned fruit and ornamental trees sometimes offer a similar effect. These can make the most dramatically figured large bowls.

Cutting logs for larger pieces of work does require a little thought. The most important consideration is the grain orientation as this affects both the final figure presented, and pre-determines the nature of movement that can be expected on drying. Remember that there will be much more shrinkage in the sap wood than there will be in the heart. Therefore a section cut with the base at the heart and with a rim of sap wood is likely to develop rim checks. A block cut on the side with one side close to the heart and the other out towards the bark will provide a bowl that will warp out of round.

When dealing with burrs and gauls, or even crotch pieces, it is often difficult to see where the solid timber will be and where there will be piercings. I have a series of ply

A beautiful bowl by Liam O'Neill turned from a log of monkey-puzzle tree where a ring of branches left the main trunk. Mary Robinson, then Eire's Prime Minister, presented a similar Liam bowl to the Queen.

rings of differing diameters ranging from 10–24in (25–60cm). One of an appropriate size is laid on the surface of the log or block, roughly positioned to where the rim might be. It is then moved around until it gives the cleanest fit. The rings each have a number of holes, and the located ring is now tacked to the wooden block to provide a rough sawing guide.

When the block is lifted on to the band saw (or positioned for chain-saw roughing if it is too large), it is blocked up so that the marking ring is horizontal. I find this an enormous help. It is all too easy to mark off the circle and then to band saw at an angle and thus lose the required symmetry. The constant reminder of the horizontal ring keeps me on track, and the moment the block dips out of true it can be corrected.

Mature branches of yew and walnut with distinctive zones of sap wood and heart

A group of small pieces by Bert Marsh. The two items in the foreground are turned from whole rounds of yew branches. Although the heart is in the centre of the wall, the thinness of turning inhibits checking. Each of these pieces is about 2mm thick.

Small items can be turned from whole branch sections, usually yew or laburnum.

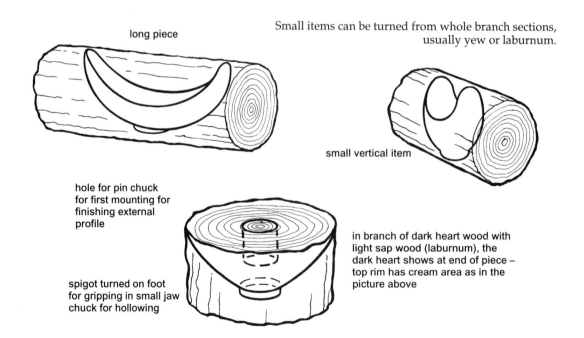

long piece

small vertical item

hole for pin chuck for first mounting for finishing external profile

spigot turned on foot for gripping in small jaw chuck for hollowing

in branch of dark heart wood with light sap wood (laburnum), the dark heart shows at end of piece – top rim has cream area as in the picture above

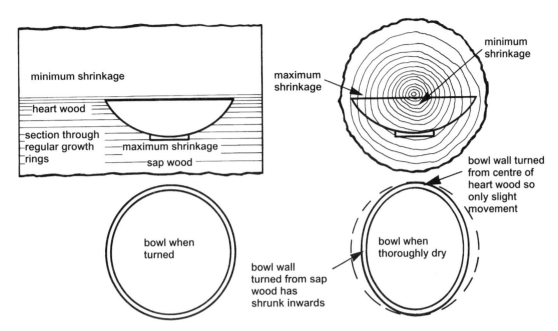

minimum shrinkage

heart wood

section through
regular growth — maximum shrinkage
rings

sap wood

bowl when
turned

bowl wall
turned from sap
wood has
shrunk inwards

maximum
shrinkage

minimum
shrinkage

bowl wall turned
from centre of
heart wood so
only slight
movement

bowl when
thoroughly dry

Drying distortion in a bowl containing heart and sap woods.

wood are often better if both the sap and the full heart are included in the finished pieces, and Bert Marsh makes the most wonderful small items by side grain turning complete 'log' sections of such woods. Here, however, checking from the pith is avoided in three ways. Firstly, the branches are from older, more mature trees with less young and sap woods. Secondly, the branches used are of smaller section; and thirdly the walls are turned very thin, which accommodates movement.

A lot can be done with two-tone woods by arranging the cut to use the light sap wood in a particular way. A platter in rich red padauk is nicely offset by a crescent 'moon' of white sap wood in one part of the rim.

A complete diameter disc of a large log may yield a number of natural-top vessels. Of course we try to avoid the heart, but we also have to recognize that any wider bowls made from such a section are likely to dry with a very uneven base.

One thing that is absolutely critical in sectioning up logs is that the chain-saw used is in prime condition with the chain freshly

sharpened. Any bluntness or uneven sharpening of the chain will cause the blade to wander just when you need it to run perfectly true to get the blocks that you are after. Chain-saws that insist on producing curved cuts have the teeth on the outside of the curve sharper than those on the inside.

We also have to think about the relationship between cut and figure. With some woods the plane of cut is critical. Oak displays good medular rays when planked 'through and through' – the normal horizontal planking done on a log. London plane becomes the lovely lacewood only if 'quartersawn' – that is, where every plank radiates out from the core. Some oak also is at its very best when quarter-sawn. Elm burrs have two distinct facets. One is, in effect, along the burr in a through and through manner. The other is straight into the burr aiming at the core of the tree. With long grain you are slicing through each of the tiny blind branches and producing a scattering of small round knots. Cut into it and you trace the branches as they push their 'root' in towards the trunk. Now you have a series of long tongues.

23

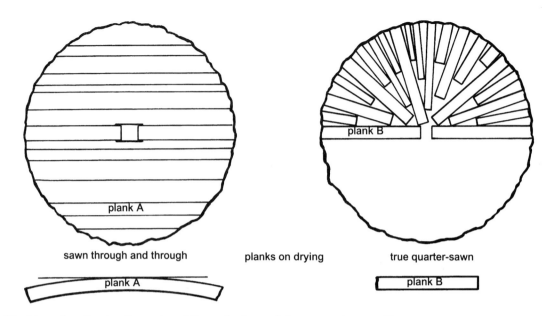

Planking a log. Sawing through and through gives minimum waste on cutting but a lot can subsequently be lost because of warping on drying. Quarter-sawing generates considerable wastage on sawing but the planks are then very stable. This cut gives the best figure on lacewood and medular rays on oak.

Once the blocks have been cut from the log, the first piece should go straight on to the lathe, and if there is likely to be any delay before the other pieces can be worked, put them in plastic bags to control/restrict the drying out process; or wax seal them for longer keeping.

BUT IS IT SAFE?

Long before the average turner has reached the 'advanced' stage, he will have experimented with many of the hundreds of types of wood that are available. It is not proposed therefore to discuss timber varieties at all, with the exception of mentioning one topic. There are scores of books on recognizing, choosing and using different timbers, but the issue that is rarely addressed is the health hazard. The toxicity of different woods for use with foodstuffs and the effect on the lungs and skin of the woodworker does need to be considered; unfortunately there has

been very little research and most of the available information is anecdotal!

Spalted woods should never be used for salad bowls. The fungus may or may not be toxic; but it does reactivate with wet salads. In no time at all a growth will develop along the spalt lines.

I earlier mentioned the skin problem I got when working iroko and it has long been known that the dust of this timber is carcinogenic. The solid wood, however, appears to be quite safe. Some woods are actually used by natives to produce poisons but it appears that only the natives know which! Yew is suspect and I would never make salad bowls from it, or anything that a baby might suck or chew. I do not know that it would do any harm but it is not worth risking.

The best advice is to stick with the woods that have been used for centuries when making food vessels. These include sycamore, chestnut, pine, oak, beech, birch, apple, pear, cherry; also olive, mahogany and teak amongst the imported timbers. Concern over

Grain patterns in burr. The normal burr roundels appear near the rim where the blind branches have been cut through their diameter. As the bowl slopes down into the centre some 'branches' have been cut down their length, giving long flame patterns. In the centre are radial checks from the heart. The main checks have been filled with wood dust and glue to match the colour of the flames.

this issue is now becoming largely academic, since we are, of course, faced with the problem that EC regulations may soon prevent us from selling items made out of wood for use with foodstuffs.

Research has shown that woodworkers are 140 times more likely to develop nasal cancers than are those who do not work in wood-dusty atmospheres, and some woods are known to be very much worse than others. There are some interesting names on the list.

Iroko is one of the worst for causing respiratory problems, with teak a close second. Western red cedars are bad, as are redwood, maple and – most surprising of all – beech.

On the skin allergies list satinwood and mansonia are amongst the worst, but many of the widely used exotics also feature.

Research shows that sanding – including hand sanding – creates seven or eight times as much atmospheric dust as does sawing – circular or band. Significant differences are immediately evident with dust collection but the ideal arrangement is to have a suction pick-up under the workpiece and a forced draught sweeping across the working zone down from the top. In other words there should be a 'forced' air draught away from the head and towards the input of the collection system.

I regard *all* dust as hazardous, and advise maximum protection whatever wood you are working. Who would ever have thought that beech could really be dangerous?

3 Preparing the Timber

Blotting paper is merely tiny wood fibres mechanically bonded together, and it will readily mop up several times its own weight of water; a tree is basically the same, but with a defined pore structure! Depending on the density and the cell structure, a log felled in the spring can have moisture content of around 100 per cent, dropping down to 50 per cent after Christmas.

Open-pored woods such as elm have a moisture content averaging as high as 80 per cent when newly felled. Some trees are even wetter.

Of course, the time of year at which the tree is felled is crucial. In the spring, sap is racing up to the young new leaves and the tree's cells are bursting. In late autumn the life of the tree has virtually sunk back into the roots and the timber is much drier. As a rough guide, the average moisture content of a number of common winter-felled species has been put at:

Tree	Heart wood	Sap wood
Ash	46 per cent moisture	44 per cent moisture
Beech	55	72
Oak	80	70
Walnut	90	75

Note that in winter the heart wood can be more moist than the sap wood.

Once the tree is felled and the source of sap has been cut off, drying starts. The impervious coat formed by the bark and the cambium layer prevents much drying off through the girth so all the moisture has to bleed out down the pores and then out through the ends of the log. This, of course, creates areas of differential drying, contraction, and thus checking.

To prevent, or at least control, the migration of sap through the pores and along the sap canals and out through their severed ends, we seal the ends, with wax until the trunk can be planked or slabbed.

When the side grain is exposed by stripping the bark or planking the log, more drying occurs. The speed at which the timber gives up its moisture is again conditioned by the cellular structure of the timber but is largely determined by the temperature and the humidity in which the timber is stored. The key factors are how quickly the moisture can migrate to the surface, and then how quickly it can evaporate off.

As timber dries, the walls of the cells, previously supported by the sap in the cell, start to collapse. As they do this the timber contracts. Drier zones shrink faster, wetter zones stay the original size, and stress develops between the zones. Eventually something has to give and the plank splits up from the ends.

To control the drying and thus the degradation of the timber, we try to remove the moisture evenly throughout the thickness of the timber at roughly the same rate.

The ideal approach to drying is to raise the temperature overall, but to keep the humidity high: this way the warmth draws the moisture out from the centre, while the high ambient humidity prevents it evaporating too quickly at the surface.

MEASURING MOISTURE

There are two or three moisture meters available in this country, but the most widely used is the Protimeter Minor. This unit has two

A moisture tester inserted into the end grain of a freshly sawn strawberry tree shows the moisture to be off the top of the scale. The log later split to resemble the spokes of a bicycle wheel.

pointed probes that are pushed into the timber and you then get a direct read-out on an LED scale of the percentage moisture content in the wood. As an accessory there is a probe with longer points and a hammer device for driving these deeper into the timber.

It is always advisable to take two or three readings. You get maximum penetration of the measuring probe into the end grain, but remember that this is where the moisture flees from first. Go for the middle of the plank and particularly the face that has been shaded or has lain against an adjacent plank. If it is a critical job, get the plank sawn in half and then test the end grain in the middle of the plank.

What should you be looking for? Again it all depends. What are you making? Where is it likely to end up? What sort of conditions do you expect its environment to provide?

In the UK, the average outdoor winter

humidity level is 22–3 per cent, which in a good summer falls to about 16 per cent. In a house heated by open fires the winter humidity could average 12 per cent; but close to the fire this may be as low as 8 per cent and a timber for use in this area would ideally need to be about 6 per cent; but the fluctuations encountered could well be extreme. Full central heating produces 10 per cent on average throughout the house, for which a timber should be dried down to about 8 per cent moisture for cabinet making; but then with our habit of switching off the heating for the summer months, the summer humidity could well rise up to 17 per cent, for which the wood only needs to be down to about 15 per cent.

It is interesting that the movement in timber may well be greatest at the very moisture levels we are talking about. Dropping the moisture content of oak from 50 per cent down to 20 per cent causes relatively little movement. There is much more movement in the fall from 20 per cent to 10 per cent: as much as ³⁄₁₆in (5mm) in a 1ft (30cm) width across the grain.

It is at this stage that you realize that you are unlikely ever to get it right! So our main interest is not in completely stopping movement, but in preventing fatal levels of movement and either wasted stocks or extremely disgruntled customers.

DRYING TIMBER

Fundamentally, we have six options for drying timber and one for preventing cell collapse without drying.

DIY Drying

The first, the most highly wasteful, is something that we all do at times. We cut the wood up into pieces of approximately the size we want. We try to avoid pieces where the differential contraction will always be high (a mix of heart and sap wood in the

27

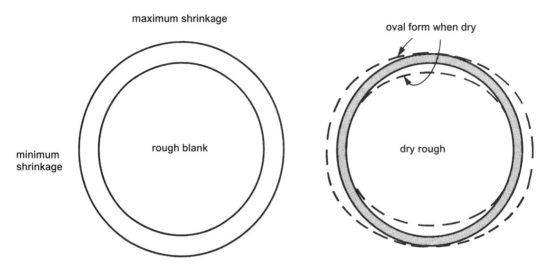

Rough turning to allow for distortion on drying. On the rough blank the wall thickness is 10–15 per cent of the overall diameter; if it is greater than this, wall checking is very likely. On drying, there is 5–8 per cent possible movement to oval form; it is possible to get a bowl with a wall thickness 3–4 per cent of the overall diameter of the original blank.

same block); then we leave it to dry hoping that it will not all split and that we will be able to rescue some usable pieces.

The second method, at the other end of the scale, is to slab up the trunk, keep it as wet as possible and turn it green within a few days. This is fine if you are into green turning where you can tolerate, or even welcome, movement in the finished piece.

Next comes a compromise. While the slabs are green we rough turn them to an approximation of the general shape we require, but leave the walls very thick, and then put the pieces to dry. However, this is not quite as straightforward as might first appear. The slabs have to be cut to minimize the amount of movement – again the mixing of heart and sap is kept to a minimum. We also have to allow for some movement. As a basic rule when working on bowls, we turn the blank such that the wall thickness is left at a minimum of one tenth of the diameter of the finished bowl. Hence a 10in (25cm) diameter bowl would be rough turned to a wall thickness of 1–1½in (2.5–4cm). Any thicker and the likelihood of splitting is increased; any thinner and the possibility is that the form will go so out of round that we will not be able to remount it and turn it into a finished bowl.

We can improve our chances by the selection of timber. Some have a very much higher tendency to distortion on drying than others:

Lower distortion timbers	Higher distortion tendency
Alder	Ash
Lime	Beech
Oak	Birch
Sycamore	Cherry
Walnut	Chestnut (both)
Willow	Elm
	Pear
	Poplar

NB This table relates specifically to distortion and not to straight shrinkage. In later shrinkage tables we will see some of the timbers change sides

There are also some differences when we start to look at the checking characteristics of different timbers:

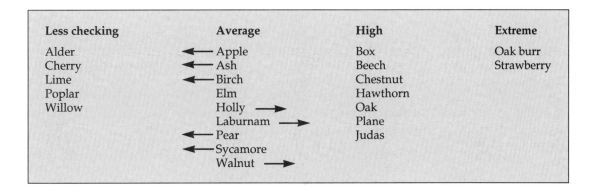

Less checking	Average	High	Extreme
Alder	←— Apple	Box	Oak burr
Cherry	←— Ash	Beech	Strawberry
Lime	←— Birch	Chestnut	
Poplar	Elm	Hawthorn	
Willow	Holly —→	Oak	
	Laburnam —→	Plane	
	←— Pear	Judas	
	←— Sycamore		
	Walnut —→		

The amount of movement can be controlled. If the rough turned blanks are put into proper drying conditions then they may dry out more slowly, and with less likelihood of checking.

Remember the optimum conditions are higher temperatures and high humidity. One way of achieving this, if throughput quantities are only small, is to put the rough turned pieces into plastic bags and to seal the necks. Put these in a warm place (the airing cupboard is ideal if your partner is away!). After three days take the bags out and turn them inside out. There will be a lot of condensation inside the bags but this will quickly evaporate away once the bags are reversed. Seal the tops again and put them back in the warm place.

Continue doing this for four or five weeks, or until the condensation ceases to form on the inside of the bag. The wood will now be workably dry and may have moved relatively little. The emphasis is upon the 'relatively', as some woods move considerably however carefully they are dried.

Taking timber as felled and drying it down to 12 per cent moisture (and you would need a kiln to achieve this in the UK) the movement figures could be as shown in the chart.

Both of the two regular commercial methods of drying work on the basic principles already outlined – a controlled temperature and humidity envelope.

Timber	Percentage shrinkage	
	Tangential	Radial
Ash	7.8	4.9
Ash (mountain)	14.2	7.2
Beech	11.9	5.5
Box	10.6	4.8
Cedar (red)	4.9	2.2
Gum	8.6	4.1
Jarrah	7.9	5.3
Mahogany	5.0	3.0
Maple	9.9	4.8
Oak	10.5	5.6
Pine (white)	6.0	2.3
Sycamore	8.4	5.0
Walnut (black)	7.8	5.5

Air Drying

Timber yards do not like to keep wood in the log any longer than necessary – logs split there just as readily as they do in our backyard! So they quickly plank the logs into the most frequently requested sizes.

The planks are then put 'in stick'. This is the practice of reassembling the planked log but spacing the planks evenly and regularly with thin battens of wood in between. A good yardman will adjust the spacing according to four factors: the type of wood, the thickness of the plank, the position of the stack, and the time-frame within which the planks are likely to be sold.

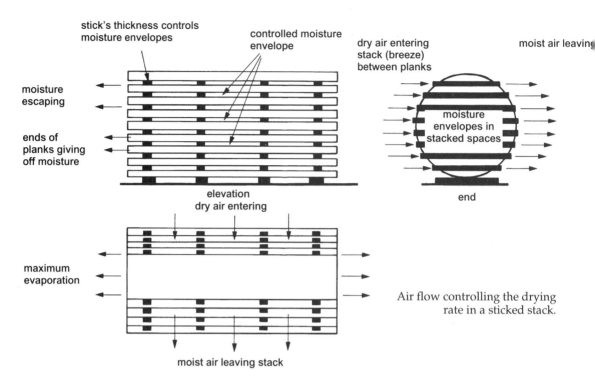

stick's thickness controls
moisture envelopes

controlled moisture
envelope

dry air entering
stack (breeze)
between planks

moist air leaving

moisture
escaping

ends of
planks giving
off moisture

moisture
envelopes in
stacked spaces

elevation
dry air entering

end

maximum
evaporation

Air flow controlling the drying
rate in a sticked stack.

moist air leaving stack

It is not a straight-line equation. Different woods take different lengths of time to give up their moisture. Under equal conditions we could get the following picture for planks 1in (2.5cm) thick taken from best felling moisture condition down to a typical UK 18 per cent summer level.

Timber	Best drying time in days for planks up to 1in (2.5cm)
Alder	20–180
Ash	60–200
Beech	70–200
Elm	50–150
Larch	60–120
Maple	30–120
Oak	100–300
Pine	40–200
Poplar	30–150
Sitka spruce	40–150
Sycamore	30–150
Walnut	30–150
Willow	30–150

However, the above table appears optimistic, and as a rule of thumb a good yardman will allow a year for each inch (2.5cm) of thickness for elm, beech and chestnut; but four years for every inch (2.5cm) of dense oak. Above 4in (10cm) in thickness the overall time has to be doubled, and oak much over 4in (10cm) never really dries. Some commercial yards try to force the pace and do what they can to accelerate the drying time.

Even with sticking, there are various ways in which control of the temperature/humidity envelope is achieved. First, the thinner the spacing battens and the smaller the air gap, the slower will be the drying. As the sap evaporates it forms envelopes of high humidity between each plank, and drying is controlled by adjusting the dispersal of the envelope. With oak and beech, both liable to surface checking if dried too fast, the sticks are kept down to about ½in (1.2cm) thick. Pines would be sticked to about ¾in (2cm) spacing, whereas with some of the denser hardwoods we might use 1in (2.5cm) thick battens.

It is important that the battens are all kept to the same thickness to prevent distortion of the plank, and for similar reasons a spacing of 18in (45cm) between sticks is about right. For thinner planks the spacing would be reduced. Thin planks can sag between widely spaced sticks and take on a prominent warp.

Controlling the humidity envelope is also a function of the position of the stack. A good draught of circulating air rapidly disperses the envelope. A higher temperature increases the evaporation. Hence a stack left in an open, breezy, sunny position, will dry very quickly – and planks from the centre of the trunk will split up the middle.

So stacks are usually placed side by side with only a foot or two gap between each for ease of access. This way you reduce cross-draught. They are always left with the bark on, and the top layer or two therefore act as a cover. Despite this, the yardman will probably cover the stacks during high summer. The cover may be sheets of corrugated iron to keep the sun off or tarpaulins both to keep off sun and retain humidity.

At best the timber in stick will only ever dry down to somewhere near the ambient humidity. Hence a stack held in a humid basin in a forest will always be wetter than would one out on an open hillside. Of course the moisture content will also vary with the seasons. In temperate countries a plank with-drawn in winter could have twice the mois-ture content of one drawn in high summer.

The label 'air dried' on blanks and planks bought from timber merchants really has little meaning. Clearly trade descriptions requirements are such that the timber should have been put into drying conditions in the air, but there are no standards for the length of time, the stacking conditions, time of year, or whatever.

Even if it has been properly dried for the requisite period and it is down to a moisture content equating with the ambient humidity of the time, this does not necessarily meet the needs of the user.

Some timbers move considerably with every per cent change in moisture content, some only little. As we saw from the earlier tables, there is going to be much more move-ment across or around the grain (tangen-tially) than there is along it (radially). And at the end of the day, while most turners (bowl enthusiasts) can tolerate a little movement in the end product, furniture makers cannot! Once they make a joint it must remain stable.

Kiln Drying

So for most of us, unless we are into semi-green turning, we eventually have to resort to artificial methods of drying. The most com-mon method is to kiln dry.

Properly done, kiln drying can take timber down to one or two per cent moisture (you don't actually need to go that low) and it will be at the same level right through the plank.

A lot of commercial kilning is really a com-promise. Yards are interested in throughput. They run the kilns hard and at higher tem-perature and take the timber out before it is dried right into the centre. And there is another problem. The yard may have kiln dried the plank, but what has happened to it after it has been taken out of the kiln? How many damp storage sheds has it been held in? Where did it winter? If you want stable timber then it is essential that you have a moisture meter, and that you use it every time you buy a piece of critical timber.

It is more than likely that you will need a kiln; and most professional and advanced turners now have their own small kiln. They are not expensive, and very quickly save their own costs.

Kilns are designed to control very precisely the rate of evaporation and this is achieved by building up a high level of humidity at a moderately high temperature, and then very gradually increasing the temperature as the timber dries out. They are also designed to be as cost effective as possible; hence the control of the humidity envelope and preventing heat loss are the main design criteria.

A unit of 8ft by 6ft by 4ft (2.4 × 1.8 × 1.2m) is adequate for the needs of the average turner working on his own. However, some set up a kiln on a co-operative basis with two or three others; or do some contract drying or dry timber for resale. If this is the plan, then a larger kiln would be required.

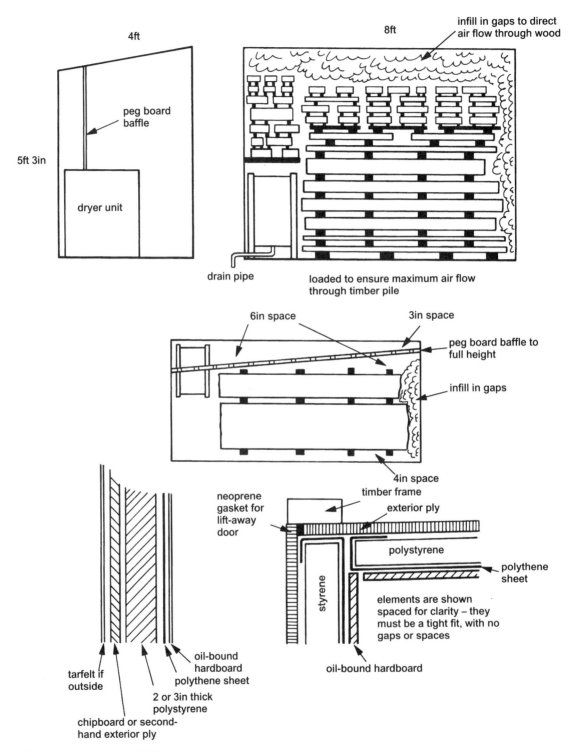

4ft

8ft

infill in gaps to direct air flow through wood

peg board baffle

5ft 3in

dryer unit

drain pipe

loaded to ensure maximum air flow through timber pile

6in space

3in space

peg board baffle to full height

infill in gaps

4in space

timber frame

neoprene gasket for lift-away door

exterior ply

polystyrene

polythene sheet

styrene

elements are shown spaced for clarity – they must be a tight fit, with no gaps or spaces

oil-bound hardboard

tarfelt if outside

oil-bound hardboard
polythene sheet

2 or 3in thick polystyrene

chipboard or second-hand exterior ply

Construction of a small kiln.

There is a very easy, cheap way of acquiring a larger kiln. This is to purchase the box of a scrapped refrigeration van. These are virtually airtight, are well insulated, and can sometimes be obtained for mere scrap value. They are available in sizes from a Luton van up to '30 ton artic', and the place to start looking is in the commercial lorry sales yards in cities. Often the yard can find customers for chassis, but not so many want refrigerated vans. If they do not have anything suitable, they can often provide useful leads. A working body of 24 × 10 × 8ft (7 × 3 × 2.4m) recently sold for £650.

Construction

Let's return to earth and think about building our own kiln of a more modest size. Your box will need to provide a timber-drying area of somewhere between 50 and 150 cubic feet (14–42.5cu m) – for which the requirement is about 8 × 6 × 4ft (2.4 × 1.8 × 1.2m). In this there will then be a small circulation cavity and a space for the small heater/dehumidifier unit.

The construction of the box needs a little care, but no more than very elementary carpentry skills. What we are doing is constructing a high-insulation (styrene-wall), moisture-proof box. The outer skin can be of virtually anything. Chipboard is quite satisfactory if the unit is to be housed inside, but for external siting, sheets of waterproof ply picked up from a building site are ideal. As a further protection some users also clad the construction in tarfelt.

Most kiln builders do not hang doors. They merely arrange for a side wall to be lifted out. This is a good option as it provides maximum access; furthermore, it is easier to fit the removable wall so that it makes a tight and leak-proof fit, than it would be to seal fully swinging doors.

The inner skin needs to be waterproof, but also reasonably non-absorbent. Oilbound hardboard is the most widely favoured, but marine-grade ply is also useful. Between the inner and the outer skins is a sandwich of a sheet of strong polythene and a 2in (5cm) thick slab of polystyrene. For kilns the size of my 8 × 6 × 4ft (2.4 × 1.8 × 1.2m) unit, some builders also provide an inch (2.5cm) air cavity, but I have a second layer of polystyrene (providing an additional 1in/2.5cm thickness). Frame members for the box are softwood fully treated against possible damp with timber preservative. A neoprene gasket may be run round the edge of the removable wall to improve the seal. I have not bothered with this level of perfection.

The internal arrangement is very basic but has two key purposes, and that is to get the best, even circulation, and to pass all the air through the dehumidifier for water extraction.

The dehumidifier units normally used have a built-in circulation fan. Some owners, however, also use a small supplementary fan to improve the overall air flow.

The secret is to spread the flow from the fan equally throughout the main box; evenly around each separate piece of timber, and then on through the dehumidifier. This is achieved using a full-sized baffle or peg board to first spread the flow.

The baffle distributes the flow, but it is the stacking of the timber that contributes most to effective drying. So layers of planks are sticked; and bowl blanks are positioned to give even gaps between each.

Use

Kilns work best when fully loaded. If the timber does not occupy the whole space then movable baffles are placed around the edges to ensure that the flow of air is through the stack and not around it.

There are two main suppliers of dehumidifiers in the UK and both provide full technical detail and support, and will design cabinets to your own specification if you do not wish to do the task yourself. Both regularly advertise, and they are EBAC of Bishop Auckland and John Arrowsmith of Darlington. John was particularly helpful when I designed my kiln (although I ended up buying a second-hand but unused EBAC unit).

The units heat the air, circulate it, and then extract the moisture, which is discharged through a drain-pipe. They are equipped with controllers, which on the smaller kilns are simply thermostats with programmed on/off phasing. The kiln is first run up to temperature and then set to operate at timed intervals, usually shown as a percentage of continuous running time. Each unit is supplied with sets of tables showing temperature setting and run-time cycles for different-sized loads of different woods.

It is normal to increase the temperature over the run as the moisture content falls, and for this reason, as well as general monitoring, the moisture content of the drying timber is checked at regular intervals – in my case once a week.

One useful approach to control-setting during the earlier parts of the drying cycle is to monitor the quantities of water discharged at the drain. My small unit draws off about 12 pints (7 litres) of moisture a day on 100 per cent setting. Once the amount extracted starts to decrease then the temperature control is notched up another 5°C (41°F). The normal working range is between 35–45°C (95–113°F), and at that temperature the overall power consumption is about 1.2kw per hour.

With this I can handle about 60cu ft (17cu m) of thin board (up to about 1in (2.5cm) thick). On 3–4in (7–10cm) thick planks of hardwood the load size is about 170cu ft (48cu m). The main reason for the enormous difference is the volume of space taken up by the quantities of sticking required with thin planks. With thin planks the sticks are about ¾in (2cm) thick rising to 1in (2.5cm) for the 3in (7cm) thick planks. A little word of caution: make sure that you choose non-staining wood for the sticks!

For cabinet work I aim for 8 per cent moisture but most of my timing and temperature calculations are based upon mixed loads of plank (usually about 3in/7cm thick) and bowl blanks, aiming for 10 per cent residual moisture.

Part of the working tables look something like this:
The softwood table shows approximately half the drying time for equivalent thicknesses.

Moisture content change of hardwoods up to 3in (7cm) thick	
Moisture content change (percentage)	Number of days
50 to 10	160
40 to 10	120
30 to 10	80
20 to 10	40

There are, however, differences between different hardwoods as the following extract from an EBAC table shows (all figures are based on the model LD82 drier that I use):

Timber	Thickness in (cm)	Charge cu ft (cu m)	Timer setting percentage	Moisture percentage from to		Days drying
Elm	3 (7.5)	40 (11)	35	25	10	40
Larch	1¼ (3)	50 (14)	90+	20	10	20
Oak (furn)	2½ (6)	100 (28)	79	20	8	41
Pine	2 (5)	40 (11)	90+	50	10	53
Walnut	¾ (2)	45 (12.5)	85	30	10	21

Microwaving Timber

A microwave cooker can be used before or after turning and we can choose either the full power or the 'defrost' option. Obviously the defrost route is much slower and more controlled, but it is not widely practised as it requires repeated heatings, each of some duration.

I believe that some turners have experimented with microwaving blanks and rough-turned items but I have not tried this. Normally it is finished pieces, usually thin-walled, and in really green timber, that are dried in this way.

Being green, finishing has to be done with wet or dry and liberal swabbing with a wet sponge. Do not use the coarser grits; it is best to start somewhere between the 120 and 180 grit and then to work right through to 400. The finished item is then oven ready.

Although the process can be controlled using a moisture meter, it is quite possible to do without. The bowl should be weighed before and after each cooking period; you know that it is dry when it ceases to lose weight on heating.

The cooking time is very short on full power: 1 minute for small bowls up to about 9in (23cm) in diameter; 2 minutes for bowls up to 12in (30cm) in diameter and 3 minutes for sizes up to about 18in (45cm). I do make bigger bowls but that is the largest that I can get into the oven! If I am interested in creating distortion (and will accept any possible checking) then 4- and even 5-minute bursts are tried.

After each cooking the piece is removed from the oven and allowed to cool right down – typically this takes about half an hour. It is then replaced for the second cooking, but this time placed upside down. For each subsequent cooking it is rotated in both the vertical and horizontal planes to ensure even exposure.

If on removal from the first cooking the bowl is hot enough it will be semi-plastic, so you can mould the shape somewhat. With some woods all vestige of a round can be eliminated and it is even possible with very thin pieces to achieve a crinkled or pie crust top rim. (Wear thick chrome-leather gloves.)

Complete drying can take anything between five and ten cycles so it can be an all-day process, and clearly needs to be integrated with other activities.

It is almost certain that there will have been some movement even if you have not tried to mould it deliberately. As a result it is usually impossible to remount the workpiece on the lathe – hence the 400 grit sanding before cooking. So the final finish is a hand job – again with 400 grit paper and 0000 wire wool. The last stage is to apply Danish oil with a pad of fine wire wool, and then hand wax.

REPLACING THE SAP

When identifying that there were a number of drying options available to us, note was also made of a sap replacement alternative. This is based upon the use of PEG, or polyethylene glycol. The principle is simple. Using the process of osmosis, wood steeped in a saturated solution of PEG slowly replaces the sap with the waxy glycol. This fills the cells, which then do not 'dry out', and hence do not collapse and cause shrinkage.

A few years ago a number of turners became interested in this approach, but although some still use it, the interest has declined. Today the biggest use of PEG is in preserving old timber ship relics (the *Mary Rose*, and several Viking ships) – and, of course, the Cheshire Bog Man.

One devotee is Ed Moulthrop, who has twenty-eight large tanks for processing the huge blocks of spalted tulipwood that he uses for his giant vases.

The advantages of PEG are clear. It enables green woods to be used relatively quickly and it saves all the costs of long-term storage or kiln drying. It also provides wood that cuts very much the same as it would if truly green. Certainly it provides full dimensional stability before, during and after the turning process.

The disadvantages are that it is a wet and messy process and the items made from PEG-soaked woods are difficult to finish. First, the sanding process involves the use of wet or dry and water as the wax quickly clogs up dry abrasive papers; and second, the surface will not take wax polishes and does not provide a really satisfactory base for precatalysed lacquers. Epoxy finishes are the most satisfactory and polyurethane varnish works very well. Against that some users say that with the matt waxiness of the PEG you do not need to apply any other finish. I have found that Danish oil is quite good provided the item is given a really heavy application and is allowed to stand for an hour. Whereas dry Danish oil will buff up to a semi-polish on ordinary wood it remains matt on a PEG-treated piece.

Using PEG

Using PEG is relatively easy for a one-off job – you can just make up the solution in a plastic container (small dustbin) and then leave the item to soak.

The moment you start to work in quantities you begin to need large soaking containers (Ed's twenty-eight tank 'farm') and you really need to consider maintaining the solution at optimum temperature. The soaking time is greatly reduced at higher temperatures. This could mean thermostat-controlled immersion heaters, and insulation around the tanks to minimize running costs. The setting up of an installation of this nature, plus the cost of the PEG, now begin to make it an expensive process.

PEG is bought in large solid blocks, and has a melting point of 40°C (104°F). The wax has to be dissolved in water, and this is not easy at the solution strengths you are aiming for unless some heat is applied.

Two strengths of solution are recommended – 30 per cent or 50 per cent –

which are best achieved by melting the wax (at 40°C/104°F) and then mixing with water. It is possible to achieve the desired strength working on weight of PEG and volume of water, but most users rely on a hydrometer, and get the balance right by adjusting the specific gravity. The following mixing proportions are used:

Weight of PEG: lb (kg)	Volume of water: pints (litres)	
	30 per cent solution	50 per cent solution
10 (4.5)	22.4 (13.1)	9.6 (5.6)
20 (9)	44.8 (26.2)	19.2 (11.2)
30 (13.5)	67.2 (39.4)	28.4 (16.6)
40 (18)	89.6 (52.5)	38.4 (22.5)
50 (22.5)	112/ 14 gallons (65.6)	48/ 6 gallons (28.1)

This corresponds to specific gravities of 1.05 for 30 per cent and 1.093 for 50 per cent; both readings are at 15.5°C (60°F).

The soaking time depends upon the solution strength, the nature of the wood, the size of the block, the temperature of the solution, and the greenness of the timber when treatment started. Unfortunately there is little published data, so determining the correct time becomes largely a matter of trial and error.

There is no doubt that the greener the wood the better the process, and it is sap green not water-soaked green that matters. Getting good penetration in a 12in (30cm) diameter by 4in (10cm) thick bowl blank at 15.5°C (60°F) (normal UK summer average) appears to take about 100 days in a 30 per cent solution. This time can be halved if the temperature is maintained at about 60°C (140°F). However, this is very wasteful of time, heat and PEG.

Rough turning makes a lot of sense, as a 12in (30cm) bowl rough turned to 1in (2.5cm) thickness requires only twenty days at 15.5°C (60°F) and a mere three days at 60°C (140°F) in a 50 per cent solution.

The PEG bath does need some maintenance. If it is heated there may be some evaporation of the water, so regular checking of the specific gravity will help to identify when a little more water needs adding. Equally, as the wood takes up the glycol the solution can become weaker, in which case a little more melted PEG needs to be added.

The bath liquid will certainly become stained during soaking, although this does not appear to affect the wood. What is unpleasant is that you can get a mould film on top of the solution; this is better skimmed off and discarded.

Once the sap replacement process is completed the timber needs drying before final turning, and this is where PEG really scores.

Air drying takes time – in fact quite as long as drying a piece of untreated timber of the same dimensions. The plastic bag process works but I find this slightly slower than with untreated wood. Of course the PEG pieces can be put in the kiln (although why you are using PEG if you have a kiln needs explaining to me). The best thing to do is to put the PEG pieces into an ordinary oven and simply cook them – without risk of distortion or checking. An overnight slow baking in a domestic oven set to 62°C (180°F) will get the pieces nicely dry.

4 Good Design

WHAT IS GOOD DESIGN?

To say that beauty is in the eye of the beholder is both a truism and, in the way it is frequently used, a piece of arrant nonsense! It is true that each of us sees things that please our eye and mind, give us aesthetic satisfaction, and are beautiful to *us*. In this sense beauty is an individual thing. But, an object cannot be described as being beautiful just because one person says that it is.

There are standards and shared concepts of beauty. There are shapes that most people who are aesthetically aware accept as 'beautiful', and such shapes very frequently conform to some basic criteria. In three-dimensional objects these will encompass generally accepted rules and principles of good design, colour, balance and form.

There are 'rules' of scale, proportion and balance that elements in nature conform to (or is it 'are driven by'?) and these have given us many of the classical rules of composition and design. In fact, all the most pleasing shapes and all the significant relationships occur widely in nature.

So when teaching design, the better arts institutes place great emphasis upon the classical concepts that have been around a long time, are widely accepted, never denied, and are widely used. Yes! if you like – good design often means *conformity*!

However, we also have to recognize that an important element in creating interesting work is the introduction of elements of non-conformity, and particularly conflict and tension; and that this is sometimes achieved by the very deliberate breaking of rules.

Discussions upon the classical concepts of design tend to focus upon form and proportion, but in fact it is a much wider topic than that. First, there are issues about basic shapes and lines and how people respond to them. Then there are factors about the interplay between adjacent shapes. Third are concerns with the centre of gravity. Fourth, there are some generally accepted and simple-to-apply rules of balance and proportion; and fifthly, and probably underpinning everything else, there are the complex and often mathematically related concepts of classical design.

The novice woodturner has enough to worry about with basic techniques and tool control, and thus cannot properly concentrate upon good design. Many aspects of working to a good design require well-developed technical skills. Undercutting rims, achieving long differentiated curves, working to fine tolerances, getting thin walls, are not skills that can be achieved overnight.

There are seven main design considerations that we have to deal with; four are more philosophical and three more concrete.

Philosophical:
Design objectives
Conventions of the profession
Fit to purpose
Respect of the material

Concrete:
Balance
Form
Decoration

Clearly there will be overlap and interplay between these elements.

DESIGN OBJECTIVES

Any piece of woodturning should be made

38

with at least two clear objectives in mind. First is what function the item is intended to serve. The second is what the craftsman wants out of it.

The possible functions are many, and the intended function of the piece has to be clear in the craftsman's mind as it sets the direction for many later considerations. Amongst the basic functions (for turned items) we could list: to support things; to contain things; to display things; to decorate in its own right; as a functional element in a process; to facilitate an activity; to demonstrate expertise.

There will then be a set of objectives that the turner will have for producing the item. These may support or be in conflict with the primary function. The objectives are usually simple: to win a competition; to generate sales; to provide a gift; to make something for the home; to make something for the workshop; to occupy time; to gain/grow in skills; to develop an idea. The generation of sales has also to be broken down into volume sales objectives or quality sales objectives.

Producing a number of items for a one-person show is a challenge. Here there are a number of objectives operating at the same time. One is the immediate generation of sales, another is the obtaining of commissions, and thirdly there is the exhibiting of a range of skills and styles. There may also be the definite objective of obtaining press coverage, and raising the public's awareness of your work.

Both the primary function and the turner's objectives must directly influence the design, and also the choice of materials.

Often two of the primary purposes operate at the same time; however, one is paramount, the other an added value. For example, a salad bowl's purpose is to contain things – salads. We would also like it to decorate, but it will probably spend much of its life in a storage cupboard. When in use the inside is mostly covered with lettuce, tomatoes, cucumber and oil! In order to make the best decorative item we might give it a flared rim; but that is not ideal for holding (and tossing)

a salad. The decorative element must be kept subservient to the main purpose.

Similarly, it is intended that 'supporting' pieces of turning such as chairs, stools, tables, plinths, candlesticks, lamp standards, and so on, may all be nice pieces of decoration, but all have their own more important primary function. Therefore they need to be of a certain minimum load-bearing capacity, that is, of some thickness; the walls need to be capable of containing weight, and so on.

On the other hand, decorative pieces are just that. They are never intended for use. They may be sculptural, even abstract; or they may have a basically functional shape, such as a bowl. Whatever the form, they are intended as 'art' pieces, and their function is simply to decorate. No answer can or should be given to the question, 'Yes! but what can I use it for?'

Why is it so important to be aware of the primary objective of what we are doing? The answer is that it should substantially affect the design we create and how we approach the making of the item.

The first major effect will be in where we focus our design thinking. According to the function of the item we can get some idea of where it is likely to be used, and where it will be placed. By their very nature some objects are floor-standing, and unless they are tall they are usually going to be viewed from above. Salad and fruit bowls will invariably be looked down upon and/or into. They will rest on the table around which we sit. The outside profile of a salad bowl is much less important than is the rim and the inside profile. Nobody, except the child with his chin on the table edge, looks at the profile of the salad bowl. The rim of a bowl designed to 'display' fruit is the only bit of the wood that is seen for much of the bowl's life. It has to frame the fruit so its design becomes absolutely critical.

A display piece of decoration may be placed down on a coffee table or be raised up on a sideboard or plinth. If it is an open bowl form it is more likely to be placed where it can be looked into; here the internal profile is of paramount importance. On the other hand, a vase or vertical form object is more likely to be placed in a raised position, so here the external profile is the critical element. Platters will always be looked into – being positioned on a table, or placed on a plate rack or hung on a wall. The external or 'under' profile is almost irrelevant.

The primary function will clearly affect the choice of wood used. We would be unwise to make a salad bowl in a piece of checked, open-pored burr. In fact anything designed to be used with foodstuffs has to be non-toxic and hygienic. Many functional and facilitation items have strength or weight requirements.

It also goes further. A vessel we look down into may have curved walls or straight, but in either case it is going to be a simple form with no incised features of interest. It therefore calls out for more decorative woods of good colour and interesting figure.

Vertical form objects, such as vases, plinths and candlesticks, present a profile that can be given many mixed and varied forms. Now the profile itself can be made interesting and the piece does not need the highly figured timbers to create effect. In fact excessive figure can detract from the profile.

Conventions of the Profession

The demonstration of craftsmanship as distinct from design skill places both real and artificial constraints upon many aspects of design. Clearly the piece must show off skills in turning technique, but it should also exhibit the highest design capabilities. Craft expertise is, however, listed as one of our primary functions in that it can force us to conform to the conventions of the craft even when these add little or nothing to the design, and may actually detract from the apparent purpose of the item.

It is only a convention of turning that the wall thickness of a bowl or vase should be the same from top to bottom – that the internal and external profiles should parallel each other. It is only a turners' convention that chuck marks should be removed from the base of objects. Super-thin walls may show off high turning skills, but they are not very durable. There are times when an item is being made for other turners (a club exhibition) where such things matter; but outside such situations should they really be allowed to influence our design – particularly when they get in the way of achieving the artist's intentions? Once in a while there may be a collector who also expects such conventions to be honoured. The vast majority of our customers do not.

If I am making an object that will sometimes be seen in profile and at other times be seen from above, it will very often, quite deliberately – and I believe rightly – have wall profiles that are substantially different on the inside and outside. They will certainly not be of an even thickness from top to bottom. Good craftsmanship requires that both profiles be 'fair' – have smooth even curves. Good design does not require that both follow precisely the same curve.

Fit to the Purpose

Choosing a suitable material must clearly relate to the purpose. Toxicity, hygiene and strength relate to specific purposes for some items. We then have to choose woods that do not stain if they are likely to be used with staining contents, or that do stain if we are looking to achieve a particular colour or effect.

There is then something that turners often overlook – we could call it 'honesty' – and it concerns the ageing characteristics of the wood we use. Is it really fair to produce an object intended for decoration that relies upon the delicate pink of pink ivory, the subtle purples of plum, or the bright scarlet of fresh padauk, knowing that they will change to a regular brown within a relatively short time? Anything with a pink, purple or red pigmentation will turn brown. Some change quickly, in under a year; some more slowly – jarrah browns only over many years in sunlight. I believe that selling a bowl in freshly turned plum with those beautiful purple bands is fundamentally dishonest.

Respect for the Material

The 'honesty' point raised above goes further. Each wood has a nature of its own. Some are close-grained, fine, with a delicate figure or colour, and capable of being worked with great delicacy. It is intrinsically wrong to use such timbers for massive rugged items. Some believe it equally wrong to hide strong figures, massive checks and worm holes in petite pieces.

Furthermore, why put applied decoration, particularly colour or substantial and particularly representational carving, on to a highly figured, significantly coloured burr? This is not to suggest that there is not a place for applied decoration. There is, and it is a growing one; and we will be considering this in detail later (*see* Chapter 10).

Good design requires that we use woods appropriate to the form of decoration that we are intending to apply, and equally that the decoration is appropriate and actually enhances the wood and the design form chosen.

It is only on rare occasions that applied colour adds anything to a strongly figured wood. Texturing and incised decoration, on the other hand, can add a new dimension.

Conflicts

At the philosophical level, design is concerned with the resolution of conflicts. We want an object which looks good, yet perfectly fulfils the purpose for which it is intended. If it is a container it has to contain. We also have to have access to the contents, which means a top opening of a sensible size.

We must also relate purpose to cost. Too many intricacies in the design may cost so much to create that the object has to be priced at a level at which it will not be bought. After

Two large jarrah burr pieces. Both have a maximum diameter of 28in (11cm) and look very dramatic in the rich red of jarrah. The Aussie worms are over an inch in diameter, making the piece in the foreground particularly attractive. It is, however, size and colour, not technical difficulty or design that make these pieces effective.

all, if we are making a fruit bowl, somebody has to buy it and use it as that before we have achieved our design purpose.

PHYSICAL BALANCE

Centre of gravity, real and apparent, is what balance is about.

Second to our concern with purpose, the next consideration in design is the emotions we are trying to trigger – whether we are trying to create comfort or tension, pleasure or shock. Conflict and tension can be created in many ways: by slashing a hard, straight diagonal across a flowing curve; by contrasting non-complementary colours, materials or textures; and by breaking design conventions.

41

A bowl with the pedestal not under the centre of gravity, but close enough to create tension rather than instability.

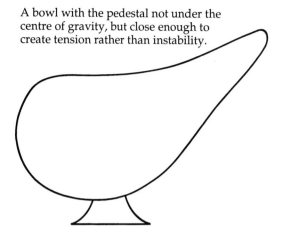

Tension can also be created by joining two masses with a thin element that looks as though it might break at any moment. Tension grabs attention and holds interest – often we are just waiting for the crash, the snapping, or the implosion.

Against this conformity, symmetry and balance can stimulate anything between comfort and sublime satisfaction.

One of the easiest ways of creating tension is to place the apparent centre of gravity such that it looks as though the object will fall over.

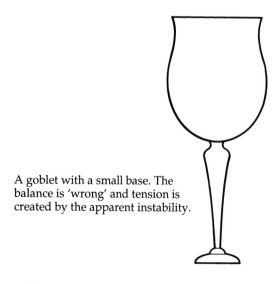

A goblet with a small base. The balance is 'wrong' and tension is created by the apparent instability.

Of course, we always have to be aware of the real centre of gravity. We do not usually wish to produce pieces that do constantly fall over, so they have to be designed with the real centre of gravity firmly over the base, and over a base of sufficient size to provide definite stability.

This leads us to another set of conflicts. Maximum stability requires large bases; yet grace and lightness – elegance and beauty – are achieved with small bases. Make the base very small and the piece has a look of instability and creates a feeling of tension in the beholder.

In turned work, the real and the apparent centres of gravity do not always coincide. It is the apparent centre of gravity that matters in visual impact, while it is the real one that is more important in utility.

There are three basic groupings of vessel design, which are created through the structured interplay of centre of gravity and base shape/size:

The 'growing out of' form.
The 'sitting upon' form.
The 'floating above' form.

The 'growing out of' form represents ultimate stability. The centre of gravity is low down and the base large. In the ultimate design the base diameter is larger than it is anywhere else in the piece. If the wall profile (internal or external) is projected downwards, the two walls never meet but go down into the earth. The object 'grows out' of the table and the earth on which it sits.

The 'sitting upon' form is achieved by getting the projected profiles to meet at a point 'resting on' the surface upon which the object is placed. It is sitting on but is clearly not a wholly integrated part of its support.

This gives a clear impression of stability, yet the object is still only an added ornamentation. Frequently it 'sets off' the support. Hence a fruit bowl can be an important decoration, but it is only a decoration of the table on which it stands.

If we arrange the design so that the projec-

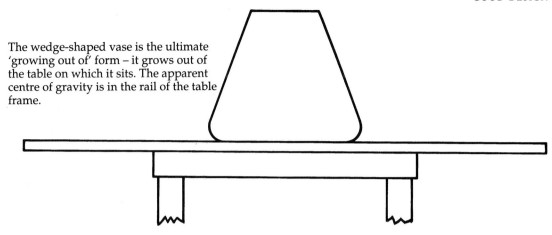

The wedge-shaped vase is the ultimate 'growing out of' form – it grows out of the table on which it sits. The apparent centre of gravity is in the rail of the table frame.

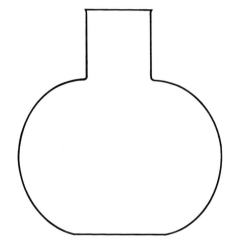

A 'growing out of' form much favoured by Chinese designers. The 'weight' is emphasized by the oval form of the flask.

tions of the wall profile meet above the support, then the object appears to 'float above' the surface. Keeping the base small emphasizes this effect. What the 'floating above' form achieves is that it makes the object independent of its support. It is now saying 'look at me – just ignore the table – *I'm* the one that matters!'

What we are doing in each of these three forms is moving the apparent centre of gravity. In the 'growing from' objects the apparent centre of gravity is even lower than the real point. In a wedge form it can actually be below the base – somewhere in the table itself. The apparent and the real centre often coincide in the 'sitting upon' form, but in the 'floating above' the real centre of gravity can apparently be as high as up to two-thirds of the way up the vessel.

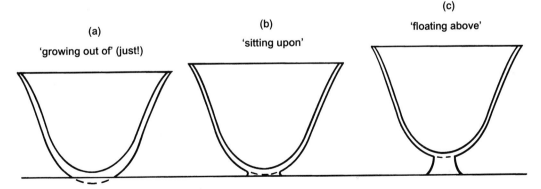

Different projections of the external profile. (a) is below the base, giving a 'growing out of' form, although the internal profile makes this almost 'sitting upon' as in (b). The pedestal base lifts (c) to be clearly 'floating above'.

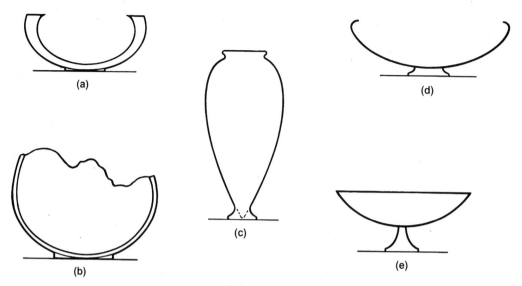

Various 'floating above' and 'sitting upon' forms. (a), (b), and (c) are 'sitting upon' forms: (a) is a bowl executed in heavy burr with a flat framing rim; (b) is a 'sitting upon' form in natural-edged burr, which, despite its size, still looks as though it could be handled; (c) is a tall amphora-shaped vase. The large fruit bowl (d) and the classic Greek calyx (e) are both distinct 'floating above' shapes.

It is not only changes in profile and size of the base that move the apparent centre of gravity; but so too do the size of the top aperture and the shape, size and decoration of the rim. Even applied decoration can by its very weight cause apparent movement.

Just why this is so is difficult to explain, but the larger the top aperture, the lower the centre of gravity appears to be. A hollow form with a tiny top aperture has a higher apparent centre; a wider, vase-like top opening immediately draws the centre down. In fact it is not quite as simple as that. If the top opening is given a return that opens out, this raises the centre point again.

While playing with the size of the base does affect the apparent centre of gravity, we can also add to the floating impression by using optical tricks.

A 'floating above' form cannot be achieved without some system of base, support or pedestal. If the pedestal can be seen it has a lowering effect; if hidden, then the floating impression is enhanced (although the apparent centre of gravity may not have moved).

We can also effect the impression by making the pedestal clearly separate. A foot turned as an integral part of the vessel ties the object to the table much more strongly than do independent legs or a supporting cage or frame.

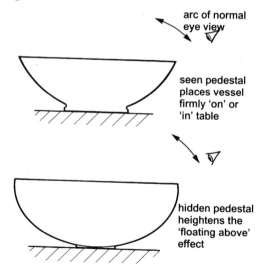

arc of normal eye view

seen pedestal places vessel firmly 'on' or 'in' table

hidden pedestal heightens the 'floating above' effect

Seen and masked bowl pedestals.

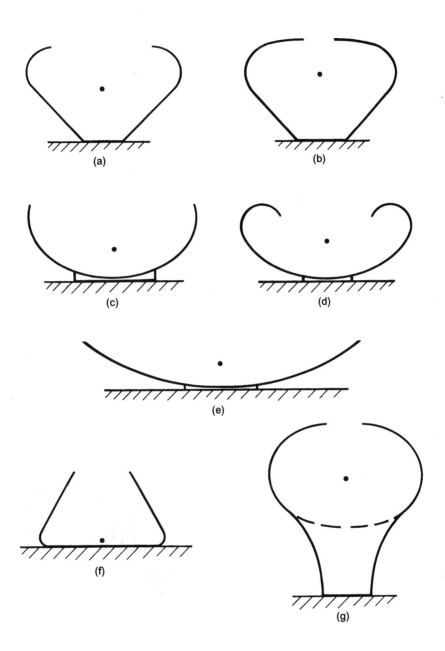

Moving the apparent centre of gravity. An open top, on its own (a) or combined with a big base (c) lowers the apparent centre of gravity; 'growing out of' forms (f) have the same effect. Shapes with very closed-in tops (b) or very wide-open ones (e) seem to have a higher centre of gravity. A rolling-in rim with a small undercut (d) puts the apparent centre of gravity where the real centre is. In a bulbous shape like (g) we only 'see' the top oval, and place the apparent centre of gravity in the middle of it.

CURVES AND STRAIGHT LINES

Clearly the extension of the wall profile will be conditioned by the line of the walls. Straight lines project to infinity, curves resolve into a circle.

While we all perceive form differently, there do seem to be some widely shared perceptions about straight lines and curves, and the interplay between them.

In almost every test that has ever been done it has shown that people prefer curves to straight lines. This is very fortunate for the turner! Uninterrupted straight lines are universally regarded as boring, undulations as interesting, curves as sensuous, and strong or over-loaded curves as voluptuous. Continuous curves of a fixed radius are, however, really little more than straight lines going round a curve; they make simple circles and even these are seen as 'boring'.

The psychological basis of such perceptions are not difficult to understand. The flat, straight line is the open landscape with no interest. Curves are the human body, and more: the round comfort of mother.

Watch people as they respond to wooden items. The flat table, they look along to confirm the flatness. They run their hand over it to find any variations – unevenness, or faults,

Both of these bowls are large, thick-walled, heavy and dramatically figured and coloured elm burrs. (The full-sized eggs give a scale.) Neither sold over a number of outings and were eventually relegated to family use. On the left-hand piece the walls are too thick for shape. The base far too wide, making it look dumpy. It is too big (and too pricey) for utility; and, despite the dramatic figure, it is not beautiful enough to be a piece of pure decoration. The right-hand piece has an uninteresting shape (and the walls not even a true vertical). It has nothing but colour to commend it as a display piece, and is far too big to have any utility. Both are a waste of wood! There is no 'delicacy' to either piece. Both were made in my days of making the biggest possible item out of the block of wood irrespective of any design consideration – and it shows!

points of 'interest'. It is more a mechanical inspection than an emotional response.

Curves are stroked and fondled. Every change in the radius of the curve is explored. They are exciting. They are caressed and give real comfort; even sensual pleasure.

The Flat Earth Syndrome

The eye moves across a surface or along a line, taking in what it sees and sending messages to the brain. The brain starts to respond and begins to see patterns.

'Ha!' it says to itself, 'this is a flat surface.' So it seeks out its programmes on flatness against which to assess the signals from this particular flat surface. It checks how flat it is – any variations, any imperfections, the smoothness and polish of the surface – and it continues to scan across the flat plane. This is fine with a large flat area such as the top of a table. To the mind flatness goes on, and on, and on. At least that is what it expects.

Now, what happens with a broad, flat rim on a bowl form? The eye sweeps across the rim but soon reaches the lip. The brain is still thinking 'flatness' as the eye plunges over the edge, and falls into the abyss. 'Help!' the brain now cries; 'Where are you taking me?'

Similar things happen if the eye is travelling along a curve – it expects the curve to carry on. So the brain becomes confused when the curve suddenly changes into a flat surface or straight line.

Equally, if the curve is 'spherical' we expect it to continue indefinitely – if logarithmic we expect it to continue until it tightens up on itself and disappears into its own interior. What we cannot live with are sudden changes in the radius of the curve – just as when going round a bend in a car and the curve suddenly, and without warning, tightens up. It is only a wrench on the steering wheel that prevents us flying through the hedge. A sudden change in the profile of the bowl and we have the same tendency to fall or fly off.

The crossing of lines arrests the movement of the eye (and hand), and dependent upon the arrangement of the crossing it may create a barrier to further motion – a 'brick wall'; or a crossroads and the question, 'which path will I take next?'

Lines, straight or curved, with breaks in them are problems; these are gaps that have to be bridged.

Comfortable lines flow one into the next. Curves of different radii can be blended into each other and the eye will make the transition with no difficulty. There are, however, transitions that we do not like – like the abrupt change from a curve to a straight line. We do not expect the curve to suddenly become an angular corner. That surprises us. Curves provide a boundary – a break between elements.

We need to help the mind to accept the change from one shape into another. We often do this by adding a little detail or some small feature of interest at the change boundary. The eye now stops and takes in this new shape and the brain pauses and appraises it for a few moments before asking: 'OK, seen that; where do I go now?'

There are often two strongly opposing views from turners assessing the same piece of work. One will admire the crisp edges – probably because they demonstrate technical skill. The other will hate the sharp edge 'just because it is sharp and you feel you could cut yourself on it'. This second turner likes to see (just a hint of) rounding over. The same pair will then agree that the design is fine when the edge is given a little detail, such as a small bead or groove.

Such matters are not just philosophical. We have to create appropriate emotions in the people whom we wish to be interested in our work. By recognizing that certain reactions are likely, we can play on them – enhance or diminish them as appropriate. If we have any objectives for a piece beyond the pure functional, we have to recognize that it is emotions that we are playing upon, and have to design the emotional appeal just as carefully as we do functional elements.

47

A 27in (68.5cm) diameter bowl making use of light sap wood (on the front face), a revealed area of natural bark and the deep colour of jarrah. A 'quirk', or bead, has been added to the inner edge of the rim to break up what would otherwise have been a stark flatness.

By gently flaring one curve into that of a different radius we facilitate the sweep of eye or hand. We increase the viewers' comfort and feeling of sensuous pleasure. We can bring them up with a jerk when we wish to introduce a new feeling. We can facilitate the transition from one line to another. When they reach a point at which their mind questions 'where do I go now?' we can introduce a detail they can consider while their mind deals with the problem of future direction. Between a bead and a cove on a spindle we put a little feature – a level zone or a groove. It helps to define the form on either side and is like a punctuation mark that either says 'Pause a second' (a comma), or 'Stop! I am now about to introduce a new theme' (a full stop).

QUIRKS

The rim of a thick-walled bowl is level. At either side it plunges down the wall. It is a straight line and the eye rapidly sweeps across. But then, perhaps, the eye does not now want to fall over the edge. A small bead in the rim provides it with something to look at while it decides whether to leap or not. It is not just an 'interesting feature', or something that 'breaks up the monotony of the flat rim'; it has a definite purpose at an important psychological/perceptual level.

Spindle turners make great use of a tiny detail between two dominant shapes. On a spindle the brain never has the chance of developing a mind-set other than that of overall direction to one end or the other. No sooner has it dipped round a cove before it is off on a climb up a shoulder, then down a long slope, and then, oops! a bead.

A spindle with quirks delineating the main design features.

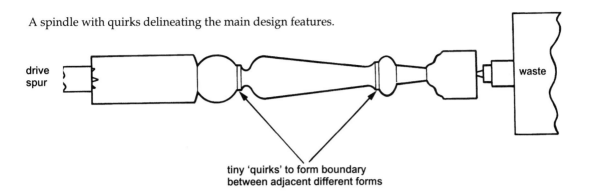

tiny 'quirks' to form boundary
between adjacent different forms

A 'quirk' is what ace spindle turner Ray Jones calls the detail that he builds in between two major shapes. You will hear other turners using the same word, and you will see similar little 'details' on the spindle work of many turners. A quirk is simply a tiny flat zone between two adjacent curves.

How the eye follows the line of the profile is very important, and it should be an essential part of the maker's design consideration to want to control the movement of the eye, and achieve a specific, required ('designed') result.

Take a table. However nice a piece of furniture you wish to make it, it is still a table: a piece of furniture intended to have things – usually meals – put on top of it. When not used for meals it is probably dressed with a bowl of fruit or flowers. You are intended to look at the top of the table. Hence the legs are designed to cause the gaze to rise to the top.

The same is true of a standard lamp. You want it to be a pleasant piece of furniture, but it is the light and the shade that are going to be the main points of interest, so you want the eye to rise to these; but in rising you want it to do certain things and behave in a particular way.

How it rises is very important. Do you want it to bump up over a series of sleeping policemen? A row of identical-sized beads is not only boring because of the repetitive sameness, but it is actually an effort for the eye to traverse because of its bumpiness.

You may want the eye to shoot to the

shade so you have a column completely devoid of interest but merely a support. A plain, unornamented, parallel-sided column of the correct proportion will do this. Give it a long taper and you sweep the eye up in comfort.

Barley sugar twists or any form of rising spiral will carry the eye upwards. Once the mind has evaluated the basic form of the twist it then moves on uninterrupted, not bored, but not particularly stimulated; unless that is, the viewer is technically minded and wonders how the hell the craftsman produced it.

Parallel grooves or fluting have a similar function of pushing the eye on along its journey. They add sufficient detail to prevent boredom in what might otherwise be a fairly long, uninterrupted and relatively featureless journey.

Once the basic design has been drawn out, trace the profile (inside and out with bowls) with the eye. Is it a fair and continuous curve you are tracing? Are there any bulges or sudden changes where we might fall off the trace? If there are, what sort of detail do we need to add to that point to arrest the trace, allow the mind to take it in, to think, and then help it into the new direction? Wherever a major change of direction is needed what have we done to help that?

Finally, looking at the whole, are there any areas where the eye does not really know what to do? Is a detail needed at this point, or even a feature? Should this be built in or

49

added on (in the form of handles or knobs, perhaps)?

We commented earlier upon the fact that there is no reason why the external profile of a bowl or vessel *has* to match the internal profile. The external profile has to be a satisfying shape in its own right. It is the external profile that has to fit in with the environment. The sweep of the line has to meet the criteria we have now raised about the sweep of the eye, change of direction, points of change, and positioning of detail.

Now thinking specifically of a bowl, the external profile eventually reaches the rim. Here we will change from a basically vertical plane to a horizontal one, and then on to a hollowed-out form.

The rim marks the transition from something that is viewed in profile to something looked down upon. It may be a transition, or it may in effect be a separation between two almost totally different things. If the bowl is deeper rather than flatter, then it is more likely to be a transition in that there will be times when the piece will be looked at obliquely and both the top and the side will be seen at the same time; in this case a detail to help the transition is more important.

With broader, flatter objects the view is much more likely to be either 'down on' *or* in profile – not both at the same time. Now the transition can be a sharp cut-off. The sharper the edge the stronger the message: 'There is nothing beyond this point, stop now!' A really sharp corner is a good cut-off.

The rim is the transition, so if the external wall has swept up and over, the curve needs to continue across the rim until the change is made to the next form – the hollowed-out zone. We have now shifted the major transition point from the outside of the rim to the top of the hollow zone – it is here that we may now need to help the eye make the change.

Remember that we design and make bowls with one of four main functions in mind:

To provide a space filler – an ornamental

sculpture that will give pleasure by being viewed in profile.
To display the beauty of a piece of highly figured wood.
To display things and to frame them.
To hold things so that they do not spill while or until they are being used.

If our prime purpose is the second one but we suspect the object is likely to frequently be used for the last objective, we have to compromise and work to the third objective.

This is important. The more significant we think the beauty of the figure or the colour of the wood, and the more likely we think that the bowl will be filled with things that hide this, then the wider we need to make the rim: it is the rim that will be looked down upon, not the inside of the bowl.

Also the more likely we think it is that the main hollow will be filled with something that will obscure the wood, the more we can think of the rim as framing the contents. Frames *are* hard-edged, and therefore helping the eye to make a transition between the rim and the hollow is not now important. A sharp cut-off becomes acceptable.

One of my own favourite features is the roll rim, which ends with a deeply undercut overhang into the hollow space. This pleases me aesthetically and is very satisfactory technically (provided I haven't produced fluffy torn grain in the undercut). Unfortunately it fails to meet two important objectives. First, to the user it creates dead space under the overhang; and second, it fails to meet my objectives of providing a frame for the contents, because most users heap up the contents, which then spill out on to the sloping rim, totally blurring the edge.

ADDED DETAIL

We also add projecting detail to some pieces – dramatic, profile-changing devices such as handles or knobs, or perhaps a supporting plinth that we can make a feature of.

Roll-rim bowls. To the right and centre the rims were deeply undercut using a round-nosed side scraper. The bowl on the left has only a slight undercutting but the roll in of the rim accentuates the effect.

The deep undercut and the broad top rim means that contents cannot be heaped up hiding the wood of the rim. This will be an ornamental piece!

Knobs on the top of lids are the easiest. These can be turned integrally with the lid or turned separately in a contrasting wood.

There is always a question about combining two or more pieces of wood, however. How much of a contrast should be aimed for? If the difference is too great – a holly knob on a dark-brown elm – the contrast is so startling that it makes the knob assume a significance far greater than its size warrants. It can easily become the thing that the eye automatically gravitates towards.

Supports

If the piece is to be held off the table to give a 'floating above' impression, it is probably going to have a foot or a plinth. Normally small feet are turned as an integral part of the main item and will therefore be of the same timber. There are times when the foot may be turned out of a contrasting wood and here a darker material should always be chosen. Dark colours are heavier and you expect weight to be low down. A dark vessel on a light-coloured plinth looks very odd. Again the line chosen for the profile is important and can add or detract from the overall message.

Let's consider two common types of foot. First there is the cove foot, which almost picks up the horizontal plane of the table and then turns the eye upwards to continue its journey on up around the profile of the pot. This is a harmonious foot where everything merges together, the piece fits into its environment, and it and the table form a whole.

The second foot is more of a pedestal. It starts with a vertical column (which may be only fractions of an inch high), then has two or three details with probably a quirk or two, before actually cupping the vessel itself. Here the foot is seen as a separate entity from the vessel. It 'presents' the object for inspection and appreciation, but is not really, conceptually, an integral part of it.

Both the integral and the pedestal foot may be in similar or contrasting timber; however, too dark a pedestal tends to intrude and can assume a significance out of proportion with the object it is displaying.

There comes a stage where the support must be very definitely separate from the vessel. This is particularly important where the item is to float some distance above the table. If you now make the pedestal in the same timber, it tends to tie the vessel to the table.

At this juncture we may care to look outside wood for our support material, for both a material and a format that are clearly not a part of the object being presented. Bent iron, metal wire, ply or thin leaves of solid wood, profiles cut in sheet plastic or metal and similar could be considered. There are, however, balances to be struck; and some considerations for which it is very difficult to define any hard and fast rules.

The base clearly has to support the object with reasonable stability, but it must not be so large, heavy, or interesting that it intrudes or detracts from the object. The profile needs to gybe with that of the object – you would not normally have jagged hard angles supporting a set of gracious curves. It needs to 'fit' with the object but not be a part of it.

Surface Decoration

So far we have been focusing upon the addition of detail that causes some change to the profile of the item. There is a much bigger field to consider when we start to look at the use of applied or incised decoration to alter the surface or texture.

Surface decoration is to be the subject of a chapter on its own (*see* Chapter 10). There are, however, a few questions of decoration that we have to consider here at the perceptual level. The weight and positioning of the decoration can affect the apparent centre of gravity, it can also dramatically affect the sweep of the eye and the stroke of the hand.

The first thing to note is that the decoration becomes a focus of interest in its own right. Although the eye will take in the sweep of the form, it will dwell upon the decoration. It will explore it, and 'feel' the ridges and grooves. If overdone, the decoration can become the only point of interest so the overall form is not even 'seen'.

The shape and lines of the decoration now become critical. Lines can be introduced that enhance or complement the sweep of the profile, or that interrupt or contrast with the form. Vertical lines or flutes on the outside wall of a vessel heighten it; horizontal lines or texturing make it more squat. Both work *with* the basically curved shape. An abstract pattern of straight lines can so contrast with the basic form that it becomes a primary feature.

Spiralling lines emphasize the turning motion of the item. Spiral grooves on the flat rim of a large platter make the object appear to be spinning still and give the piece a dynamic of 'energy'.

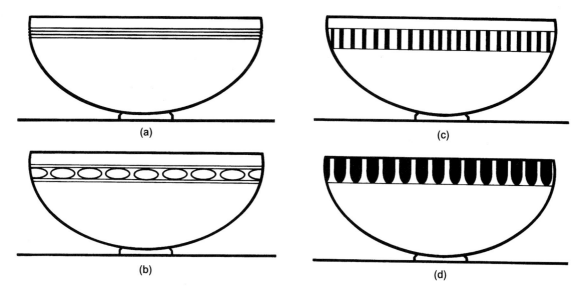

The effect of vertical and horizontal forms of decoration. Narrow radial bands incised with the point of a skew chisel (a) make the vessel look wider and more delicate. A decoration band inlaid with composite banding (b) gives a mixed message to the viewer; it is horizontal in structure, but the broken pattern is more akin to vertical decoration. A vertical pattern carved with a veiner or V-router (c) adds height to the vessel. The heavy vertical pattern in (d) is fluted carving made with a power router and then coloured; it has the effect of narrowing the width of the vessel and adding to the height and weight.

Surface texturing needs to be controlled. It can add weight to lightly figured/coloured wood, but can make a heavily figured piece look fussy.

Applied colour decoration also has to be thought about very carefully and again we will be considering this in Chapter 10. Strong, hard-edged or angular colour decoration is its own statement and may even be using the wooden item as little more than a shaped canvas. Colour washes blending one in to the other, and spray-applied paint with blended edges are more soft, and therefore more comfortable and compatible with turned shapes. So if the required effect is that of pleasure, comfort and beauty, the choice must be for merged, soft-edged and naturally complementary colours.

A vase with a lot of angular, dramatic shapes in vivid contrasting colours can be shocking. There is an immediate conflict between the angularity of the applied decoration and the curve of the form, which is heightened with strong colour. The result is to create tension in the viewer. You will hear people describe the piece with words like 'bizarre' or 'jazzy'.

Even after all this psychological mumbo-jumbo (my wife's comment), we have still not got down to the real kernel of design – form, proportion and dynamic symmetry.

5 Dynamic Symmetry

THE GROUND RULES

Studying design by way of examining the work of others has long been the traditional approach at art school. At some schools today, however, this is discouraged, and students are prompted to do their own thing: 'It is what you feel that matters!', they are told. I firmly believe in the approach adopted by an art master whose classes I attended. He was a highly accomplished and original abstract painter, but he started the class off by saying: 'Learn what the masters have done and why they did it before you decide to go off and do your own thing.'

Obviously, if we only ever copied what has gone before, we would never see any development or new ideas – no innovation, no Picasso, no Sureat. But even Picasso had many years of study and practical experience in more traditional fields before he launched off into cubism. Unstructured creation, freed of a grounding in classical rules, most often results in cerebral popcorn. It is usually also self-indulgent, appealing only to the creator – a case of beauty being *only* in the eye of the one beholder!

In this chapter we are going to consider two practical approaches to design. One is wholly analytical, substantially mathematical, and is based upon concepts developed in ancient Greece. The other is a more spontaneous approach, trying to create pleasing curves using various simple aids.

Tracing some of the work of the Greek masters we will see how two fundamental and timeless rules of design were devolved. The 'golden mean' and the 'rule of thirds' are in fact crude representations of highly sophisticated ratios based upon mathematical and geometric models. The analysis done all those

years ago has never been bettered; in a sense it was complete and perfect! The studies of over 2,000 years ago combined the philosophical, mathematical, natural and biological, and the aesthetic; and names that we do not associate with art will be found in early design literature – names such as Plato and Pythagoras.

It is not the function of this broad treatise here to re-explore the mathematics, nor do we need to go through all the proofs of the original geometric theorems. There are, however, some important key concepts, and a brief dip into these will help us to develop a much deeper understanding of good design. In fact our later spontaneous creation of good designs will be greatly facilitated if we first go through the rigours of studying the analytical concepts of form. This traditional, art-school approach to developing design ability has never been bettered.

'Natural' Structure

One of the Greek starting points was nature itself. They looked at the growth of cell structures, of patterns of leaves in trees, and of the shapes of individual leaves. They found that many exhibited interrelated, simple mathematical ratios.

A single cell grows in a very structured way. Across given periods of time (and the period differs from cell to cell) the growth is continuous and proportional. Of course it is subject to external influences – the leaf responds to the elements such as heat and cold, aridity and moisture – but if examined sufficiently closely, discounting all variables, fundamental patterns can be found.

Each leaf, from the largest nearest to the trunk out to the tip of the branch, gets pro-

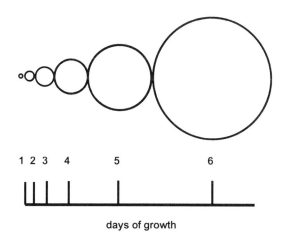

1 2 3 4 5 6

days of growth

Development of a single cell over given time intervals for a conical shape.

gressively smaller. The multi-leaflet patterns of the leaves of trees such as the rowan also have a regular grading of sizes from base to tip of each leaf.

But of course the leaf is an assemblage of many, many cells, and each cell will be found to follow this grading of size. If we take a single cell and draw it out as it would be at given stages in a set time-frame, the development will be seen to be exponential. Placing the stage drawings in line we would see overall a clear conical shape.

Some life-forms trace this pattern of development and reflect it in their overall structure, even assuming a conical profile. Several sea shells are like this. On British beaches we

Spiral and conical shell forms follow logarithmic growth patterns. Note the beautiful natural curves of the mouth of *Hemifusus*.

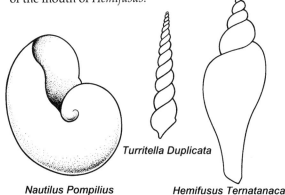

Turritella Duplicata

Nautilus Pompilius   *Hemifusus Ternatanaca*

get the shells that as kids we called ice-cream cornets. Here there is a straight, vertical spiral, which appears as the *Odostomia* shell. In tropical seas the cone pattern becomes a flatter true spiral in the *Nautilus*.

If we lay out the drawing of the conical development of the single cell into a spiral form we create what is called a logarithmic spiral. Growth develops at a logarithmic rate – again the *Nautilus* is a superb example. This precise set of relationships in cell development and overall growth provides one of the strongest themes in classical design.

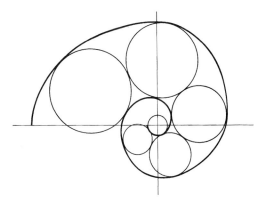

Logarithmic growth pattern of a single cell shown in spiral form.

The Root Two Rectangle

By taking the true spiral and superimposing across it a right-angled triangle with the hypotenuse horizontal, such that the right angle at the top lies directly above the eye of the spiral , we find that the spiral forms the basis for a series of overlapping right-angled triangles, each with a fixed ratio to the next. The complex of triangles also provides the basic framework for an important rectangle, known as a 'root two rectangle'. Root two, three and five rectangles form the basis of much of what is known as dynamic symmetry. And for us these are the most important design concepts that we need to consider.

We do not, fortunately, have to go through

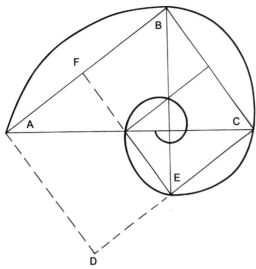

Right-angled triangles within the spiral provide the basis of a fundamental rectangle.

the very difficult process of drawing out logarithmic spirals to produce dynamic rectangles. The process of laying out is simple; it is merely the derivative and relationship with nature that is complex.

A root two rectangle contains a right-angled triangle ABC, which then becomes the rectangle ABCD. A perpendicular from the right angle at B is scribed to intersect AC at right angles at point X. BX is continued to intersect CD at E and the rectangle is bisected by line EF, which is parallel to BC and AD. However, for this to be a dynamic rectangle, there needs to be the 'natural' ratio of AB to BC, which is derived from the logarithmic spiral. The ratio of the long side to the short side of the rectangle is 1.4142 to 1. This is, in fact, the square root of 2 ($\sqrt{2}$) – hence a root two rectangle. A root two rectangle produced in this way will always have EF divide it into two identical half rectangles.

If we take a root two rectangle, and draw a square on the short end (BC) and another on the long side (CD), the smaller square (MNBC) will be exactly half the surface area of the larger square (COPD).

By placing two logarithmic spirals side by side and taking the diagonals across the combined figure, we get a root three rectangle,

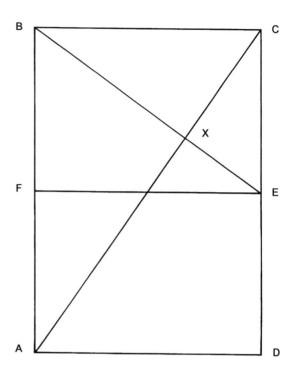

The triangle ABC from the logarithmic spiral forms a basic root two rectangle.

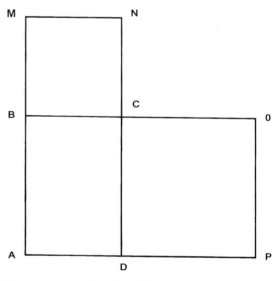

The squares on the sides of the root two rectangle have a fixed ratio to one another: the surface area of square COPD is twice that of square MNCB.

THE RULE OF THIRDS AND THE GOLDEN MEAN

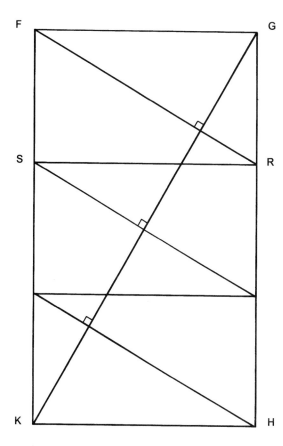

A root three rectangle, derived from two logarithmic spirals placed side by side. This is the basis of classic design. The ratio of the short side KH to the long side FK is 1 to root three or 1:1.732. The ratio of FG to a third of the long side FK (FS) is also 1:1.732.

where the main rectangle divides into three exactly equal sub-rectangles, and the ratio of the long side to the short is the square root of three, or 1.732, to 1.

The ratio for a root four rectangle is obviously the square root of 4, that is, 2 to 1; and for root 5 it is 2.236 to 1. We rarely become involved with higher root forms in turning design.

The root three rectangle has provided us with one of the most basic of all design rules – the rule of thirds. Expressed in its most simple form, this rule states that in any frame (square, rectangle or circle) the point of greatest interest is one-third in from the side, and one-third down from the top. A feature placed at this point will create maximum impact. Furthermore, the profile itself will be best balanced if the main features are placed upon the thirds. The most sophisticated use of the rule of thirds is to work precisely to all the dimensions of the root three rectangle. Artists make considerable use of this rule and if you look at many of the old masters, features of significant interest are placed upon one or other points of intersection of thirds.

As we have already implied, perfect symmetry may itself become a little dull, so we have a second ancient rule – that of the golden intersection, which I like to think of as the rule of thirds deliberately broken to introduce an element of dynamic tension.

The golden rule and the rule of thirds are not the same. In fact, the golden mean is almost half-way between root two and root three.

To establish the golden mean ratio, start with a perfect square – KLMN. Let's use line NM as the base. The base line is bisected at the half-way mark, which is point P. Now, using the length of PL as the radius of a circle, describe an arc to intersect with the projection of line NM. The point of intersection is Q. Complete the rectangle KRQN. The corner of the original square now becomes point M on line NQ and is the golden intersection on that line. The actual ratio of the shortest segment to the longer, MQ to NM is 1 to 1.618. The interesting point about the golden intersection is that the ratio of the shorter segment, QM, to the longer, NM, is the same as it is for the longer, MN, to the whole, NQ.

In the seventeenth century an Italian mathematician, Fibonacci, developed a number

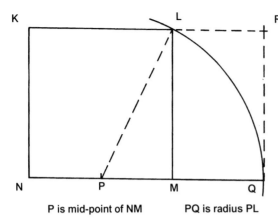

P is mid-point of NM   PQ is radius PL

The golden intersection, or golden mean.
The line LM is on the golden intersection of
the rectangle NKRQ. The ratio of MQ to NM
is 1:1.618 and the ratio of NM to NQ is also
1:1.618.

progression system that approximates to golden mean ratios. Starting with 1 + 1 and then adding each pair of adjacent numbers you develop the following sequence:

$$1 + 1 = 2$$
$$+$$
$$2 = 3$$
$$+$$
$$3 = 5$$
$$+$$
$$5 = 8$$
$$+$$
$$8 = 13$$

Above 8 on this sequence the ratio between adjacent numbers is close to 1.618 – the ratio of the golden mean.

The mathematical base of the root rectangles and the golden mean are useful if you wish to design forms to precise classical principles. They become an essential starting point once you move into computer graphics and computer-assisted design programmes to generate shapes.

On a day-by-day basis the actual ratios are taken for granted. All we need to do is to block out a root two, three or five dynamic

rectangle and use this as the framework within which to sketch out the vessel we wish to produce. In time, by examining the classic works of the past and frequently using the rectangle frame, we become so familiar with the proportions that use of the concepts becomes second nature.

Let's now consider how these ratios may work in practice. Certainly working to the rules of dynamic symmetry produces forms of satisfying proportions. Absolute adherence to the rules will produce pieces of classic simplicity – even, at times, uninspired purity. However, from the classic starting point we can move elements around and easily produce extremely interesting shapes using touches of rule deviation in order to generate tensions.

The first application of the rules helps us to determine the best relationship between width and height. We then use the ratios to position points of interest or to highlight and accent features.

Look at works of plastic art. Much Greek, early Turkish and Roman pottery will be found to have forms of classical proportions. Draw these out on root two, three and five rectangle grids.

In turning, most of us start with blanks that are cut to standard diameters (6, 8, 10 inches or 15, 20, 25cm) and from planks of standard thicknesses (2, 3 or 4 inches or 5, 7 or 10cm). We then try to make the largest possible item from the given dimensions of the blank so that there is minimum wastage. Rarely do blanks to these sorts of measures facilitate the making of pieces to classic design proportions. Poor design often starts with the timber yards and the sizes to which they make their blanks.

IDEAL-SIZED BLANKS

We would probably all produce more pleasing work if we started with blanks of 'ideal' proportions – that is, discs that conformed to the rule of thirds or one or other of the root rectangles.

Table of root three rectangle bowl blanks												
(Diameters are shown to the nearest usable first place of decimals. The units could be inches, centimetres, feet or whatever you like)												
Diameter	6	7	8	9	10	11	12	18	20	24	26	30	36
Thickness	3.5	4.0	4.6	5.2	5.8	6.3	7.0	10.4	11.5	13.9	15.0	17.3	20.8

This same table is appropriate to vase blanks by simply making vertical (rectangular) blocks to the same dimensions.

These dimensions would provide a good starting point for either large open bowls or even tall, hollow vessels.

Table of dimensions for root five blanks												
Diameter	6	7	8	9	10	11	12	18	20	24	26	30	36
Thickness	2.7	3.1	3.6	4.0	4.5	5.0	5.4	8.0	9.0	10.7	11.6	13.4	16.1

APPLYING THE PRINCIPLES – DESIGNING A VASE

So let's now build up a vase form from a root three rectangle using the concepts of dynamic symmetry to define both key dimensions and the positioning of additional design features. For this exercise we will produce a vase 15in (38cm) high.

We are going to draw this out, and the first step is to build the basic rectangle. It will be shown as ABCD. The height of AB is drawn in at 15in (38cm). The ratio of a root three rectangle is 1.732, so the 15in (38cm) is divided by 1.732. This gives us a base, AD, of 8.66in (22cm). So ultimately we will require a block of timber of 15 × 8¾in (38 × 22cm).

On the drawing we could construct the sub-rectangles as we did earlier using a diagonal CA, and dropping a perpendicular down from B to a point F on CD complete the sub-rectangle EBCF, and so on (see diagram on p. 57). However, we know that the long side will eventually divide into three exactly equal parts. So it is quicker to divide the 15in (38cm) by 3 and so get three sub-rectangles of 5in (12.66cm) by 8.66in (22cm) each.

Next do the same with the uppermost of the three sub-triangles. 8.66in (38cm) divided

by 3 gives us 2.9in (7.33cm); having divided each side into thirds, we now have a set of mini rectangles each 5 × 2.9in (12.66 × 7.33cm).

Note the ratio of the sub-rectangles is still root three. The 5in (7.33cm) sides of the three sub-rectangles (BE) give a ratio to the short end of the whole rectangle (BC) of 5 to 8.66 (7.33 to 22) or 1 to 1.732.

We now have the grid on which to work. We will place the widest part of the vase upon the line EF – the top third. Make the neck opening one-third of the maximum diameter. For the moment we will make the base the same size as the open mouth. The walls will follow continuous curves but we will avoid the dullness of constant-radius curves.

The result is a simple shape of pleasing line. At this stage it is satisfactory but a little uninspired. This would be a nice piece to use for spray painting: the use of subtle colours could make it very appealing and add great interest to an attractive form. However, before we resort to colour, let's see what happens if we move one or two points and add decorative features.

First, make the base a little narrower than the full third. It does not change the overall

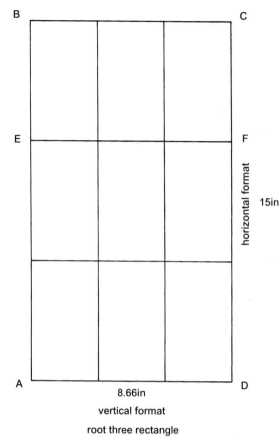

B   C

E   F

A   D

8.66in

vertical format

root three rectangle

horizontal format

15in

Matrix for root three objects laid out for a
15in high vase.

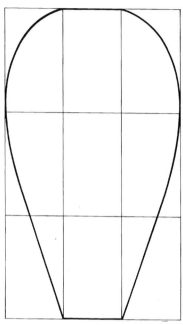

Basic design conforming precisely to all
critical dimensions of root three.

shape and balance but does lift the vessel and
gives an impression of lightness. We are also
going to add a little return on the top opening. Here we will not alter any important
dimension. The overall height will remain at
15in (38cm), and the open top of the aperture
will be kept at one-third of the diameter.

We have retained all the critical dimensions and overall form, but with a couple of
small changes have created a much more
interesting piece. Now try covering up the
lowest third. In effect you have reduced the
overall rectangle to a rectangle closer to root
two, but have built a design that incorporates
several dimensions based upon root three. It

has given us a vessel that is still acceptable in
form, although a little squat and dumpy, and
requiring some ornamentation, possibly
applied decoration from the centre line up
towards the neck.

There are many variations we could have
introduced into the root three vessel. The
neck could have been made narrower – possibly to root five proportions. We could have
retained root three top diameter but brought
the neck in to a very narrow throat, giving a
wide flair. The maximum diameter could
have been reduced and two handles added to
restore the apparent diameter to the full
8.66in (22cm). At this stage I might have
wished to reduce the base even further and
create a 'floating above' effect by having a
small pedestal foot. By modifying the curve
of the wall in the upper third we could have
'hunched the shoulders', thereby raising the
apparent centre of gravity.

The root three rectangle could also be used
by placing the greatest diameter on to the

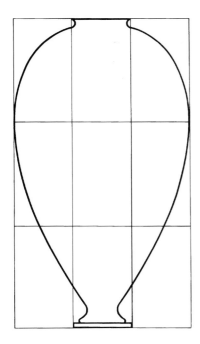

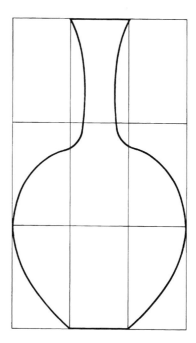

A vase drawn to root three with detailing features added. The curve of the lower walls makes the object a little penguin-like but does allow a clear 'floating above' form. Some more detail would be possible in the plinth without becoming 'fussy'.

A root three decanter (or small bud vase). A piece 15in tall could just be hollowed out with offset bit turning tools.

lower-third line. This would be moving towards a decanter.

Root three rectangles are probably the most satisfying framework to start with. Root three (and the rule of thirds) tends to produce marginally more satisfying shapes than does root five, and root three appears in Greek pieces more than does any other set of ratios. Root four, of course, gives quarters and the focus of a middle centre-point. Dead boring!

Root seven and beyond start to come into play with pedestals and table lamps. I once calculated that a four-poster bed leg that I was examining was a root 377 rectangle (approximately 6½ft (2m) × 4in (10.5cm) × 4in (10.5cm) square).

Working within the dynamics of a root three rectangle does not confine us to tall vases or even to the vertical format. The rectangle can be laid on its side with equal effect.

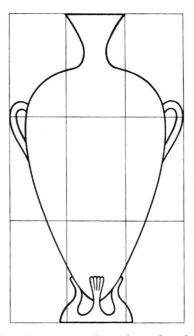

Still working to root three, the neck and waist are now narrowed. Handles bring the waist profile back to root three. The vessel is just turnable because of its flared neck, if you use a Stewart hooker. The base is turned on and then hand carved.

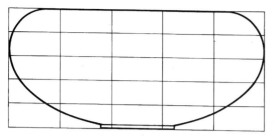

Bowl drawn to root five.

HORIZONTAL FORMS

Here, too, we do not have to take major features exactly to key lines, nor use the maximum space within the rectangle. Many Greek calyces use a horizontal root three rectangle as the basis. Here the vessel is in the upper triad; a narrow pedestal traverses the middle section; and the base occupies a small part of the lower third.

I found one simple calyx in Cairo Museum. The delicate pedestal rose through the lower two rectangles. The dish filled the upper. The curve of the dish was of very large radius, and the dish was therefore shallow; but the curve was just logarithmic or asymmetrical (of continuously and proportionally changing radius), steepening ever so slightly up the side walls. I spent almost thirty minutes gazing at it and then even longer trying to sketch it. It really needed careful measurement, it was so perfect; but the display case could not be opened. It was the most perfect and beautiful thing in the whole museum – which, it must be remembered, also houses all the King Tut treasures!

In a thesis analysing the mathematical relationships of dynamic symmetry in Greek vases, the authors show how in some classic pieces there is a clear ratio between each and every element of the design. Even the undercut under the rim of the lip has a precise set of dimensions, as does the placing and shape of the handles, and even the radius of each curve. When it gets to that stage of precision, I prefer just to doodle!

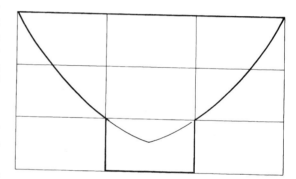

A simple root three calyx, drawn to classic lines.

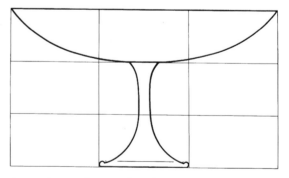

A simple root three calyx, drawn to contemporary lines.

A root three calyx in tall pedestal form. The thickness of the stem is critical: if it is too thin, real and apparent structural integrity is lost; if too thick, proportion is affected.

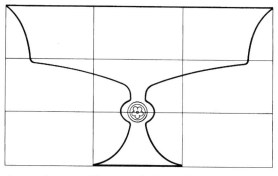

Pedestal vessel. The main body in the top third is offset by the carving in the centre of the lower-third line.

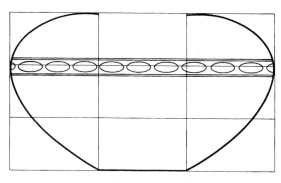

A root three bowl with a band of inlaid decoration on the top third.

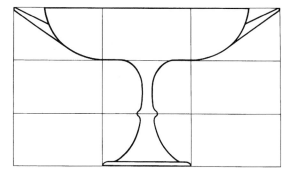

Pedestal with handles to give full root three dimensions to the profile. Other features are positioned on key dimension points.

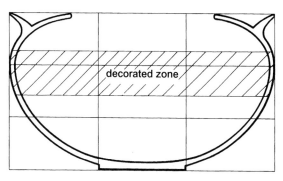

A double-profile bowl. The lower third of the wall is too rounded and heavy. A broad band of decoration might make the piece a more desirable item.

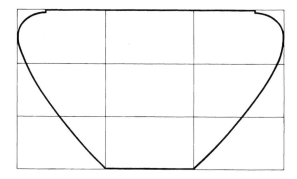

A simple bowl drawn to general root three principles; the top shoulders in at one-third of the outer third.

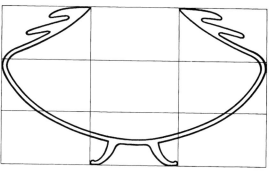

UFO bowl based on classic root three dimensions.

Maple leaves follow a basic pentangle format.

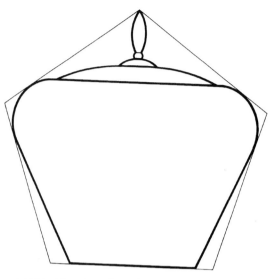

A lidded box based on the pentagon form.

Another form that was used in early times, and this can be found in Egyptian and Mayan cultures as well as the Greek, is the regular pentagon. In nature the best example of this form is the leaf of the maple family. From this we also get the pentangle – the dynamic symmetry and 'mystical' power of which has long been recognized. Several mystical, religious and votive symbols and many pieces of bas-relief carving spanning almost all civilizations have used the pentangle as the basis of design, and particularly as a structure to fix points of emphasis within a broader design. The pentagon form provides a useful basis for the design of lidded boxes.

Working on analysed design with the careful application of classical principles requires first calculating out the basic profile and then introducing modifications to create interest or tension. It starts with the drawing of the basic root rectangles or pentagon and then dividing these up into some proportional grid. On this a shape is sketched. It means working with a drawing board, probably squared paper, pencils, rulers, rubbers and also a calculator.

In the past, I would take a piece of interesting timber and place it in the workshop at a point where I would see it every day (and probably fall over it more frequently). After a time I would begin to see a shape in the block. Usually that shape would use as much

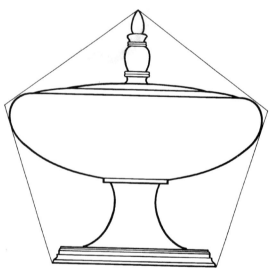

A lidded vase based on a Greek perfume vase. It uses a pentagonal form overall with root three placing of key elements.

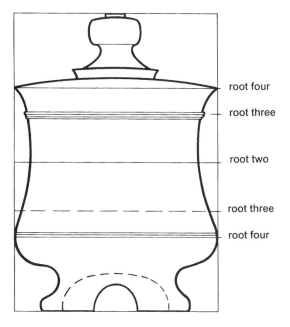

root four

root three

root two

root three

root four

A lidded bowl based on a Greek pyxis using basic root two dimensions but placing features on root two, three and four base lines.

as possible of the available wood. I know that many turners follow similar approaches.

What happened was that the shape of the block as purchased became the overriding criterion in determining the design that finally developed. Achieving a good design was almost incidental – certainly accidental! It was also a clear product of working mainly with dramatic burrs, which always come in random and awkward shapes and sizes.

Once in a while the blocks were cut at the saw mill to better dimensions and gave the facility for working out a required design. The resultant pieces were quantum jumps better. So the next stage was to design something that I wanted to make and go and look for pieces of timber that would accommodate this. Again the improvement in output quality was noticeable. It also, incidentally, became clear that suppliers are in league against good design! They cut up trees to a set of design-resistant principles and ratios!

During this middle period I started to find it useful to draw out the rough profile of the block that I had and then to play with lines within this framework.

My growing appreciation of dynamic symmetry came at a time when I had large stockpiles of random, and often badly sized blocks and blanks, and I am still working through some of these piles. Once in a while, however, I find one where it *is* possible to work from basic principles and the results are so satisfactory that I know this is the way to go. Thus I am now slabbing up my logs so as to give a number of blanks of root three proportions.

DESIGN AIDS

Computers

It started when I upgraded my office computer and began crude experiments using the basic Microsoft Paint software that came as a part of a DOS system. Paint allows you to produce curves and lines and draw shapes. There is then a limited facility for copying, inverting and reversing the shapes. It was, however, too difficult to control the elements to the degree required, and I found drawing with a mouse almost impossible. Then I was introduced to CorelDraw, a fascinating graphic software package. Unfortunately my computer could not handle it. Now I have one that can, and for some months I will probably be spending more time experimenting with design than I will on producing turned items. What graphics software does is to allow you to produce profiles and then modify elements. You can also manipulate and rotate designs, and view them from different angles.

I plan to draw a series of templates for vases, bowls, calyces and goblets. There will be a number of basic variations on each, but they will all conform completely to the basic rules.

Once these have been saved I will be able to call up a template and push and poke the profile with the Corel line modification tools.

Details, features and decoration patterns can be added, tried, and erased. Once I like the result, a sketch will be printed off (even a table of dimensions if wanted). It will be quick, and a short session in the evening could set up the work for a whole day on the lathe. It will certainly be cheaper than doing the design experiments on the lathe using rather costly pieces of figured wood.

I hope later to produce designs in which the basic planes are modified.

There is one other possible development. If plan and elevation view photos of the block are scanned into the computer it will be possible to juggle with the shapes and work out the best marking-up arrangement for the block.

But this is in the future. For the moment we have to content ourselves with more traditional methods, and use some of the everyday aids that are available. Beyond proportional drawings there are various approaches to design that we can use – some which are totally unstructured, some using supporting mechanisms.

Simple Tools

Two very useful tools are the flexible ruler, and a long necklet chain. These can be laid on a drawing board and then be pushed, poked and curved until a satisfactory profile is produced. At this stage the outline can be traced with a felt-tip pen. Sometimes I use these aids 'freehand', and sometimes within the confines of a drawn-out root rectangle.

A large mirror is also very useful. Drawing half a profile – one side of a bowl – is not difficult. Repeating this to get a complete profile is a job for an artist, and my drafting skills are appalling. The answer is to draw out the half profile, in pencil first so that it can be erased and modified; once correct it is inked over with a felt-tip pen. Now, holding the mirror in a vertical plane to the paper and at one end of the half profile, the mirror can be moved to produce a complete profile – half on the paper and the other half its reversed reflec-

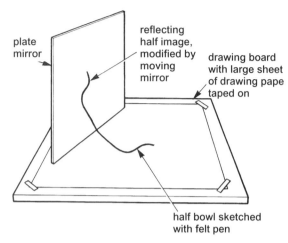

Using a mirror to produce basic designs.

tion in the mirror. The mirror can be moved along the base of the half profile to produce broad, open bowls; or squashed up for more vertical shapes.

Another invaluable tool is a set of French curves. Unfortunately those available in most stationers are too small to be really helpful. Architects have larger versions and railway engineers had magnificent ones that they used for designing track layouts. With a set of these and a half-elephant drawing board you could have endless fun!

Playing with the profiles that can be drawn with the French curves can produce quite elegant forms. Later again I hope to be able to scan these into the computer for further manipulation. (I gather that someone has now programmed the complex maths to do this electronically.)

French curves provide one feature that transcends all others. They are based upon a continuous logarithmic development of the radius of the curve, that is, progressive and continuous slight change. In fact it is impossible to draw even a small arc of a curve of fixed radius with French curves. Any vessel drawn with the curves will have a good line – the skill is in building that line into a complete profile. It is exactly that which the craftsman had achieved with the Cairo Museum calyx that I commented on earlier.

French curves, the most important design tool of all. The logarithmic curves almost invariably produce pleasing profiles and avoid the dreadful'roundness and slavish symmetry seen in some work.

Root rectangle grids and a suitable-sized set of curves can often be used together very successfully. A small drawing produced in this way can then be gridded off and redrawn larger, but an enlarging photocopier can also be used if available.

THE 'ART PIECE'

Great emphasis has been placed in this chapter upon drawing out constructed profiles. Some people may feel that this is mechanizing design and taking away all creativity. The advanced woodturner does plan and draw things out before the timber is mounted on to the lathe. The really advanced turners probably do less of it. It is not that they do not accept the principles, rather that they have totally assimilated them and use them automatically and subconsciously.

The final concept of design that we will look at here is really only available to the very, very advanced turner. Only such a person is likely to be commissioned to design and make a really significant piece to be set in a specific position.

We started to think along related lines when we earlier talked about internal and external profiles in relation to how the object would normally be viewed – from above or in profile.

What we are now addressing is the piece of work that is going to be treated as a 'sculpture' – a piece of plastic (as distinct from graphic) art that is to be precisely placed in a particular environment to create some emotion or aesthetic satisfaction. It probably has to operate in three dimensions.

An art teacher I had once regularly used a phrase that at first meant nothing: 'Don't look at the profile of the object – look at the spaces between!' I came across the same phrase later in photography classes. It was once simplified by one artist who said: 'Draw in the background, and that will automatically define the object.' In the end (I think) I understood. I painted an electricity pylon against a gale-torn, rain-sodden sky. Nothing of the pylon was painted in, but its form was clearly there, traced by the triangles, rectangles and diagonals of the patches of sky. The picture was eventually hung in a major gallery.

When designing an art piece we have to consider size and proportion; and take account of the spaces, lines and decoration that the object has to offset, conflict with, or subjugate. The colour has to complement or

The spaces between. An impression of an electricity pylon breasting a storm is created by painting the light seen coming through the spaces. Often it is the environment or background that gives the piece its form rather than its own basic profile.

contrast; certainly ambience and appropriate style is important. Many Barbara Hepworth and Henry Moore sculptures have holes through them so that you can see the landscape within which they sit. The hole is not there as a circular decorative feature – it has a much more important function. The jagged edge of a natural-top turning is not just an interesting variation on a straight line but creates a special interplay with the space around it.

When taking on a commission for such a work the important questions are not 'how big do you want it?' or 'what is the budget?', rather 'what effect do you wish to create?', 'what emotions are you trying to trigger in the viewer?' Quite often you have to prompt the initial answers and then probe to test their honesty – few people will come clean and say 'we want it to look arty, impressive, and expensive.' But that is sometimes just what they *do* want, and that brief would have a major effect on what I might produce.

Making a piece to fit in a particular space requires that we take into account all the formal aspects of design that we have been looking at here; but also that we think just as much about the object's final environment, both physical and psychological! Even when it is on the lathe, you have to keep a clear mental image of where it is going to sit and what it has to achieve.

In America there is a particularly good idea at some 'crafts fairs'. Once in a while they have one laid out as a series of environments. Instead of each craftsman having his own stand, there are groups of products. So you get a rug, two or three pieces of furniture, a picture or two, and other decorative objects set out in positions where you would expect to find them (including a jumper thrown across the arm of a chair). A fruit bowl would have fruit in it, a sculptural piece would not! Customers can see objects in the sort of situation they are intended for. No longer do you get stupid questions such as 'Yes! but what can I use it for?'

6 Holding the Wood

MOUNTING PROBLEMS

We have now designed our piece, found and prepared the wood, and are ready to start turning. The first problem is mounting the wood on to the lathe, although at times, with some of my pieces, it is actually lifting up the wood that is the first obstacle!

Most lathes come with a basic range of accessories. Usually there will be a face plate, a drive spur and a tailstock point. This may suffice for a time, but very soon we will need to add a fancy multi-chuck and probably a three- or four-jaw one to our kit. Later, as we turn much bigger or much smaller items, or work with difficult types of wood, the basics become less than half the 'essentials'.

Almost everything on the market is useful; certainly to every known problem someone has worked out a solution. The fun, however, is often to work out your own gismos.

Let's start by listing the main shapes that we will have to hold.

1. Long, medium-diameter pieces that can be driven from one end and restrained at the other (spindles, chair legs, tool handles, candlesticks, lamp standards, banister spindles).
2. Items to be production-run to regular shapes and sizes. Often these are small thin pieces that can be held one end and restrained at the other (lace bobbins, pens).
3. Long pieces that can be held at one end but not restrained at the other – you may actually be working on or into the outboard end (tall, hollow vases).
4. Long items that need drilling out (candlesticks, lamp standards).
5. Medium-length pieces that can only be held at one end (goblets, eggs, fruit, boxes).
6. Hollow tubes (pepper mills).
7. Tiny and relatively short pieces that can be held at one end only (chess pieces).
8. Large blocks requiring double mounting that can be driven from one end and initially restrained at the other (large rough bowls, starting hollow vessels).
9. Large blocks that can only be driven from one end on a single mounting (deep bowls).
10. Discs that can be driven from each face and will be double mounted (most bowls).
11. Discs with thin bases (platters).
12. Items that are offset driven at one or both ends to produce out-of-round turnings (chair legs and ornamental turnings).
13. Finished turned items that require the bases cleaning up to remove chuck marks – 'reverse chucking' (bowls, vases, goblets).

We also have to take into account other factors that have a direct bearing upon the method of mounting. These include the nature and condition of the wood, the amount of waste wood that is available, and the grain orientation.

Wherever we support the work from the outboard end we use the tailstock. Under most circumstances a simple point will be used, and unless you are a died-in-the-wool pole lathe user this will be a 'live point' – a rotating point running in a ball race. Grease-lubricated, fixed-point tailstocks are a thing of the past. As we examine each holding requirement in detail we will also encounter one or two special types of tailstock.

Stair Spindles, Candlesticks, Chair Legs

This is the main body of turning normally classified as between centres or spindles. The tailstock end will be supported by the tailstock point but there are two basic options for the drive end. Most frequently we use the simplest form of drive: a prong drive or cross-head drive point. The alternative is to use a four-jaw chuck.

The cross head is quick to set up and is best suited to medium-density woods. The wood is first marked off to find the centre. For speed and accuracy a corner marker is used. A spare drive bit is hammered into the wood to mark it before putting the wood on the lathe. Do not drive the point too hard into the end grain of dense wood as this may split the timber; and *never* hammer the wood on to the point mounted on the lathe as this soon damages the spindle bearings.

If the timber is very soft, as with some pines, and if any resistance is met during turning, a cross-head drive can spin in the end of the timber, 'drilling' out a deep recess. An inadequately seated prong can also skate on the surface and spin with very hard, dense woods. Under these circumstances the four-jaw chuck is preferable.

Four-jaw chucks are the most positive means of holding timber for turning. They have two disadvantages. First, you cannot work the timber right to the inboard end, and second, the projecting jaws on the chuck can wreak havoc with the knuckles of the left hand.

Lace Bobbins and Similar Repetitive Items

Here a standard size of square-section blank is used continuously. The drive-end spur has a square hole into which the wood blank is pushed to a tight fit. At the outboard end the tailstock point may be used, but it is better to use a revolving socket in place of the normal point; this is much less likely to split the blank. Again the socket has a square section set to the standard blank dimensions, and

provides a very positive location without applying lateral pressure.

A similar drive arrangement is often useful for production runs of stair spindles, but this is something that you would have to make for yourself, or have made to order, as there are no off-the-shelf units available. Most stair spindle producers use a conventional cross-head drive bit and tail point.

Hollow Vases and Tall Goblets

There are a range of options available here. One of the determining factors is how much waste material you have. Certainly the two most secure methods of attachment are by the four-jaw chuck gripping on to the waste, which is the most positive method, or by a small face plate screwed on to the waste zone. The face plate fixing is less positive in some end grains. In both cases a length of waste between the base of the piece and the mounting device allows free working. The finished item is finally parted off this plug.

The essence of turning items where you cannot provide outboard end support, is, obviously, to have a really firm fixing at the drive end. The sideways pressure exerted when working up near the top of the object is quite considerable, even with the lightest of cutting strokes. Relying upon a drive fixing at the base alone is not really safe, and yet you cannot restrain with the tailstock as you will be working across the end face.

So the method of holding the base is only half the story. A second support is needed somewhere near the outboard end and this is best provided with a long-work steady. Old-time steadies had wood or brass fingers, which were clamped to bear on the rotating timber. These marked the surface, sometimes quite badly. Modern steadies have three ball races mounted to bear on the workpiece, but even these can cause some marking.

The ball races have to bear on a relatively flat surface. A sloping contact point will cause the bearing to apply a pressure that can draw the base away from anything but the

Turning a long-necked vase. The blank started as a grasstree log held between centres. A flat base area was cleaned for the face plate, which is screwed on to a waste collar. This will be finally turned away by reverse chucking.

firmest base mounting (or push it harder on to the base if the slope is in the other direction). When making tall grasstree vases I leave a collar on the outside wall for the steady to bear against. When the hollowing is finished, a plug is fitted into the open neck and the tailstock point is brought up on to this so that the collar can be turned away, the outside finished and the item parted off from the base.

Hollowing out. A running track is left for the long-work steady to run on. A Stewart slicer is being used to start the hollowing process. Once hollowing is complete a wooden plug will be fitted and the tailstock point be brought up so the running track can be turned away.

When using the long steady on spindles – either to turn off the outboard end or to drill out a centre – there is not the same lateral pressure as there is in hollowing out a vase. A collar of wood is no longer necessary, and a few wraps of masking tape will provide a track for the bearing races to run on without marking the surface.

Candlesticks and Standard Lamps

The profile turning will probably be done using cross-head drive and tailstock. If the item is of any length the long-work steady can minimize flexing and also vibration.

The drilling-out process requires exactly the same fixing as for hollowing vases and goblets. The best method is to allow a length of waste wood and clamp this in to a four-jaw chuck.

Again a very firm clamping is necessary as drilling into dry end grain with a saw tooth bit exerts a lot of pressure and friction drag. Despite the fact that it is torsional load rather than lateral pressure, the long-work steady is still required to hold the piece central for the initial drilling. Once the drill has penetrated, it provides its own centring and stabilization.

Drilling out is done with a saw tooth bit, and the normal mounting for the drill bit is a Jacobs chuck mounted on a morse taper and fixed into the tailstock quill. The tailstock is clamped off and the drill is advanced by winding in the quill.

For this task always use the slowest speed that the lathe is capable of. Higher speeds do not drill any faster but create much more friction. This task will also show you just how dry the timber really was. I have had 'air-dried' timbers that generated so much steam that the drill was hidden in the cloud.

To get any depth of drilling, the headstock will have to be repositioned two or three times. Wind the quill in, move up the tail-

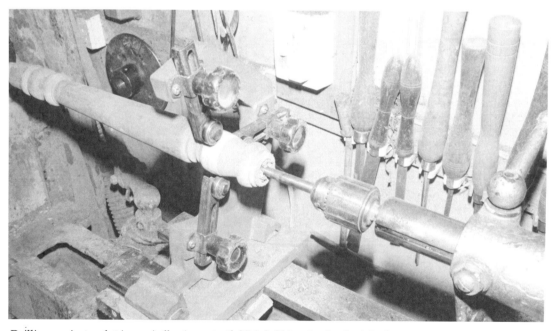

Drilling a spigot socket in a spindle. A saw tooth bit is held in a Jacobs chuck in the tailstock. It is kept in tension so that a cross-head drive spur can be used in the headstock. Stability is achieved with the long-work steady, which runs on a track of masking tape to avoid marking the finished surface.

stock, reclamp and drill in again. It is advisable to withdraw the drill head completely between each repositioning and allow a few moments cooling. This also serves another function. The build-up of swarf behind the drill can sometimes lock it in, particularly if the timber was in the slightest degree moist.

Always, when re-entering with the drill, do it with the lathe motor stopped. Even being a fraction off-centre can cause the drill bit to bite on the lip and wrench the workpiece off its mountings.

At one time the maximum length that could be drilled was determined by the shank length of the drill bit, and the possibility of working with the Jacobs and the quill down inside the turning. Now kits of saw tooth bits are available with sections of extension shaft, and it is possible to work to 9–12in (23–30cm) deep. Beyond this, it is a little tricky and so drilling should be done at the slowest possible speeds – 60–100rpm is ideal – and the drill should be completely withdrawn every 2in (5cm) to prevent the build-up of swarf.

Deep drilling generates very considerable friction and heat – quite sufficient to split some of the denser hardwoods. A 12in (30cm) hole may require several entries with a long cooling-off period between each.

When making the cable ways in standard-lamp columns, a long-hole auger is used. Most of these are 30–36in (76–90cm) long, and so for a full-height standard lamp you may have to turn the column in three separate sections; these are drilled out and then finally assembled to provide the full length.

Most lathes have a hollow tailstock spindle designed so that a long-hole auger can be fed in, and therefore steadied through the body of the quill. Where this is not a feature of the lathe, it is possible to make or obtain a boring jig that can be fitted into the tool post.

Again, proceed slowly with frequent withdrawals to remove swarf.

Cross-head spurs are now available where the centre point has been replaced by a metal dowel, which fits into an augered hole. With these the cable way can be augered from one end, the dowel spur fitted and the spindle turned round to complete the drilling from the other end. This way, a 36in (90cm) auger will comfortably drill a 5ft (1.5m) spindle.

Goblets, Fruit, Eggs and Boxes

Here again there are several mounting methods available.

Many of the tasks of holding medium and smaller pieces for the first stage of turning can be achieved using one of the combination chuck systems that are currently marketed.

The precision combination chuck that I use offers a number of approaches to holding cylinders, and most other makes of chuck offer similar facilities. The cylinder is first turned between cross-head and tailstock point.

One arrangement is a spigot collet that grips a small spigot turned on the end of the cylinder. Sometimes the spigot makes an effective foot for the finished piece; at other times it may be cut away as the item is parted off from the waste. A second and slightly firmer method of holding is to use a three-piece collar dropped into a spigot groove in the cylinder. The collar is then clamped up by the chuck ring. Again this method requires that there is some waste from which the item can be parted. Both alternatives require initial mounting, probably between centres, while the spigot or grooves are cut.

Some turners use cup chucks into which the end of the cylinder is driven. These also require a length of waste and are not very effective in resisting sideways pressure over any length. I do not like them and have not used mine for several years.

There are times when a single hole in the main drive end is not objectionable. It may even be useful if the piece is later to be hollowed or drilled out. Under these circumstances a screw chuck can be useful. Driving a screw chuck into the end of a cylinder is fine so long as the cylinder end is absolutely square. You can get away with being off-square when turning a spigot collar, but not

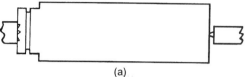

(a)

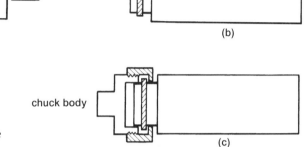

(b)

chuck body

(c)

screwed
collar

Split ring collet for firm end mounting of cylinders. The zone to be mounted is cut down to the diameter of the chuck body (a) with a ring groove cut for the split ring collet. This then sits in the groove (b), but has to be removed to slide on the chuck's screwed collar. The screwed collar grips the split ring against the chuck body (c). This provides the firmest of all grips for goblet and box turning, being even more stable than a four-jaw chuck.

with a screw chuck. And don't think you can compensate for an off-square cut by backing off a little on the screw and then centring on the tailstock point – it does not work and usually results in a broken screw.

Pepper Mills and Like Items

Again, the first stage may be cross head and spur, or straight into a jaw chuck. Hollowing is done with the saw tooth bit working from each end.

Hollow tubes are best held on a mandrel with one end of the mandrel clamped in a jaw chuck. Many makers of small mills drill out the centres of the rough blank using the pillar drill, and then do all the roughing and finish turning of the exterior with a single mounting on a mandrel.

My mandrels are lengths of screwed rod with turned plug collars, washers and lock nuts. Various lengths of rod and a series of tapered collars accommodate a range of standard tubes.

The inboard end is clamped in a four-jaw chuck. There are three alternatives for the outboard end, which has to be accurately

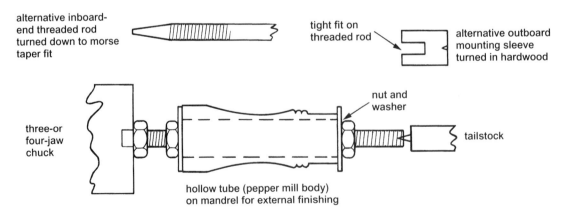

alternative inboard-end threaded rod turned down to morse taper fit

tight fit on threaded rod

alternative outboard mounting sleeve turned in hardwood

three-or four-jaw chuck

nut and washer

tailstock

hollow tube (pepper mill body) on mandrel for external finishing

Turning tube forms on a mandrel. The centre-point can be fixed with an HSS drill in a Jacobs chuck with the mandrel held in a tight-fitting sleeve running in a long-work steady.

74

positioned with the tailstock point or similar item. One way is to drill a centre hole in the mandrel rod, but getting this accurate is not easy; the second way is to turn the end of the rods down to fit into a ring centre; the third, and simplest, is a drilled wooden boss that fits over the end of the screwed rod, and then has an outboard end centre-mark for the standard tailstock point.

Chess Pieces and Small Items

Turning small items such as chess pieces and lamp pulls was always a four-jaw chuck job. I would normally mount a blank long enough to make three or so items, parting each off from the end as it was finished. The trouble was that the third one was so dwarfed by my 5in (2cm) diameter chuck with its massive jaws that it caused me to tense up, often resulting in the wrecking of a near-finished piece.

Then Craft Supplies introduced a tiny four-jaw chuck insert for their precision combination chuck. This was precisely what was needed. However, I still use long blanks and rough out a number of pieces as a single spindle before separating them and finishing each off on the combination chuck with the jaw set fitted.

The vast majority of advanced work done on small pieces does not use commercial chucks at all.

Bonnie Klien, the American turner who specializes in beautiful tiny objects turned in a wide variety of materials, has a large number of very small face plates. The piece of material to be turned is glued on to a small block of wood using either gap-filling grade superglue or an epoxy resin glue. The wood blocks are fixed to the face plates with fabric-based double-sided sticky tape. This arrangement is perfectly adequate for turning even the hardest of materials. The objects are turned right down to the wood block and are then parted off by cutting through the base block. One base will make four or five items before it has been parted right away!

Inserts turn the combination chuck into a miniature four-jaw unit – ideal for turning chess pieces.

Some makers of small boxes – particularly those who specialize in globe form boxes – use standard between centres methods to produce the first cylinder, but thereafter work entirely with cup and spigot chucks turned out of scrap wood. A recess (cup) chuck holds the cylinder while the external walls are worked and the lid is formed and parted off. The main body is then hollowed out. Next the lid is refitted and the joint faired off. The lid is then inverted into another cup chuck made to give a tight fit; then it too is hollowed out. There are times when this second cup chuck can also be used to hold the inverted body while the lower wall and base are cleaned off. An alternative is to make a spigot on to which the box can be pushed for base cleaning.

Obviously the making of wooden chucks, cup or spigot, requires that they be an accurate and tight fit.

Some pieces require the gripping of a rounded shape – such as turned eggs or bowling balls for end finishing. If there is a variation between eggs then a slotted cup chuck with a clamping band (large jubilee clip) is used to adjust between the different egg diameters. When turning skills are such that each egg is always to the same diameter the expert has a single cup chuck into which every egg can be pushed in turn.

Bowling balls have to be of exactly the same diameter so we have a fixed, single-sized cup. Cup chucks for balls work on the principle that the workpiece bottoms on the inside base of the cup preventing it falling right in. There is probably free space around the rest of the inside of the chuck, but the mouth of the chuck has a tight-fitting rim that grips on to the item to be turned somewhere close to the point of greatest diameter.

Ball cups have a spigot ring fitted to the base for easy mounting, and there is a ¼in (6mm) hole up through the centre with a small spigot plug normally in place. The hole is sometimes necessary when the ball is a snug fit and refuses to be withdrawn from the open mouth. A dowel pushed through the hole will normally dislodge it. The spigot plug is to keep the chuck body relatively air-tight, which provides a vacuum to help hold in a ball that is a fractionally 'loose' fit.

Large Natural-Top Bowls, Deep Bowls and Hollow Vessels

Usually, although not always, large items of this nature are going to require more than one sequence/method of mounting. Sometimes four different approaches will be used before the single vessel is finished.

Very, very few turners have band saws large enough to preshape all of the blocks that they wish to turn. Even some smaller, awkward-shaped blocks may not sit well on a saw table, so the roughing to a round is still done on the lathe. We will look at this problem a little more closely in Chapter 9.

With smaller blocks for roughing round the profile and foot, I frequently use a pin chuck as the driver, and support the outboard end with the tailstock point. Pin chucks are simple to fit, requiring only a single hole drilled with a saw tooth bit. They are, however, only reliable in reasonably dry, denser clean wood, free from rot and faults. In bad, soft or wet timber the pin sinks into the wood

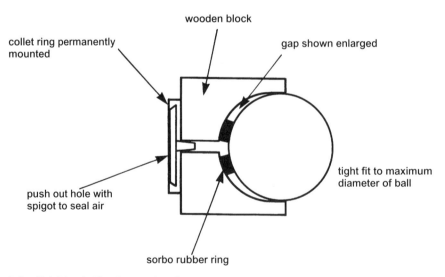

Cup chuck for finishing balls of a regular size.

and fails to provide the necessary wedge to transmit drive.

A recently introduced alternative is the two-prong bowl drive designed to work with the Precision chuck. The large prongs on this are of sufficient size to bite well into most blocks and provide an effective drive for roughing to shape (between centres).

When it comes to larger blocks, the only real solution is a small-diameter face plate placed on what will be the top of the vessel and fixed with long screws or coach bolts. This allows the outside of the vessel to be turned, the base to be formed and cleaned, and provision to be made for the second stage of drive attachment. Suitable plates have to be custom made or adapted from commercially available face plates, as they require more screw holes than are normally provided. The ideal is 4–6in (10–15cm) in diameter, probably of ⅜–½in (9–12mm) plate and drilled close to the rim to accept a number of ¼in (6mm) diameter, 2–3in (5–7cm) long, square-headed coach bolts. If you have an air supply in the workshop these are easy to drive in with a pneumatic gun; otherwise a couple of hammer blows, followed by tightening in with a cranked ring spanner should do.

There are times when a large block is going to be shaped inside and out from a single face plate mounting, and this is often the approach used to work deep vessels. This can be done in one of two ways. The first is similar to some of the one-point mountings we have already looked at. The vessel is turned, leaving a waste block, which is finally parted off. The second method is to have a slightly larger face plate with the screws in the outer ring of holes. The screw holes are now in the

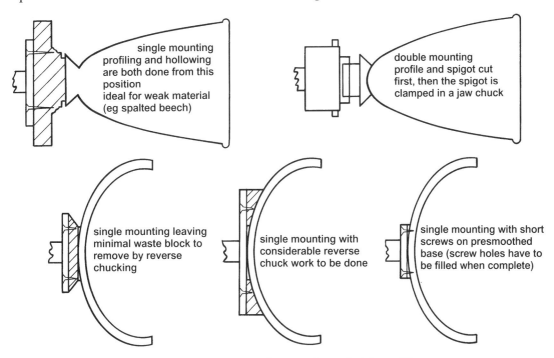

single mounting
profiling and hollowing
are both done from this
position
ideal for weak material
(eg spalted beech)

double mounting
profile and spigot cut
first, then the spigot is
clamped in a jaw chuck

single mounting leaving
minimal waste block to
remove by reverse
chucking

single mounting with
considerable reverse
chuck work to be done

single mounting with short
screws on presmoothed
base (screw holes have to
be filled when complete)

Various mountings for large blocks. With a single mounting as in (a), profiling and hollowing can both be done from one position. This is ideal for weak material, such as spalted beech. When two mountings are necessary, the profile and spigot are cut first, then the spigot is clamped in a jaw chuck (b); this is not ideal for large pieces.

dead wood outside the profile of the vessel. Again, to start with, the tailstock outboard end support is brought into play until the worst part of the outer shaping has been completed.

Once the main part of the outer wall has been shaped and smoothed and the inside shaped and totally finished, the face plate is removed from the base and the vessel is remounted on the lathe with the base outwards so that the waste can be turned away, the full profile achieved, and the outside and base of the vessel finished. This is what is known as reverse chucking – the last of the basic approaches we will be outlining.

Salad and Fruit Bowls and Deeper Platters

Although these are primarily driven with a face plate and are not supported by the tailstock, they do still require at least two mountings.

First they are attached to the lathe with the base outwards. This can be done using a small face plate, a robust screw chuck or a pin chuck depending upon the eventual depth of the bowl. For bowls with a diameter greater than 10in (25cm) (or less in extremely hard woods) a simple screw chuck is not recommended. Mounted this way the external profile is worked and finished and the base is prepared to take the secondary mounting.

Several alternatives are now available. Before demounting, the outline diameter of the face plate can be scribed on the base using scribe callipers. Once demounted, the face plate is then fixed to the base with short screws. Using the scribed ring the plate can be positioned very accurately. The second method is to fix a dovetail ring for attaching to an expanding spigot of a combination chuck. Again the ring is accurately located by tracing on its outline with callipers before demounting from the lathe.

The most widely used approach is to inset into the base of the wood a dovetail groove for direct mounting on to an expanding spigot. By keeping the recess shallow it is still possible to work to a thin base. This is a secure mounting, which will tolerate heavy work during the hollowing-out process. It does, however, leave a dovetail recess, which many find undesirable.

On smaller bowls and dishes a spigot groove may be cut into the base for gripping with a spigot collet chuck.

A three- or four-jaw chuck may also be used on larger items. By cutting a recess into the base, a jaw chuck fitted with expanding jaws can provide a moderately secure mounting.

For a completely smooth and unblemished base the three- or four-jaw chuck may again come into play. The simplest route is to leave a spigot of 1–1½in (2.5–3.7cm) in length, and part the finished piece off from the waste later.

Another alternative for smaller items is to incorporate a small foot into the design. The foot is turned and finished and then becomes the spigot for remounting. It is pinch clamped between contracting jaws. By wrapping three or four turns of masking tape around the foot it is possible to prevent jaw marks marring the finish.

The third alternative is set up before the piece is demounted. A wood block is glued to the base, probably with hot-melt glue. This is then turned to provide a spigot for gripping in a jaw chuck.

Whether the spigot is solid or glued on, it has to be removed later by reverse chucking.

Thin Platters, Game Boards and Similar Items

Here the problem is that you do not wish to drive any screws into the wood at any stage.

First glue a spigot block on to what will be the top face. This should be positioned as close to the centre as possible. The block may be round or square, and will probably be glued end grain on. Some turners use gap-filling superglue for speed, others a hot-melt glue from a glue gun. I prefer the latter as it tolerates some surface unevenness. Obviously you have to allow a short while for the glue to set, so the hot-melt method is best suited to batch runs.

The spigot is clamped in a jaw chuck (if it is square section it has to be a four-jaw). The base and outer profile of the workpiece are finished and a second spigot block is then glued on the centre of the base. It is not necessary to position this precisely, nor do you need to allow full hot-melt glue setting time for this fixing, as the tailstock can be brought up to keep the block in place while it is turned to a round and trued.

If this second wood block is glued side grain on, fix it with the grain at right angles to the grain of the platter blank. If it is glued on end grain, the orientation does not matter so much. The reason for this positioning will emerge shortly.

The workpiece is taken off the lathe and a swift sideways blow with a hammer will remove the original base block. The new spigot block is now clamped in the jaw chuck and the top profile of the platter is worked.

When finished, the piece is demounted, the block removed and any traces left behind are sanded clear. It is usually possible to knock the second block off as we did the first with a swift sideways blow with a hammer. However, make sure it is hit in the direction of the grain of the platter so that it is less likely to raise splinters off the finished base. It may be possible to hand or power sand the base effectively to a good finish. If there has been any grain pulling as the second spigot block was knocked away, the platter will need reverse chucking for the base cleaning.

There is a traditional method of preventing the problem of possible tear-out. It is what is known as the 'glue sandwich' method. Here the waste block is glued to the workpiece using any suitable glue, but between block and workpiece is a sandwich of paper. Sugar paper is ideal, as are postcards or similar card. The joint is quite strong enough to permit full working on the piece, but can be broken fairly easily with no danger of tearing

fibres from a finished surface. If using traditional hot glues the parting can be assisted using a long, thin, flexible knife blade that has been heated. This is pushed into the joint and melts the glue.

Mounting for Off-Centre Turning

Full entry into the world of ornamental turning will introduce you to beautiful, machine-made chucks that are designed to produce measured levels of offset. A lot can, however, be done without going to such lengths.

Some furniture legs – such as the cabriole legs for chairs – require turning on two centres before finishing off by hand carving. This is normally achieved with the conventional spur drive working to a set distance either side of the centre axis. Some designs also require driving from one end of one axis and then turning the piece round on the lathe and driving from the other end to an offset axis.

With bowls and open forms a very useful chucking device can be made for producing oval recesses. The device has a face plate mounted between two rails. The rails are fixed to a board, which in turn is mounted on to a spigot chuck. The rails grip the face plate in position and by slackening the rail screws the plate can be moved laterally.

The sliding face plate is fixed to the centre of the blank to be turned and the centre of the bowl is hollowed out. The face plate is then moved in the rails to the required amount off-centre and the bowl is again hollowed. Next, the face plate is given an equal offset to the other side of centre and the third hollowing is undertaken. The small shoulder between each ring is carved or power-filed away. A very attractive arrangement is to take three or four positions either side of centre, each one with a smaller diameter.

The same device is also used for producing patterns of concentric decorative grooves with each set of grooves at different, offset centres.

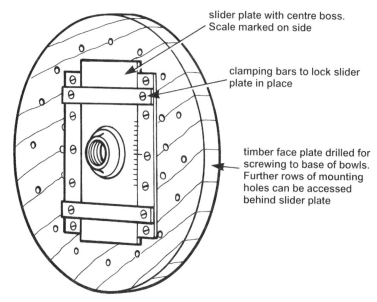

slider plate with centre boss. Scale marked on side

clamping bars to lock slider plate in place

timber face plate drilled for screwing to base of bowls. Further rows of mounting holes can be accessed behind slider plate

backing plate for oval turning of bowls

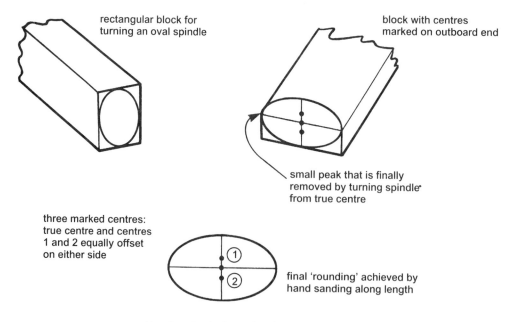

rectangular block for turning an oval spindle

block with centres marked on outboard end

small peak that is finally removed by turning spindle from true centre

three marked centres: true centre and centres 1 and 2 equally offset on either side

① ②

final 'rounding' achieved by hand sanding along length

oval turning of spindles using three centre

Off-centre turning.

Finishing the Bases – Reverse Chucking

The title reverse chucking specifically applies to chucking the workpiece for final base shaping and finishing. As will be seen from the foregoing, it may be the second chucking of the piece. It may equally be the fourth.

Two basic approaches are used. One is to grip the top of the workpiece in some way. The other is to clamp the piece between a padded, friction-drive boss, and an outboard or tailstock end support.

The first method is fine for clean-grained timber, for even, level rims, and, particularly, for items that are fairly shallow, and ideally have vertical walls, such as level-rim bowls and dishes. When the bowl is finished, mount a piece of clean scrap wood on the lathe, true the face and then cut a spigot recess into which the bowl' will fit. The recess should have vertical walls and it should be 'box-lid

tight' on the bowl or platter, that is, the work-piece should be held in place by vacuum and come away with a plop of inrushing air.

Although a tight fit, you may wish to play for safety and bring up the tailstock. If you do, slip a small disc between the point and the bowl base to prevent marking. Most of the base area can be cleaned and certainly the dovetail shoulders can be cut away with the tailstock support in place. It does, however, have finally to be withdrawn for the last bit of finishing. Now the tool rest is brought up close and parallel to the base, which will prevent the bowl flying off. Alternatively, the left hand bearing lightly on the vessel will hold it in place for the few seconds required to clean away the centre.

The trouble with this method of reverse chucking is that you may need a new scrap timber face plate for each bowl, and, particularly . if your work is fairly large, this can

The step block for reverse chucking. The point has been removed from the tailstock to avoid marking the bowl. The shoulders of the bottom spigot will now be rounded off.

A large vase in spalted beech on the last step of the step block. The waste wood block on which the vase was mounted for hollowing has now been turned away.

mean the use of more 'scrap' timber than you have!

The second variation again uses scrap timber and is also used specifically on regular-rimmed bowl forms. Here the 'scrap' timber is a large, deep bowl blank. This is best permanently fixed to a dovetail ring so that it can be remounted accurately over and over again on a combination chuck. The blank is turned to give a series of steps, each about ½in (12mm) deep. The diameter of the steps should be set to the various diameters of your most popular range of work. In cutting the steps, work rough! Use a blunt tool and tear the wood as much as possible. I have used a piece of dry elm (non-burred) and really torn it. The rougher it is the better friction grip it will give in use.

While an airtight fit is not required, for some jobs you may still need a fairly precise fit. You can always reshape one of the steps.

(Eventually you will turn it all away but it takes a long time.) The inverted bowl is fitted over the appropriate step and the tailstock is brought up to hold the workpiece in place.

If the step does not provide a precise fit and you do not wish to turn a new step to exact size, then to help in centring, position the tool rest close to the rim of the vessel and turn by hand, watching the gap between rim and tool rest. Using the size of the gap as a tell-tale indication, adjust the position of the workpiece; by constantly readjusting and reducing the gap to a hairbreadth you can achieve near exact centre location.

For natural-top vessels you cannot have the rim bearing down on to a face plate. We now need something that will fit right down into the vessel.

Sometimes it is possible to turn a large, rough-tapered plug on to which the vessel can be push-fitted, using a twist or two of

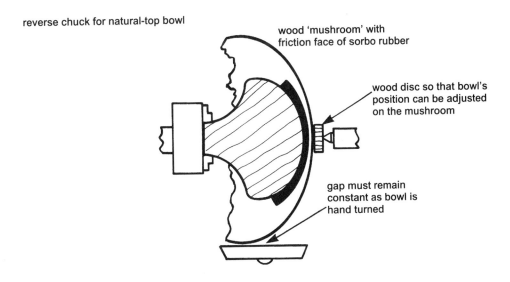

reverse chuck for natural-top bowl

wood 'mushroom' with friction face of sorbo rubber

wood disc so that bowl's position can be adjusted on the mushroom

gap must remain constant as bowl is hand turned

short spindle mounted for drilling

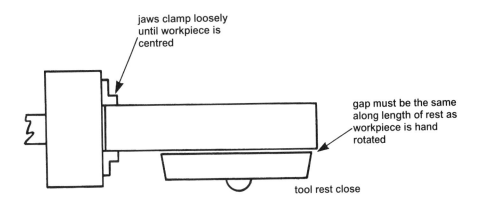

jaws clamp loosely until workpiece is centred

gap must be the same along length of rest as workpiece is hand rotated

tool rest close

Using the tool rest to centre jaw-chuck mounted items.

foam rubber both to provide friction and to prevent damage to the finished inside of the workpiece. Here again the plug has to be turned to the specific diameter and form that you are working on.

The plug itself would normally be driven through a spigot clamped in a jaw chuck.

Care needs to be taken with taper plugs. If the tailstock quill is tightened up too hard it can cause the walls of the vessel to split. Much better is a 'mushroom', which fits right down into the base of the object. Probably a range of four mushrooms will accommodate the typical run of work; two long and two short, with one of narrow, sharp radius, and the other of broad, flatter radius in each length.

Mushrooms are held in a jaw chuck and they have to turn the vessel, which is usually already oiled and polished, relying on surface friction alone. Hence they are best covered with a high-friction material – a layer of sorbo rubber turned right over and stapled under the rim of the mushroom is ideal.

83

To help mount the mushrooms with reasonable accuracy, the outboard end has a recess for alignment against the tailstock point until the jaws of the chuck are clamped up. Once the workpiece has been nipped in, the final positioning is done using the tool rest to tell you when it's right. Using this arrangement the tailstock has to be left in position at all times.

SPECIAL CHUCKS

Let's come back to turned rim items rather than natural tops. Friction-fits work, but they can sometimes slip and occasionally mark a finished surface. There is also the problem we have twice highlighted: you need a new disc or taper for each size of item. The solution to this problem is to use wooden jaw plates that extend the capacity of a four-jaw chuck. Most jaw chuck makers can now provide chuck plates for mounting wooden jaws on their chucks.

With my four-jaw chuck I use two sets of wooden jaw plates, one for a contraction or clamp-fit mounting, and one to provide an expansion grip. Both have wooden jaws made from a quarter-segmented disc of 14in (35cm) diameter. The wood jaws are permanently fixed to their own plates. This two-set approach is necessary because of the hassle of unscrewing and refixing wooden jaws to a single set of plates each time I want to change from internal to external clamping. The cost of the extra set of metal jaw plates is more than worthwhile. I must admit that there are times when I would even welcome the availability of two or even three chuck bodies for super versatility.

My first set of wood jaws were in oak. One soon split in use and the flying platter whistled past my ear. Now they are in beech. The disc was band sawn to a round, mounted on a small face plate and the back face was cleaned and trued. The centre was carefully marked. Once the face plate had been removed, the disc was sawn into accurate

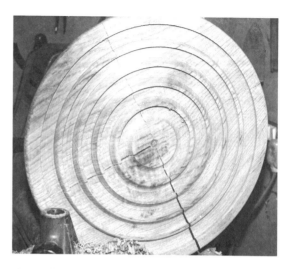

Grooved wooden jaw plates can be fitted to a four-jaw chuck for contraction gripping the rims of bowls. This set was made in oak but flew apart at speed. Later models were made in beech.

quarter-segments and fitted to the steel jaw plates with bright zinc countersunk screws. The chuck was now fitted to the lathe, the rim and front face of the wood plates cleaned and the grooves were cut. In this way the grooves were accurately centred.

On both expanding and contracting chucks the bowl-holding recesses can be spaced at 1in (2.5cm) intervals as there is sufficient movement to then give infinite variability. The outer recess is just ½in (12mm) in from the outside rim. The smallest recess is 5in (12cm) in diameter, as anything below this can be handled by the basic jaw chuck itself.

On the externally gripping chuck, the recesses are undercut on the gripping face, have a ½in (12mm) wide flat bottom to the groove, and then slope up to form the next shoulder. Clearly this profile is not suitable if you make bowls with walls considerably over ½in (12mm) thick, nor can it be used to grip the solid bases of vases or the like. But then it is not intended to – it is designed specifically for reverse chucking bowls.

The second set of wooden jaws grip from the inside of the workpiece by expansion. The

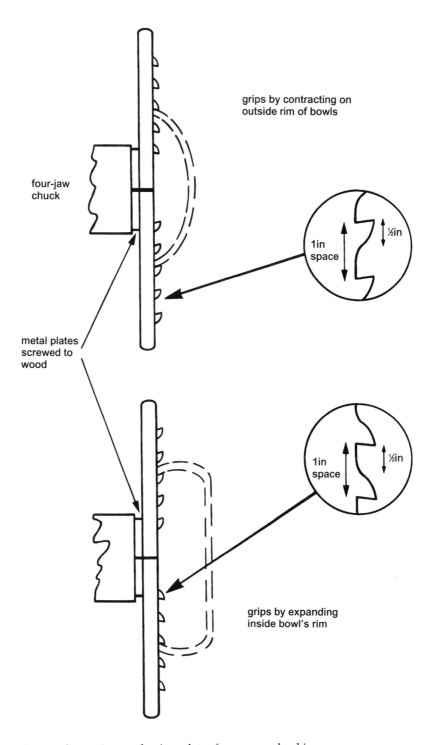

grips by contracting on
outside rim of bowls

four-jaw
chuck

½in

1in
space

metal plates
screwed to
wood

1in
space

½in

grips by expanding
inside bowl's rim

Contracting- and expanding-grip wooden jaw plates for reverse chucking.

The wood jaws in use. This bowl turned in green elm had moved considerably on drying. Here the base is being levelled off.

principle is exactly the same as the contracting jaws, except that the recesses are reverse profiled. By using a 2in (5cm) thick disc the recesses can be a little deeper to give a slightly longer spigot.

In both cases the recesses, including the undercut zones, have been scraped to leave a rough 'friction' finish.

There is a third clamping option which is of occasional use. For this, a 14in (35cm) diameter, 1in (2.5cm) thick disc was used. It was turned roughly true, and a dovetail ring was permanently fitted. Now mounted with the ring fixed on to the spigot chuck, the disc was finely trued and a series of pencil lines were marked to give location circles at ¼in (6mm) intervals from the centre right out to the rim. Using the point of a skew chisel, the pencil circles were incised to give permanent positioning guides.

Next, working on the quarter-segments, four radial grooves were cut. These pierce right through the discs and were cut with a ¼in (6mm) router cutter. They are for locating the mounting cramps.

Various cramps have been made and these are held in place using lengths of threaded rod and butterfly nuts.

One set of cramps fit close to the disc and can be used for gripping the rim of platters and similar objects. Another set of close-fitting cramps will grip bowls with sloping walls.

There is then a set of rings that can be slipped over the base of different diameters of bowls and vases. The rings are discs of 8mm ply. Longer lengths of threaded rod grip the vessel between the rings and the disc.

One lesson quickly learnt was that the length of rod was fairly critical. A simple nut with the rod peaned over at the outer end is less likely to catch clothes, hand or tools. This means that the butterfly adjusters need to be inboard. Too long a length of exposed rod now fouls the headstock. The kit has 4, 6, 8 and 10in (10, 15, 20, 25cm) rods. I found that greater lengths than this provided a unit that was altogether too 'floppy'.

This 'monstrosity kit' is frightening at anything over the lowest lathe speed and therefore tends to be a tool of last resort! Where the cage has really paid for itself is when a piece of less sound timber is being hollowed on a dovetail spigot and the dovetail breaks away. Mounted in the cage a new dovetail can be cut.

Although in working through the main chucking methods we have taken each one separately and tied it to a type of turning or a specific pattern of workpiece, they are not exclusive. Often they are used in combination to overcome a particular problem.

The basic principle of making a grooved plate or a tapered plug can, and has been, modified in 101 ways. Finishing off the bases of unusual items has been facilitated by a range of odd spigots and cups. Differences in sizes between two similar items may be accommodated by tapers, but strips of friction materials or wraps of masking tape are often used to get a good positive drive. Frequently the tailstock point does not bear

The 'monstrosity' kit. The kit is used to hold vases and natural-top pieces for reverse chuck work.

The cage in use. A vase is in the cage for the base to be finished. There is a shaped block inside the vase to help stability. It is turned at the slowest possible speed.

A shallow bowl in the cage. In this format the cage is very effective and quite rigid. Here it is being used on a broad, roll-rim bowl that cannot be gripped in jaw plates.

directly on to the workpiece but on to some pad or spigot. Once the candle hole is drilled out of the top of a candlestick a wooden plug is pushed into the hole, and the tailstock supports this while finishing and polishing proceed, and certainly while the item is being parted off.

What of the hazards? Clearly the first one is the four-jaw chuck itself. A ring of car inner tube helps to mask the edge of the jaws and gives some protection; but as I said earlier I have the scars to prove that it is no real answer. Care has to be taken in mounting shaken timber – it can fly apart, or the dovetail can give way and the vessel take off. Screwing face plates into end grain can be dodgy, particularly when you are using brutal methods of hollowing out deep forms: before now I have used a dozen 3in (7cm) coach bolts to fix a block to the face plate. The number of holes on many standard face plates is not sufficient and extra holes can be useful. The use of the outer holes on a face plate is more secure than using the inner ring. The moment that the tailstock can be brought into play as outboard support, the problems of security of mounting are lessened. It never ceases to surprise me how four tiny cross-heads will drive huge lengths of large-diameter spindles.

Some people have a fortune tied up in a vast array of mounting devices, and my own investment is not insignificant. Others have one spur drive and one face plate, backed up with a cupboard full of home-made cups and spigots – but then some people have a lot more ingenuity!

Perhaps Bonnie Klien is right. A face plate, a wood block and a glue pot is all that you really need.

7 Tools and Techniques

CUTTING WOOD

Most woodturners eventually acquire a complete range of basic tools, although many are not used often as the turner tends to focus upon a particular specialization in turning. However, it does not matter what you have been turning, or whether you are beginner or expert, the basic principles of cutting wood are fundamental – whatever the tool and whatever the item being worked upon. With an understanding of those principles you can apply them to any and every tool, and start to design tools for yourself. It has to be said that almost every advanced turner has made some tools for himself, even if only reprofiled scrapers.

It is interesting how often when demonstrating turning, someone with some years experience will bring up a workpiece with a defect and ask how to deal with it. The most common issue is fluffy torn grain on the inside walls of bowls. The cause of this problem is well known (and is something we all get at times); what concerns me is that an experienced turner should ask what to do about it, because in asking he indicates that he does not understand the basic principles of cutting wood.

Basic Principles

All turning tools are derived from one fundamental requirement, and two key modifiers. The requirement is to cut the grain cleanly; and the modifiers are the profile shapes we are working to at the time and the best possible angle of attack or tool presentation within that form. These two factors determine the tool form, shape and profile, and the ideal bevel angle.

All turning tools are merely means of *cutting* wood. Basically they have different shapes to accommodate the different profiles that we will be working on, and in each case the tool profile roughly mimics and therefore determines the profile we are trying to create. A skew is straight for cutting straight-walled cylinders and vertical faces; a gouge is rounded for hollowing out rounded curves; a domed scraper is domed for producing long, flowing concave curves; a diamond point is used for angular insertions, a ring-cutting scraper for cutting rings, and so on.

Provision is often made for increasing the efficiency and utility of the tool by small modifications to the basic profile; and use is facilitated by eliminating dangers – for example, corners are cut back to reduce the risk of them catching and causing a dig-in.

Wood cuts best when it is attacked along the grain, and when the ends of the fibres are planed off where they are still firmly supported by the fibres underneath. The cutting blade is so angled just to take off long thin slivers or the ends of fibres, and not to cut too deeply into them. Let's call this downhill cutting. The wood comes away in long, broad, thin shavings and leaves a smooth, unblemished surface.

The moment you start to cut 'uphill' into fibres that are unsupported, the chances are that however carefully the blade is angled it will dip under a fibre that will be pushed up; as it is unsupported, it will lift off and tear away as a splinter. Often the splinter will go from a sharp initial point into a wedge, getting ever deeper until it ultimately breaks off, leaving a jagged tear in the main timber. The shavings are often shorter, and while still broad, tend to be thicker. Any curl in the shaving is formed by a series of cracks.

If we now cut across the grain, still trying to make a planing cut, we may sometimes get away with it if the tool is sharp enough and angled just to skim off the top. We may, however, get under the long side of the fibre and roll it off. The splinter will probably be cigar-shaped, pointed at each end, while the mark in the main body of the timber is a shallow, narrow trough lying along the grain. The shavings are much shorter and break up to the touch.

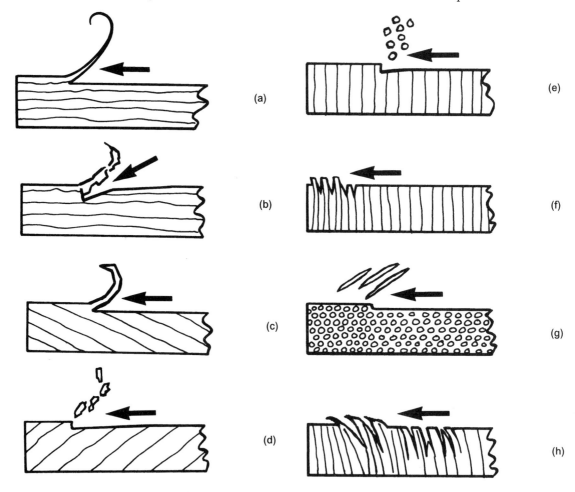

Cutting along, down and across grain. (a) shows a horizontal cut along the grain; this gives an even depth, long, curly shavings and a smooth surface. An angled cut into the grain (b) produces broken, wedge-shaped shavings and a smooth surface. A horizontal cut into rising grain (c) gives split shavings but a smooth finish. When falling grain is cut into horizontally (d), however, there is a tendency for the fibres to push apart and the surface is torn. A horizontal cut across end grain (e) gives a smooth finish but requires a lot of effort; while a horizontal cut across unsupported end grain (f) pushes the fibres apart, causing break-out and a rough surface. A horizontal cut across the grain (g) gives long fibres that roll off as splinters and a ridged surface. Cutting into near-vertical grain (h) separates fibres and causes breaks over fibre ends; the finish is torn and fluffy, notably with less sharp tools.

When we cut across the end grain at right angles we shear off the ends. There is more likely to be dust than shavings, although in wet or resinous timbers the dust hangs together in small flakes. Because each fibre of the grain is tightly held in place by the fibres surrounding it, there is no tendency to tear or splinter – until you come to an edge where the grain is no longer supported. Now the last few fibres are pushed away from the main body and the ends do not shear off, but are pushed over so that a broken surface is created. Of course, if the tool is not really sharp it pushes the fibres apart, and does not shear off the ends but breaks them apart, giving fluffy breaks and deep crevices between adjacent fibres.

Theory into Practice – Turning a Bowl

Now think about these basic principles in terms of turning a bowl. We will use a conventional approach with the grain lying parallel to the face plate.

Let's start by cutting this blank with a cutting edge offered at right angles to the lathe's axis.

On the outside of the wall as the blank rotates we pass through a continuous sequence of planing downhill, shearing supported end grain, shearing unsupported end grain, planing uphill into unsupported grain, and finally back to the beginning and the next cycle of planing downhill, as we start on the second half of the first full rotation, and so on.

Of the eight basic segments of each rotation, only four would give us a clean

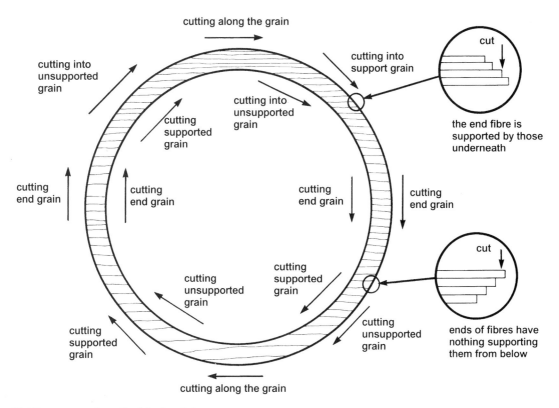

Cutting segments as the blank rotates.

finish and four would probably result in tearing – two of the four in really fluffy tearing of the worst and sometimes irreparable kind; and two where splinters are likely to be torn out leaving jagged holes.

Clearly this is not on, so we always try to cut into supported grain. This is done by working the tool from the centre axis of the lathe out towards the maximum diameter of the blank. This is a cut over which there is some confusion in the turning literature. I call it cutting downhill because you are going from the smallest diameter to the largest (the base out towards the rim). It is also downhill if you think about the grain orientation. Cut in this direction, you are going down into the grain by shearing off the exposed ends of fibres. Unfortunately, because you are working from the *base* of the bowl 'up' to the rim, some people refer to it as cutting 'uphill'. It is therefore always safer to talk about cutting from the smallest diameter to the largest.

However, this refers only to the outside wall of the vessel. The position is very different when we start to hollow out a bowl, and particularly when we scrape the inside wall. We are now doing what we said we should not do when considering the eight segment cycle – going into the grain head on, and thus cutting into unsupported fibres twice in every revolution.

So now you should cut from the larger diameter to the smaller. The gouge has a shallower angle of bevel so that the angle between the tool handle axis and the surface of the bowl in the cutting area is fairly shallow. The actual cut is on the side of the gouge tip. Cutting in this direction and with this angle, you are keeping the maximum support for the fibres being cut for as much of the cycle of rotation as possible.

When teaching basic turning it is appropriate to tell students to enter at 9 o'clock with the tool handle held slightly below the axis and make the tip trace an S-shaped arc. As they progress, you no longer give set routines and formulae but explore grain orientation and cutting principles so that each person can

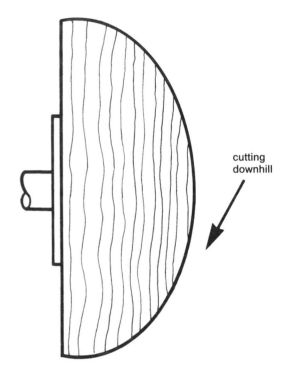

cutting
downhill

Cutting downhill. The cuts are made from the smaller diameter towards the larger, hence 'downhill'. The grain is supported the whole way down provided that the tool handle is angled over the lathe bed.

build up an understanding and can then adapt his technique to the layout of his own lathes and the profiles that he wishes to turn.

I tell students: 'Whenever you create a torn area on a piece of work in progress, stop: clearly identify the orientation of the grain and the level of grain support in the torn area, remember how you offered up the tool to that area, and you will very quickly identify how the poor finish was produced. Now work out how you can present the tool to minimize the assault on unsupported grain; and do better next time!'

Of course there are situations when you just cannot present the tool in a theoretically correct manner, when the profile and the position of elements of the lathe totally prevent it. Furthermore, there may be no alterna-

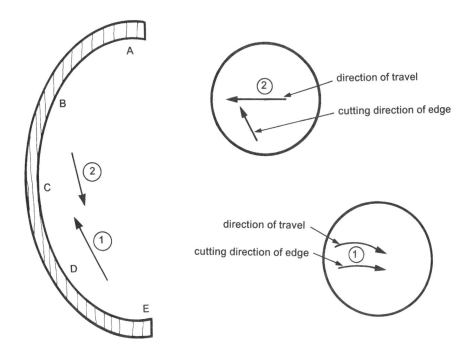

Cutting angles inside a bowl. Zones A and E are end grain and therefore easy to cut; zone D is supported angle grain – again, no problem. Zone B is the worst angle of unsupported angle grain during half rotation when the end grain is descending on to the cutting edge; here a badly torn surface is difficult to rectify. Zone C is either along or across the grain (this will alternate), provided that the cut is·straight across and is not angled. The direction of cut 1 is from 9 o'clock in towards the centre with a U form bowl gouge; the open top of the U points towards 2 o'clock. The direction of cut 2 is from the centre out to the rim with a modified gouge, the U pointing to 12 o'clock. This gives effectively a vertical cut, thus reducing the problem of lack of fibre support. When cutting zone D there is thus much less tearing potential. The shoulder cutting edge of the modified gouge also gives a much finer bevel angle and a sharper, cleaner cut.

tive tool that could be angled better. The first thing to check is whether you could cut in the opposite direction – back towards you instead of away, for example. If this is not possible, then all that you can do now is to get the angle as good as possible, make sure the tool is sharp, and take the most delicate of cuts.

SCRAPERS, CHISELS AND GOUGES

Although all tools are designed to *cut* grain fibres – even scrapers – there are two different principles involved; and below we will describe how different types of scraper are distinguished. We can identify two categories of turning tools:

1 Those that cut with the bevel rubbing
2 Those that cut with the bevel unsupported

These are chisels and scrapers respectively.

All non-scrapers are designed to cut with the bevel rubbing on the timber. This stabil-

93

izes the blade, and accurately controls the depth of cut. The firm pressure exerted to keep the bevel rubbing helps the edge to shear grain – even unsupported grain – rather than break off the ends and tear. The bevel angle precisely fixes the angle at which the edge presents to the grain. The bevel angle also determines the angle at which the tool has to be held to get correct presentation. Because the bevel controls so much, chisels are very forgiving and require less ultimate skill and tool control than scrapers do. This is also why the correct bevel angle is so critical, and why for different profiles and tasks we need a range of bevel angles.

I wish scrapers were not called scrapers – this gives entirely the wrong impression. Admittedly, this is the way that some turners use them – they see them as a crude tool for just tearing away wood to achieve a rough shape (which then requires hours of heavy sanding to produce an end result). Perhaps if we called them 'peeling cutters' or something similar, they would be given the respect due to them.

Here we have a tool without the crutch of the rubbing bevel to control the depth of cut – we have to achieve this with our own unaided skill. The scraper also tends to do its main cutting at right angles to the surface

off the grinder

burr raised on end of scraper

grinder finished, then honed on slip stone

scraper with burr honed away

Cutting edge of scrapers. A cutter that is sharpened on a grinder will have a burr raised on the end. This feather edge cuts the ends off grain and improves the cut on unsupported grain. If the burr is then honed away on a slip stone, the smooth scraper will shear the ends of fibres, provided they are supported.

(actually at a slight downward tilt) – it cannot be substantially tilted or angled as can a gouge, and will, therefore, more frequently be working on unsupported fibres – cross or end grain.

Some turners sharpen the scrapers on a grind wheel, raising a burr on the edge, which they then clean away using a slip stone. This does give a good strong cutting edge, but it is not quite so sharp as an edge with a well-defined burr – particularly when cutting unsupported grain. It has to be recognized, however, that the burr quickly wears or breaks away; for really fine cutting, the touching up of the scraper on the grind wheel is an almost continuous process.

Vibration

There is another problem. The one thing we wish to avoid in all tools, chisels or scrapers, is flexing and vibration. Various things are done to minimize this. The whole process of planing with a skew is unlikely to cause any vibration in the tool tip. The whole tool is firmly supported on the lathe's tool rest, and the cutting tip is also supported by a tool rest immediately behind it – the tool rest formed between the wood and the bevel. Hence skews are made light, and look delicate.

I can hear someone saying 'Nonsense, you often get vibration when planing spindles, causing little ripples on the wood surface.' True, you can get ripples, and true, you get vibration; but it is not the tool that is vibrating. It is usually the wood that is flexing (whipping), and is vibrating under a fixed blade. The ripple or waves occur because at one instant the spindle has flexed towards the tool edge and then at the next flexed away from it. If you continue planing in the same area the tool bevel will start to rise and fall on the waves and will then plane each trough deeper – now (and only now) the tool starts vibrating. The cycle has to be broken to get a smooth finish and this is done by altering the angle of attack, drawing the edge back so that the bevel is just touching the wood rather

direction of vibration-inducing shocks
– along blade and absorbed in handle

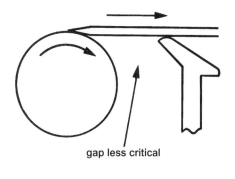

gap less critical

planing with a skew chisel

direction of vibration-inducing
shocks – a direct chatter-
inducing motion

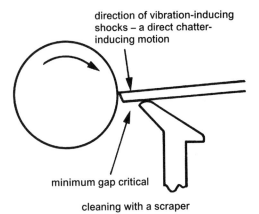

minimum gap critical

cleaning with a scraper

Vibration-inducing moment in skew and scraper cutters.

than resting on it, and making sure that the tool is held rock steady.

Just to complete the argument, bear in mind that the angle of attack of a skew chisel when planing is such that there is virtually no vibration-inducing moment on the blade – the shocks are always back down the axis of the blade, they are not blade-flexing down-

length of overhang of blade X and of rest Y give total possible vibration amplitude $VX + Y = \log V$

bowl rest angled inside but cannot support while cleaning lower arc

in position 1, direct attack. By position 2 and lower; scraping is off side of tool rotational forces are increased

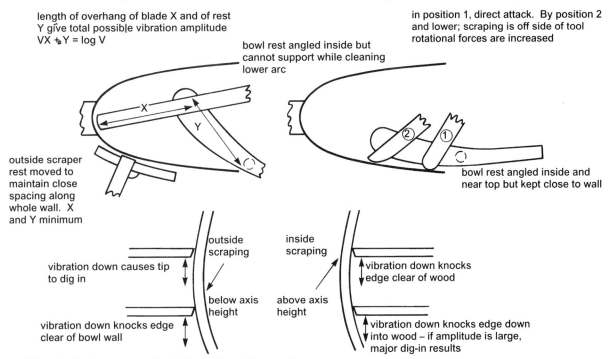

outside scraper rest moved to maintain close spacing along whole wall. X and Y minimum

bowl rest angled inside and near top but kept close to wall

vibration down causes tip to dig in

outside scraping

inside scraping

vibration down knocks edge clear of wood

below axis height

above axis height

vibration down knocks edge clear of bowl wall

vibration down knocks edge down into wood – if amplitude is large, major dig-in results

Vibration in the scraper tip inside and outside vessels.

95

ward blows. It is for this reason that modern skews are made of much lighter, thinner section blanks.

Gouges are skews with the sides bent up, and all that we have said about the skew is equally true of spindle gouges. On top of this, the U form of gouge blades gives a structure that really cannot flex or vibrate. So again they can be made of relatively light section.

Of course bowl gouges are different – we now have a steeper bevel angle and downward blows, and thus vertical flexing forces; hence the need for a stout gauge bar to reduce vibration forces.

Because it is known that scrapers often have to work with long overhangs, and the flat structure of the blade is an optimum vibration-producing device (overgrown chatter tools), scrapers are invariably made heavier than an equivalent-sized chisel. They look heavy, we think of them as heavy, and therefore tend to use them in a heavy-handed way. It has taken me a long time to learn to hold and use my 2in (5cm) wide, domed scraper with even greater delicacy than I would a ¼in (6mm) bowl gouge. Yet that is what is required!

Scraper blades are always vibrating, and the further the tip is from the tool rest the greater will be the amplitude of vibration. There is no rubbing bevel just behind the edge providing a second tool rest. So we have to use the tool in such a way that the vibration is likely to take the edge further away from the wood when in the trough of the vibration cycle, and hold it at optimum cutting position when at the peak of the wave. Hence we scrape the outside wall of vessels with the scraper just below axis height, and move the blade to above axis height when scraping the inside walls.

Dig-In

There are two problems that many turners encounter when scraping the insides of large bowls in rough, burred or pippy timber. Both are dig-in problems, and both can be of some

magnitude. One occurs when smoothing off the inside base – a flat zone at right angles to the lathe axis. The other arises when working the lower section of the inside side walls. Both are understandable when worked out from first principles.

The inside base is likely to be at some distance from the nearest point of the tool rest. Hence scraper blade vibration will be at its greatest. Furthermore, you are cutting across the long grain – rolling up long fibre splinters by pushing them from the side. The scraper gets under a fibre, is pushed down, flexes, then bounces back up to encounter fibres that have now rotated to present the rising blade with relatively unsupported end grain. There is a tiny dig-in, but immediately the raised fibres build up on top of the cutting edge, drawing it deeper into the wood: in milliseconds the tiny dig-in becomes a major plunge and a huge chunk is lifted out of the workpiece.

The side wall principle has similar characteristics but with one or two additional problem elements. The tool rest is set to the optimum position for cutting inside. As the scraper moves in towards the lower side of the wall (nearer the base of the vessel), the length of tool overhang is again increasing. So too is the distance between the part of the tool rest being used for support and the tool post itself. Both scraper blade and tool-rest blade now have long overhangs, and both will flex and vibrate.

Something else is also happening. The blade will inevitably be angled downwards, so by now the tip is cutting below the centre axis. When vibration occurs and there is flexing and a mini dig-in, the fibres on top of the blade push the blade down and wedge it in the reducing gap between bowl and tool rest.

The first answer is to use a heavy-duty (vibration-free) bowl-scraping rest, which can be positioned as far as possible inside the vessel.

The clue to the base-cleaning problem is to use narrow-tipped cutters of massive thickness, such as the front tip of a narrow-blade left skew scraper or diamond cutting side scraper.

Cleaning the walls is also less problematical if a similar thick tool is used. A diamond side scraper with the corner rounded off is quite effective. The problem is also less likely to arise if the cut is made from the base up towards the rim by drawing the tool slowly backwards.

With these thoughts in mind we begin to realize why the tool rest is raised and lowered and why, when scraping the outside wall, the tool tip is presented just below the axis line, while for cleaning up the interior it is raised to just above the centre. We can now also see why, when planing with a skew, the tool rest is set just under the height of the top of the cylinder. I have emphasized the importance of the uphill/downhill concept, and also shown why there are times that we just can't cut the inside walls of some bowls cleanly.

You should also now realize why some turners have a multitude of tools in their armoury. As we identified earlier, all tools have the same simple purpose – that of cutting wood. The different shapes of the tools are simply there to make some tricky tasks easier. It is interesting that some advanced turners have fewer tools than others. (Some gimmick-happy individuals like me have more!) There are turners with only half a dozen – a couple of skews, a bowl gouge, a finger-nail gouge and a couple of scrapers. One Scandinavian master boasts only three tools.

The fewer tools you have the more skilful you have to be. Perhaps I am lazy; if there is a tool that facilitates something that I do regularly, then owning such a tool seems to me to be cost-effective. At least, that is the argument that I put to my accountant.

BUYING TOOLS

Within the range of standard tools there are two points worthy of note. To an extent both come down to one thing: you gets what you pays for.

Handles

Let's start with the easy bit – handles. In the last couple of years some manufacturers have begun to get the message: we want handles that better balance the blades to which they are fitted. This usually means longer handles. Of course most turners make their own handles as a matter of pride. Why pay someone else to turn something as simple as a tool handle? I found that I had to make my own handles because the standard ones were all too short and were poorly shaped. As a general rule I like to see handles about twice as long as the blades for everyday work, and three times the blade length for heavier pieces.

Commercial handles are usually also shaped wrong. Under normal circumstances you are holding the tools somewhere near the back of the handle and steadying the blade against the tool rest. On heavier work you also lodge the centre of the handle on the top of the hip bone for extra stability. This further reduces vibration and particularly shock loading and flexing of the right elbow. Then, when you are using just the one hand for tool control – as in parting off – or using the left hand to apply anti-vibration pressure to the rear of a spindle, you hold the handle at the top just behind the ferrule. Hence the top and the butt need to be 'holdable' and the middle can be thinner – the very reverse of some bought-in handles.

Both length and placement of the main areas of mass affect the tool's balance. A long handle, probably weighted at the butt, is needed for larger tools. For big bowl turning my wooden handles are now four (or more) times the length of the blades, and some are ballasted at the outboard end.

There are now tools available, mainly from America, with metal handles; and some are arranged with cavities in the butt that can be loaded with lead shot to balance the weight

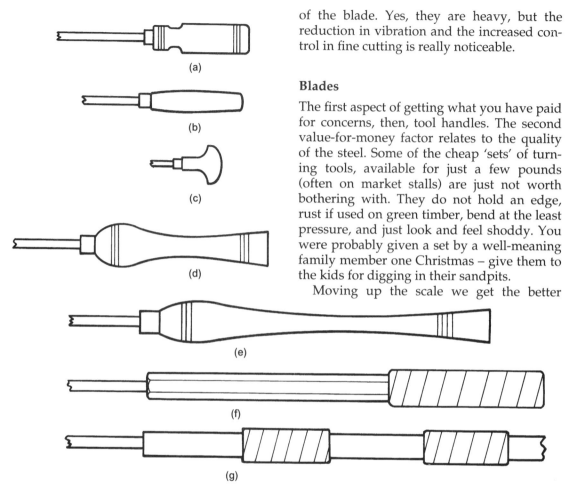

of the blade. Yes, they are heavy, but the reduction in vibration and the increased control in fine cutting is really noticeable.

Blades

The first aspect of getting what you have paid for concerns, then, tool handles. The second value-for-money factor relates to the quality of the steel. Some of the cheap 'sets' of turning tools, available for just a few pounds (often on market stalls) are just not worth bothering with. They do not hold an edge, rust if used on green timber, bend at the least pressure, and just look and feel shoddy. You were probably given a set by a well-meaning family member one Christmas – give them to the kids for digging in their sandpits.

Moving up the scale we get the better

Tool handle profiles. (a) is a chisel designed to be hit with a mallet; it is used for standard woodwork and large sculpture and is held by one hand round the centre zone. (b) is intended for cabinet making and carving and is only occasionally hit with a mallet; it is held by the main hand round the centre, while the lay hand rests a finger on the blade to hold it steady. A carving chisel like (c) is never hit with a mallet; it is held in the main hand with the palm over the knob; a lay finger could be used to help steady the blade. (d) is a small turning tool used for detail work; it is held just behind the ferrule while the lay hand supports the workpiece. The rear of the handle is rarely held – it is there to provide balance and is 10–12in (25–30cm) long. A large turning tool like (e) is held near the butt while the lay fingers hold or steady the blade at the tool rest; it is rarely held behind the ferrule. The handle will be 2–3ft (60–90cm) long. A larger turning tool like (f) may have a metal handle (often hexagonal section) with a tape or rubber grip at the butt, which is sometimes ballasted; this tool is never held at the ferrule. The lay hand steadies at the tool rest. An even larger turning tool (g) will have a metal tube handle with tape or rubber grips. Both hands will be needed to hold the handle; this tool is often used with pivot pins on a tool rest. The handle will be 4–8ft (1.2–2.4m) long and the blade 2–4ft (0.6–1.2m).

grades of carbon steel. You can immediately tell it from the tatt. It has a brighter finish and looks almost as though it has a finer grain! Actually, this is just the quality of grinding and polishing at the factory. Different manufacturers use different specifications and you will have to find your own preferred maker. Even amongst the well-known names, I find some very much better than others and now tend to use only Isles or Sorby, although in the last year or two other manufacturers have caught up. Some old tools are marvellous; I have a massive, very old, carbon steel roughing gouge by Marples and some wonderful old, thin-section, broad-bladed skews. They are high quality, carbon tool steel and are marvellous.

The beauty of carbon steel is that it will easily grind to a very fine edge. The problem is that it does not hold its edge for very long.

Most turners now use High Speed Steel (HSS), and again different manufacturers use slightly different alloys and hardness. There are a number of advantages to HSS: it holds the edge well, it is almost impossible to burn on the grind wheel, a tool lasts four times longer than an equivalent one in carbon steel (and is therefore much more cost-effective), and it is more predictable in that there is less variation between manufacturers' HSS steels than there is between different toolmakers' grades of carbon steel. The main disadvantage is that whereas carbon can be quickly ground to a very sharp edge on the grind wheel, an equivalent (or even better) edge can be produced on HSS only by following the grind wheel with stoning and honing. Most turners do not bother; they just use the edge produced by the grind wheel.

Then there are various tools using cobalt steels or chrome molybdenum and vanadium alloys; and some of these are significantly harder than normal High Speed Steel. I cannot say much about them, never having used them, but there are turners who speak very highly of them. Neither do I know what the alloy is that is used on solid steel metalwork lathe cutters. They are, however, very useful

and one of the special tools that we will look at can use suitable-size lathe bits.

At the extreme end of the range we have to put tungsten carbide. 'TC' tips are used on some tools – the Stewart system uses them on its slicer (more of this below). Generally these are very good, hold their edge for a long time and are not difficult to sharpen, rarely requiring more than a mere touch-up; but sharpening does have to be done with either a diamond sharpener or a soft green grindstone. TC is, however, very brittle (it does not like being dropped on the workshop floor, nor catching the corner of a jaw chuck) and it has to be cast to the shape required – you cannot just grind it to a profile. Normally, therefore, it comes as a point or narrow chisel bit, which has to be brazed on to a steel shaft. Many metalwork lathe bits have TC tips, and the better-quality small router bits are now made of solid tungsten carbide because of the long edge-holding capability of this material.

Such obvious quality issues apart, the old adage has it that it is a poor workman who blames his tools; the advanced turner cannot accept this, however. As skill grows and more ambitious projects are undertaken, the limitations of some tools become increasingly apparent – in fact, with some tools, absolute!

MODIFICATIONS TO THE BASICS

Many novices have trouble with the skew. At first, they find difficulty in keeping the cut in the centre of the edge, and they then catch one or other of the points. Later, as they become more skilled, they begin to find the skew enjoyable for its ease of control and the fine finishes that it produces. So they start to use it for more ambitious things such as rolling beads and fairly sharp radius curves. Now, despite their skill, they do still sometimes get a catch; particularly on the short point end. They also find that they undertake tasks where it is no longer practical to keep the blade at the ideal 45-degree angle to the lathe's axis.

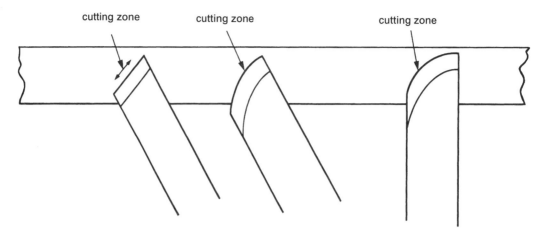

Ideal skew presentation. The handle has to be angled to a standard position to give a 45-degree presentation of the cutting edge to the axis of the lathe. It can, however, be presented at other angles if you use different parts of the arced cutting edge while maintaining 45-degree presentation.

I do not know who it was who first thought about grinding the edge of the skew to a curve rather than a straight line; but I thank them for the brilliant idea. Some turners now grind skews to a small arc of a circle, some to nearly a quarter circle. With the latter, should you so wish, you could have the handle pointing straight towards you while still presenting the edge at an optimum 45 degrees. The versatility of a curve-edged skew is enormous and most of my skews are now ground to arcs of differing radii.

Couple the curved end with the oval blade and it becomes one of the easiest to use of all tools. If it is also kept sharp I find that I can even work uphill without changing sides. The thin section of the oval blades also adds a dimension.

There are two main contributions that this development has made. First, with the thin section and the cut-back lower point, it is much easier to roll over a tight curve into a very narrow groove at the inboard end, for example when shaping the back end of an egg just before parting off. This is the condition under which I used to get most dig-ins with a straight skew. The second is that the thin sections make it easy to use broad-bladed skews on quite fine work. In fact, my

thick-section ½in (12mm) and ⅞in (21mm) straight-ended skews have been unused for the past two years.

The next tool modification that I have to cheer about was developed by Liam O'Neill from Galway and Mick O'Donnel from Thurso. They took conventional deep-fluted bowl gouges, slightly increased the bevel angle at the snout, but then carried the cutting edge back and along the top of the U gouge for up to 2in (5cm).

Again, this has created an enormously flexible tool. Using the nose and a millimeter either side, it can cut off the snout almost like a conventional bowl gouge. Working a little further along the far cutting edge and with the tool handle pointing to the far side of the lathe bed, it can make quick, large cuts in a forward motion.

Similar deep cuts can be made by drawing the blade back towards you and cutting off the nearside shoulder. Also, by angling the handle across the bed, it is possible to cut right up under an inboard rim. In fact, Liam produces hollow spheres with relatively small top apertures using only one of these gouges.

Thinking about it, I realize that I now use bowl gouges ground to this profile more than

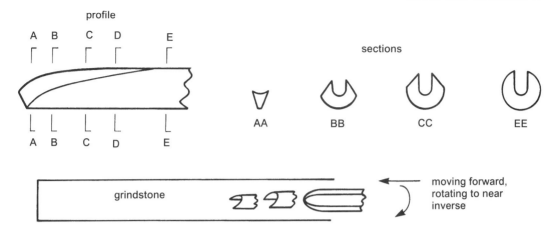

The Liam O'Neill bowl gouge modification. To shape it, the tool is pushed up a grind wheel while being rotated at the same time. The bevel angle at the nose is about 55 degrees; it is then shallow at BB before gradually increasing to DD.

I use my straight bowl gouges. I also use them a lot with pivot pins, an idea that will be investigated later in this chapter.

KEEPING SHARP

In *Woodturning – A Manual of Techniques* I stated that I always use tools straight off the grind wheel; this is still substantially true, but not totally.

Sometimes, for a little fine detail, a little extra sharpness is required. To achieve this the edge is given a few strokes with a hand-held stone. I find this particularly important with gouges when a shaped slip stone is used to remove the burr on the side of the edge that has not been ground.

The second deviation from the rule is necessitated entirely by the carving work now applied to some pieces. No grind wheel produces a finish that is quite good enough for carving chisels.

In the earlier book I talked at some length about the grind wheel that I had made, which had a series of fixed-height platforms to achieve different standard bevels. I received considerable flak for that. Nobody criticized its effectiveness – in fact, many have told me that they have copied the idea. However for

the pictures to show how it was assembled and worked, the safety cover had been removed. That caused mayhem! First I was

My home-made grind wheel. The leaves allow tools to be presented to grind at the optimum angle. The cover has been removed to show the layout.

101

Tormek grind wheel and jig. This arrangement gives good angle control and a superb edge for special applications, but these slow-rotation wet grinders are far too slow for production use on turning tools.

Scandinavian and Scandinavian production costs are amongst the highest in the world.

My Tormek has a large composite stone, and this certainly is worth the extra cost compared with their other stones. At the other end of the shaft is a rubberized honing wheel, and while this is useful it is not brilliant.

Even with the wet grinder and rubber wheel I was not getting the sort of edges that are ideal on chisels to be used on soft woods, as in carving decoy ducks in lime, for example.

So my power grinder with the 80 grit wheel at 1,000rpm produces the basic profiles and removes broken and serrated edges (some brittle chisels break and one does occasionally miss the rubber mat when items drop to the floor).

The Tormek then gets a good edge before I

Essential ancillaries. Clockwise from 9 o'clock: two Japanese water stones for carving chisels; hollow coarse stone for gouges; slip stone for removing burrs inside wheel-sharpened gouges; abrasive compound for use with the hard felt wheels (centre), which produce a high burnish and long-lasting edge on all tools – always used on power chisels; long abrasive stick for the teeth of the Arbortec.

sent lists of the regulations (many EC) that I was breaking. Then came letters saying that I should be setting an example! Fortunately, as I do not employ anyone else in my workshop I got away with it and still use my grinder. I now also have a conventional, legal unit – somewhere!

Snide aside, there have been other developments, firstly with the Tormek wet grinder. It is marvellous, painfully slow, and far too expensive. Marvellous because it produces a good basic edge and never, ever burns the tips; marvellous because it produces an even and near-flat edge (it does not wear into a groove as does an oil stone); painfully slow because it can take ten or more minutes to produce an edge on a 1in (2.5cm) wide blade so if you used it for turning tools, you would spend your whole workshop time tool sharpening; and too expensive because it is go on to an 800 and 1200 Japanese water stone – these really are wonderful. The final edge produced in this way will do a good day's work before needing resharpening.

Then I acquired a Bourdet power carver (*see* Chapter 10) and with this came a hard felt wheel and a stick of buffing compound. Originally the wheel came for fitting on an arbour for the power drill.

This proved to be marvellous. I can even by-pass the water stones if I wish (I rarely do), and within a few seconds a bright polished edge is achieved. This again gives a full day's work, but since it is so easy to use, I give the edges a quick burnish on the felt wheel several times a day.

I said that the wheel was originally on a power drill arbour. At the moment I am assembling a grinding and buffing unit with a main shaft and a number of wheels, and with mops running off it. Several elements of this will be difficult to guard, so I am sure that it too will attract adverse comment.

With all grinding systems there is the same problem. We know what angle of grind we would like for the bevel of each different tool – the difficulty is achieving that angle easily and regularly. The Tormek, bridge, slide clamp and rocker are fine. They are accurate, and as almost all carving tools have the same bevel, there is no resetting to be done between one tool and the next.

I still believe that a series of pivoting platforms each set to produce a specific bevel is the only answer for turning tools.

However the bevel side has been sharpened, there is still a burr left on the other. For turning chisels I have a little shaped slip stone beside the grinder. For all other tools the felt wheel has a second shaped wheel alongside. This is used inside the gouge (and similar tools), and with the buffing soap takes the burr away in seconds.

TOOLS TO SOLVE PROBLEMS

This brings us to the special tools that have

Nesting bowl tool. This is a brilliant piece of kit from Craft Supplies; it takes a multiset of nesting bowls from a single blank. The inside is finished before removing each bowl, and the outside of the parted item is then cleaned by reverse chucking and a small flat base is worked. Unfortunately the bowls are hemispherical and symmetrical – not my style!

appeared in recent years. Some really are gimmicks – they are marvellous for what they were produced for, but their use is so specific that the average turner has to question their real utility. The nesting bowl tool is excellent, but how often do you wish to produce nests of bowls to similar profiles?

Others, particularly those that have been built up into systems, are both effective and a real investment. It was the slicer that first attracted me to the Stewart tool, but now I use all the other parts of the system almost as much as I use the slicer itself.

Many turners have designed their own tools and then either fabricated them themselves or had them made by an established tool maker. Some of these tools have then been picked up and have been put into regular manufacture by some suppliers.

Mathew Calder is a very talented young turner producing large, often rough-textured, hollow-form art pieces. He has a set of tools that look like a bag of junk. They are all made by Mathew himself. Most have long blades with HSS or cobalt steel cutting tips clamped or brazed on to the ends. The handles are various metal pipes and steel tubes. They are long, to get the control and leverage required; weighted, to get the balance right; and then wrapped in plastic tape or bicycle handle-bar tape to provide grips. They look awful but do superb work in Mathew's hands. They were produced because there was nothing suitable commercially available in the UK.

In Morecambe, Terry Harvey also uses some large special tools. They are hooks and special cutters. He designed them himself

A hook tool in use. A properly used hook tool is probably the most versatile device in the turner's armoury. It can be presented at almost any required angle and cuts swiftly and cleanly, once you have mastered it. Hooks are much more versatile and forgiving than are ring tools.

and had them made specially by a well-known tool maker. The cost of doing it this way is not prohibitive, but tool makers are not too happy about undertaking such commissions, or having their name attached to the tools. The reason is simple. With these larger tools we do tend to push the boundaries and take risks. In this increasingly litigious age the makers are not prepared to risk proceedings for injury suffered by a user of one of the specials that they have made.

Both the commercially and the home-made 'unconventional' tools have been produced for one of four reasons. First, they may use or have adapted a material not normally available (such as special machine-tool tungsten carbide cutters). Second, they may have a special cutting end or profile to achieve a particular effect or solve a specific problem such as hollowing deep vessels; third, they are of an extreme size, either very large or really minute; and fourth, although there may be commercially sold ones available in some parts of the world, people may not know where to find them.

Making Your Own Tools

There are clearly some limitations on what the home tool maker can do; forging a round gouge from a flat bar and/or massive amounts of cutting and grinding of High Speed Steel, are beyond the capabilities of most. However, forging a cutting tip is not difficult. Ed Moulthrop makes massive tools for his massive bowls. It is not unusual to see him with a tool with a 5ft (1.5m) long handle and a 3ft (90cm) long blade. There are two tips that he uses, both of which he forges himself. One is a lance – a sharp spear-like point, which is used in the vertical plane, and the other a hook, which is virtually a lance bent round to about three-quarters of a ring. The lance is mainly used to form the outside of vessels and the hook is used for hollowing. With both, Ed tends to employ massive bowl-turning rests and almost always works by levering the tool against pivot pins.

Ring tools are a poor man's hook tools with L plates. Not just for end grain turning!

Sometimes on special tools the tip is integral and merely an extension of the blade itself. Sometimes the tip is fixed to a long, steel bar blade. With many of Ed's tools, the tip is integral with the blade and these are made from old machine taps. It must be a good scrap yard that can provide 2–3ft (60–90cm) long machine taps of 1–1½in (2.5–3.7cm) diameter! The end is heated in a small blacksmith's forge (these are not difficult to construct yourself if you do not have a friendly smith in the area). It is then hammered out on an anvil until the required profile is achieved. The most critical stage is to get the temper right, but even this is not difficult. The tip and an inch or two below is heated in the forge until it is cherry red. It is

then quickly quenched in oil, waste sump oil being quite adequate.

Incidentally, old files should never be used to make turning tools unless they too are tempered. File steel is too brittle and is only case-hardened. It snaps and splinters very easily, sometimes with lethal results.

Hook and Ring Tools

Hook tools are widely favoured in Scandinavia, but have never really caught on in the UK. Today they appear more frequently in the kits of most top turners. Some time ago, Sorby produced a ring tool, which is little more than a completed hook. Many people bought one and then found that they could not get on with it. Some did find that they could use it in end grain but not side grain, hence it became known as an end grain tool. The question has to be asked, why should the ring tool be an end grain tool if a hook can be used on side grain? It has to be acknowledged that Ed Moulthrop uses his lance and hook almost exclusively on whole tree trunks working into the end grain; but the Scandinavian turners use them for all grain orientations.

The clue comes in how the ring tool is used. If you try cutting on the side of the ring – apparently quite a natural angle of attack – the face of the ring acts as a bevel and gives some control over the cut (it is ground to an angle to do just that). However, once the cut starts, the swarf going down through the ring tends to rotate the head, and in an instant bevel contact is lost and the cutting edge bites ever deeper into the timber. In no time at all there is a deep gouge, and probably the lathe has stalled or the workpiece disintegrated.

If, on the other hand, we cut at the end of the ring, there is not the same turning pressure as on the side of the cutter. There is no tendency to rotate and therefore to dig in.

In fact, there are a number of secrets to effective use of a ring or hook tool. Firstly, it is best suited to green timber as this slices more easily and is therefore more forgiving.

Secondly, yes, it is better suited to end grain, where you are slicing the ends of fibres rather than trying to plane along the grain. Thirdly, work off the end of the ring and not the side; and, of course, fourthly, keep it sharp. And fifthly, I might add, use the smaller rings. They are much more controllable, and if they do dig in, the damage is usually repairable!

Cutting off the end is relatively easy when working inside a vessel and along its base. Trying to use the end of the tool as you come up the wall means that the tool handle is getting further and further away from you. Eventually it ends up across the lathe almost at right angles to the axis. This means that the ring has real limitations for closed-in hollow forms. You will certainly need adequate clearance on the far side of the lathe to allow free tool swing, and you just cannot get the necessary swing if you are trying to work through a narrow-top aperture. I also find that the use of a heavy-duty bowl rest with pivot pins gives a lot more control over the ring tool.

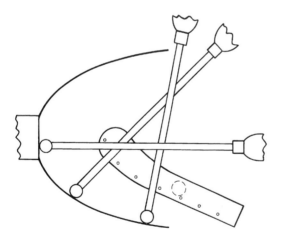

The swing of the handle necessary to retain end cutting of the ring tool to avoid rotational moment and dig-in.

Sharpening is done using a cone-shaped stone from the inside. Clean up the outside face if you wish, but do it with a hand stone, not on the grind wheel.

With some hollowing-out tools you just have to learn to cope with the rotation problem; other tools have various methods to reduce the difficulties incorporated into them.

Hollowing-Out Aids

David Ellsworth's Tools

The ultimate master of the hollow form is probably David Ellsworth. He uses small HSS cutters mounted on the end of steel shafts in such a way that they can be set to work straight forward, or at any angle to the side. At his demonstrations he often sells a moderate-sized tool that has a 1in (2.5cm) long cutter of ¼in (6mm) square section. It is set at 40 degrees to the shaft and is ground to a rounded scraper tip. The blade that I have is 12in (20cm) long and I have mounted it in a robust, 2ft (60cm) long wooden handle.

The first lesson that I learnt was that when working blind (inside the vessel), it is very difficult to judge the angle of presentation of the tip; so I put a spot of paint on the top of the ferrule to indicate that the cutting edge was then at right angles.

The cutter being only 1in (2.5cm) long, the turning moment is not too great and with a stout handle it can be resisted with little effort. The shaft is relatively light, being only ½in (12mm) in diameter. This does, however, seem quite adequate because of the very small contact area created by the ¼in (6mm) wide tip. The short tip has another advantage. By leaning across the lathe bed and carefully aligning the eye along the handle and blade, it is possible to judge where the tip is, and thus how thin the wall is getting. I now find it relatively easy to get walls down to about ¼in (6mm) thick with this tool. Unlike David I am unable to judge wall thinness by the sound that the cutting tip makes; but by tapping on the wall with a finger nail you can get a reasonable idea. There is a distinct thin, hollow sound the moment that you get down to the ¼in (6mm) thickness.

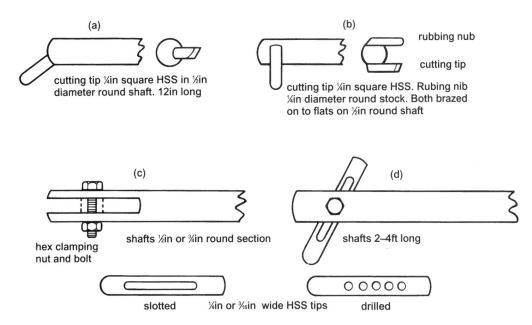

Tools used to produce hollow vessels. The Ellsworth tool (a) and the Firmager tool (b) are usually obtainable from their designers at demonstrations. The special tools (c) and (d) are based on those used by David Ellsworth; these are commercially available only in the USA.

The tools that David uses himself are much bigger: he tends to have a range from 3ft (90cm) long upwards. On these he makes use of ballasted metal tube handles. The shaft is a long steel bar of about ¾in (18mm) diameter. The end is slotted, and into this he clamps (with a small nut and bolt) a ¼in (6mm) square HSS cutter – again usually ground to a round scraper end. The beauty of this tool is that the cutter can be set to cut in any position from straight forward right round to back along the shaft. It can also be set to stick out from a mere ½in (12mm) up to about 1½in (3.7cm). The weighted, sometimes hexagonal, section handle makes control of the cutting edge quite positive and the rotational forces can be resisted easily.

There are three difficulties with all of David's turning tools. Firstly, there is the rotational moment already noted; secondly, the difficulty of knowing the orientation of the tip in terms of cutting presentation (my paint dot helps); and thirdly, being such a small cutter I find it difficult to get a ridge-free finish with it. Some turners are not concerned about this as it is inside a vessel that probably has a narrow neck and therefore nobody will know. However, this is not the case with David. Cut open one of his large, hollow vessels (and he has done this to prove it) and the walls are an even ⅜in (9mm) thick all round, and are nearly perfectly smooth.

Melvin Firmager

Melvin Firmager, the English master of the hollow form, has addressed the rotational moment problem, and at the same time solved the presentation aspect. He has produced tools similar to David's smaller version, with a welded-on HSS cutter underslung below the steel shaft; and on the top of the shaft he has welded a small, steel, round-nosed rubber. The rubber is ground as the tool is sharpened so that the cutting edge just trails the rubber by a thou or two allowing a perfect, just off the horizontal, tip presentation.

The tool is fed into the vessel and brought up to the wall so that the rubber makes contact. The nose of the rubber now acts as a bevel and is kept in firm contact with the timber. The tool handle is rotated clockwise until the cutting tip comes into contact with the wood and starts to work. It is very easy to come to grips quickly with this tool. Without the worry of presentation since there is no risk of digging in, the turner can concentrate on judging where the tip is, and thus how thin the wall is getting.

The Stewart System

The Stewart system has come closest to solving most of the problems of turning hollow vessels. Developed by Dennis Stewart of Oregon, it comes as a kit of elements, which can be assembled into a number of different forms. It provides either a simple pistol grip handle for light work or a massive arm brace with an elbow pad. The tool is so rugged and fits so well that, with a long lance mounted, you can actually lock up a rotating lathe with no injury to the turner. (Not a good practice, but I had to try it!)

The second feature is that by using extension bars, a strong shaft of about 4ft (1.2m) can be put together for getting deep inside the workpiece. It is also sufficiently robust to allow you to work with most of its length overhanging the tool rest without vibrating.

There are then four heads. First a slicer with a 5⁄32in (3.75mm) wide tungsten carbide tip, then a hooker – a curved slicer with a bend – which effectively overcomes the rotational problem. This also has a TC tip. Then there is a similar hooker on to which can be bolted a range of small, shaped scraper blades; a straight shaft with an inclined head to which the scraper blades may also be cramped for shear scraping; and finally a straight shaft into the end of which can be clamped either square-section HSS cutters, or

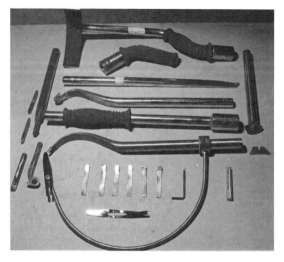

The full Stewart kit. From the top: the arm brace and hand grip; tungsten carbide-tipped slicer; round-tip hooker; extension piece; TC-tip hooker with thickness gauge and finger; chatter tool bits. To the left and right are various scraper bits, extensions and mounts.

one of a number of profiled spring steel blades which are used for chatter finishes.

The first joy of this tool is that the slicer can be used to remove a cone (even a nest of cones) from the centre of large bowl blanks. As a bowl turner, I am enormously worried by the amount of the timber that I buy that ends up as shavings on the garden bonfire. Using the slicer gives me at least a dish, possibly two, out of the centre of the blank. On more than one occasion the two dishes have just paid for the timber, which has nicely increased the profit margin on the big bowl.

There is a knack to taking out a cone, and it is to keep the cut fairly wide. I therefore start by cutting in at right angles to the face of the blank and then making a second cut out towards the rim so that I can remove a wedge-shaped ring. This then gives working space. As the groove gets deeper, the slicer blade is moved from side to side so that the groove is always about twice the width of the cutting tip. If the groove is not kept open, the shoulder of the slicer will eventually bind up, and you too will test the tool's ability to stop

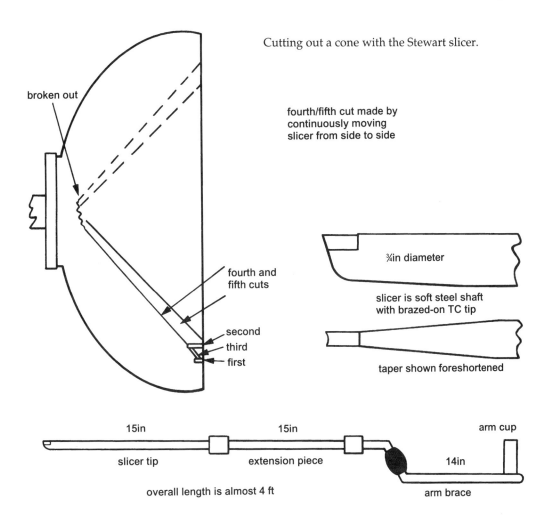

Cutting out a cone with the Stewart slicer.

broken out

fourth/fifth cut made by
continuously moving
slicer from side to side

fourth and
fifth cuts

second

third

first

¾in diameter

slicer is soft steel shaft
with brazed-on TC tip

taper shown foreshortened

15in

15in

arm cup

slicer tip

extension piece

14in

overall length is almost 4 ft

arm brace

the lathe. Make sure that you are holding on tight!

Quite often the groove begins to peter out and the tool tip bind up before the cone is finally parted. At this stage it is often possible to break the cone away using a tyre lever. This is easier with clean-grained wood if you split it across, rather than along, the grain. Only once has a cone split away pulling so much of the blank that the bottom of the bowl ended up too thin.

The hooker is a bent slicer. It is designed so that the tip cuts to the side of the tool's axis, but the inclusion of the curved section allows the cutting tip to lie actually on the axis of the shaft. This does create one anomaly. You normally position the tool rest as close to the cutting point as possible. When cutting near the top of the vessel with the hooker this could mean that the curved section is on top of the rest, which would make the rotational moment quite high. So the tool rest should be drawn back from the workpiece so that it always supports the straight shaft section of the tool.

Using the hooker with small scrapers is the best way I have found to finish the inside of hollow vessels. The blades (believed to be of cobalt steel on the original model) are big enough to remove the ridges and provide a

109

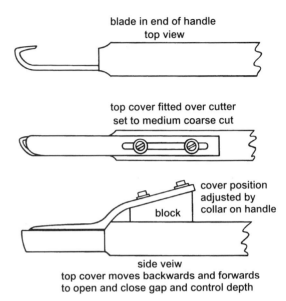

blade in end of handle
top view

top cover fitted over cutter
set to medium coarse cut

cover position
adjusted by
collar on handle

block

side veiw
top cover moves backwards and forwards
to open and close gap and control depth

*Scraping with the hooker. It is not normally used
in this way but it demonstrates the heavy
cutting ability of the round tips on a hooker arm.*

The DAHT (deep adjustable hollowing tool).

fair curve, but small enough to cut and not dig in if a flaw is encountered. The shaft is robust enough not to vibrate, and the control possible with the arm brace really does reduce (even eliminate) the risk of accidentally cutting in too deep.

Some of the other features of the Stewart system (the depth gauge, chatter fingers and so on), will be mentioned elsewhere.

DAHT

The next special tool is again concerned with hollowing out. It is the DAHT (deep adjustable hollowing tool) that has recently been brought on to the UK market by Craft Supplies, but originally hailed from New Zealand.

It is always said that a problem identified is a problem half solved, and the DAHT tool provides the next stage of solutions.

In essence it has a lot of the qualities of Ed Moulthrop's hook (and the many hooks of Scandinavia). It does, however, offer a longer

side wall, anticipating more side cutting than end turning. It provides a bevel and a vertical cutting edge as does the hook or ring tool. However, it has a device that limits the depth of cut; if the tool starts to rotate, it just ceases to cut, instead of digging in. This is achieved by giving the normally open top of the hook a lid. The lid can be accurately positioned to control finely the space between the lid and the cutting edge, and in this way acts like the sole plate on a hand plane.

It is a sophisticated piece of kit in that the position of the lid is controlled by a rotating collar on the handle. It can be set to give a very fine finishing cut or undertake much coarser timber removal – and all without danger of dig-in. There is a very nice ballasted handle, and extension pieces; and as part of the kit it is possible to obtain a mounting cradle, which fits into the tool post and which then has the same function as pivot pins in a tool rest. After a few weeks of trial I have been unable to fault it.

SOMETHING TO REST ON

On frequent occasions mention has been made of two devices. Firstly, heavy-duty scraping rests, and secondly, pivot pins.

Most bowl-turning rests are curved to follow the profile of a bowl. Some have the rest so positioned on the post that it can be set well inside the bowl to assist hollowing. The best bowl rests will position well inside a vessel, but the rest arms can only be of a certain length before they have too long a cantilever and will flex under load. To give a reasonable length without flexing requires a massive construction. Hence good bowl rests have curved arms, are of considerable length, need to be mounted on a heavy-duty post, and must be of very substantial section and construction. They should be of a vibration-resistant cast metal. Curved, steel bar tool rests are inadequate.

A tool working with a long overhang is

The Treebridge rest inside a bowl. The curved rest allows minimum space between rest and wall – ideal for internal scraping.

Bowl scraper rests. On the left is the Poole Wood bowl rest, right is the old Treebridge model. A loose pivot pin lies between. The Poole Wood rest is not normally supplied drilled.

much more stable if it is supported off a flat table. Therefore bowl rests are flat topped and are called scraper rests. At one time Treebridge made a real beauty, but the company ceased production and nobody else offers anything nearly as good. The closest alternative is the heavy bowl rest available with the Poole Wood 28/40 lathe.

The Treebridge rest incorporated the second of our devices – pivot pins.

The tops of all of my flat bowl rests have now been drilled with ¼in (6mm) diameter holes every 2in (5cm) along the length. I then have a number of pins that are ⅝in (15mm) in diameter with ¼in (6mm) lower sections. The pin end is pushed into a hole and then tools can be held against the main section of the pivot pin.

A cutting tool can be levered into the wood in either a forward or rearward motion. It cuts in an arc as it pivots around the pin. While the main advantage is that of powered leverage, allowing deep cuts for rapid waste removal, the pivot pin also gives a high degree of positional stability so the tendency to jump, vibrate or dig in is much reduced.

111

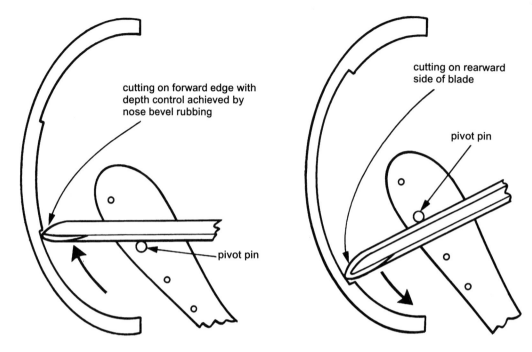

Aggressive forwards and backwards cuts with a modified gouge.

Some hardwoods cut only slowly with even the sharpest of bowl gouges; when the pivot pin is brought into play, the cutting rate is increased five- or sixfold.

For power cutting the pivots work best with a modified-end bowl gouge. Ed Moulthrop uses these throughout with both lance and hook. When he applies leverage with a 7 or 8ft (2.1 or 2.4m) long tool the shavings really fly.

At the other end of the scale is the extremely delicate control that pivots give. They are useful for getting clean sweeping curves by careful control of a scraper. I find them good for better control of a ring tool when cutting off the side, and very valuable when using the DAHT tool. They also provide optimum control when scraping with a Stewart hooker.

I do not propose to detail the micro turning tools that are now available. Suffice it to say that we now have sets of miniature tools duplicating all the conventional gouges, skews and scrapers – even a mini hooker for hollowing bud vases. In every case the design principles adopted are the same as for their big brothers. Some miniaturist turners make their own tools using sections of machine hacksaws (for parting and grooving tools) and masonry nails for skews and scrapers.

8 Between Centres Turning

CINDERELLA NO LONGER

For some time it appeared that all the turners in the country were bowl turners. Go to any local woodturning club competition, and that was all that you saw. Even at the major exhibition held by the Association in conjunction with their biennial international seminar, bowls predominated – even swamped.

In the last two or three years this has begun to change. Now we see composites with elements of face plate and between centres work combined. We also now see a few items that are totally between centres pieces.

Of course there have always been spindle workers beavering away quietly, but it has been massive, art-piece bowls that have taken the thunder.

It is not difficult to see why. It is not that spindle turning is any easier or less skilful than face plate (in fact it can be much more technically demanding); but spindles rarely exist as finished items. They are usually a part of something else: legs of a piece of furniture, rails for banisters, handles to a mirror, columns for standard lamps and so on.

To make matters worse, the first thing that most of us ever turned at school was probably a spindle, often a tool handle. We probably then did one or two fancy spindles to practise rolling beads, hollowing coves and to achieve nice graduated ogees. Then we made our first bowl and after that, for many years, we hardly touched another spindle. Because for us spindles were connected with starting to turn, we downgraded spindle turning in our minds.

Some did go on to make the occasional handled mirror, and maybe tried an hour-glass or two. A few were even tempted to enter competitions for a matched pair of candlesticks. Then one day we had the idea of making a spinning wheel, and suddenly we began to appreciate that spindle turning is fun. More, it can be quite demanding. Elements of the wheel did not quite fit together, but, after a bit of bodging, the end result was pleasing. At this stage some get hooked and probably move into a little furniture making in which turned work is combined with skilful cabinet making. Suddenly, spindle turning ceases to be Cinderella and blossoms into a fully fledged princess!

It is probably true to say that the majority of people who regularly turn spindles do so for one of two reasons. First they are professional jobbing turners who rely on regular contracts for quantity items such as banister spindles to make their bread and butter; or they are not content with the skill levels required to turn bowls and need the additional challenge of cabinet and furniture making. A few wish to specialize in a product range that involves substantial spindle turning – such as, for example, spinning wheel building.

So it is from the professional end that we need to approach spindle turning as it relates to the advanced woodturner, where the key factors are the need to work quickly, replicate items, make things that fit together, and achieve precise measurements.

There is a problem right at the beginning. So far I have used the phrase 'spindle turning', but many refer to this area of activity as 'between centres' turning. I find the semantics of this a little difficult to cope with as I frequently rough-round large bowls between centres, and almost always complete the outside profile of deep vases between centres. I also make goblets, the stems of which are really spindles, using a single mounting off a four-jaw chuck.

Spinning wheels are one of the ultimate challenges to the spindle turner. There are copy elements; joints that must fit; elements that must align; measurements that must be accurate; and in the end it all actually has to work. This, my first try, did not quite fit together!

What about balls? The main work is done between centres – often using a cross-head (or 'four prong') drive and tailstock point. But they are then parted off at the outboard end and remounted in a jaw chuck. Finally the inboard end is parted off and the piece is finished in a cup chuck. I still regard ball making as being primarily between centres and it is therefore detailed in this chapter.

A Norwegian pattern wheel – the most complex of all designs, but what a joy to make and to use.

Almost all spindle work, certainly advanced between centres turning, is very concerned with dimensions. Very often we are working to precise tolerances because we are making a number of elements that have to be fitted together and assembled into a whole finished piece.

Secondly, we are often faced with the need for duplication, producing two or more items each to exactly the same profile and dimensions.

The further we get into the duplication aspect the more we also become concerned with speed – usually there is a production run to be completed against a tight deadline.

There is another aspect that concerns some of us at times, and that is the problem of size. Some jobs exceed the capacity of our lathes; so let's start by looking at large spindles.

LONG AND LARGE SPINDLES

The main difficulty encountered in turning large spindles is in mounting them on the lathe. The only long-bed lathes available today are probably very old and are often engineering lathes. Wadkin made a few longer beds and there are still some old Britannia and Colchester lathes with 12 and 15ft (3.5 and 4.5m) beds to be found; occasionally you may find even longer lathes lurking in the back of old ship-building workshops.

There was an old turner in the shipyard at Sunderland. He had a 12ft (3.5m) Colchester lathe. Sometimes he was commissioned to produce shafts of up to 20ft (6m) long. His solution was simple. He took the tailstock off the lathe, removed a few bricks from the wall of the workshop, inserted a greased cradle in the hole, and rested the outboard end on this. There could be anything up to 5ft (1.5m) of rotating spindle outside the workshop.

Today, most long large pieces are made in sections and are then joined.

The actual turning of large spindles requires just the same high level of skills as does the turning of small between centres pieces. Some turners scale up the size of the main tools, gouges and skews. For almost all between centres work, I prefer largish skews (old pattern makers' tools of 2in (5cm) width and thin section) and have ground most of them to the half-moon arc.

The making up of long 'spindles' by joining up shorter segments is probably the route that most of us have to take. A 6ft (1.8m) standard lamp column is going to be made in two sections – sometimes even three.

The problems come less in turning the components than in jointing them. The quickest method, which most of us adopt, is to drill a hole in the end of one segment and turn a dowel or spigot on the end of the other. The two are finally pushed together and held with glue.

The first set of difficulties relate to the compatibility of the pieces to be joined. It is very difficult to get colour and finishing to match between two jointed sections. Then, if the two pieces are not of identical timber, and are not at the same moisture content, we can get differential movement with the glue joint breaking down. For this reason the slightly more flexible PVA glues are preferable to brittle-drying adhesives such as Aerolite (a wood glue that is otherwise absolutely marvellous for permanent bonding). The best answer of all is to make the elements screw together.

Cutting Threads

Now there are two issues to consider – first, positioning the joint in the least conspicuous place, and secondly, cutting the actual thread.

The best place for the joint is immediately under an overhanging feature. Hence in the 'right angle' just where a bead meets the main column, or at the bottom of an ogee curve.

The conventional way of cutting threads is to use a screw box and tap, but there are three problems with this. First, most boxes will not cut a thread right up to a shoulder, and you often need to do this for a jointed spindle. Secondly it is only the best and most expensive of the generally available screw boxes that are any good; there is absolutely no point in buying a cheap box. And thirdly, there is the difficulty of keeping the cutters ground to the right angle and really sharp.

A compromise solution can be adopted. First, get a good pair of taps and handles that hold them firmly. The first will be a taper tap to start the thread cutting in the hole, and the second a bottoming tap that will cut thread right down to the bottom of the hole. Do not bother with a screw box – cut the thread on the dowel spigot by hand.

Hand-chasing a thread on the spigot end is not difficult. The first one or two you will need to mark out carefully, thereafter a free-hand approach is usually quite accurate enough to give a good fit. As you are making a joint that you do not expect to be made and broken frequently, a certain level of inaccuracy will actually ensure a tight fit.

A word of warning at this stage – *before* you complete your socket and spigot! It is said that you cannot cut a thread into end grain (*see* the instruction literature published by screw box manufacturers). Possibly because I do not know what end grain is in this respect I have never found this statement to be totally true. If you are putting thread on to a dowel are you not working down from the end grain? Isn't the thread itself being cut across side grain?

However, I do have to acknowledge that it can be difficult taping out a thread into a socket drilled in end grain, so it is always worth taking a scrap piece of the wood in question and trying it out before finally committing yourself.

If it works, then fine. If it does not, all is not yet lost. There are two options. The first is to drill the socket well oversize and turn, fit, and glue in a sleeve of cross-grain timber into which you can then tap the thread. The second is to design an element that is turned in cross grain and which then acts as a link between the two spindles to be joined.

To Hand-Chase a Thread

First mark off the thread pitch of the tap on to the spigot, tracing the thread around the spigot with a pencil.

To mark out the thread, measure the pitch of the tap – say four turns per inch on an inch diameter spigot. Mark an inch (four thread peaks) on the spindle spigot starting hard up against the shoulder. Now starting on the opposite side of the spindle half a pitch distance from the shoulder (⅛in), mark off another four thread peaks. Trace the first inch of thread by joining the marks. Absolute accuracy is *not* essential. Make sure that the twist of the thread mirrors the direction on the tap! This is the opposite way to that normally used for barley sugar twists. The groove is cut out with a small V gouge or Veiner. Keep the gouge sharp and turn the workpiece by hand.

Obviously you will try to keep the thread pitch even and the groove of a constant depth. However, there is a lot of tolerance and a workable but tight fit will be achieved even with an indifferent thread. The end result will probably be better than you would achieve with a screw box, particularly on 'end' grain; it will go right down to the shoulder of the spindle; it will have saved you a lot of money; and above all it is satisfying to achieve it 'by hand'!

Drilling a Socket

Normally a spindle will be held between a cross-head drive prong and a centre-point tailstock. This becomes something of a problem when you need to drill out a socket for the jointing spigot. We can no longer rely on a prong drive if we cannot use the tailstock point for pressure.

One alternative for smaller-diameter spindles is to drive through a screw chuck. My preferred alternative is the four-jaw chuck. The spigot end of the spindle is held in the jaws allowing about 1in (2.5cm) of waste. The tailstock point is used as a steady while the

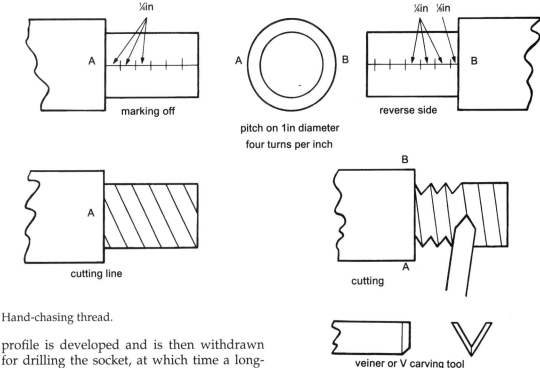

¼in

marking off

A   B

pitch on 1in diameter
four turns per inch

¼in ⅛in

reverse side

A

cutting line

B

cutting

A

veiner or V carving tool
used to chase thread

Hand-chasing thread.

profile is developed and is then withdrawn for drilling the socket, at which time a long-work steady is used to stabilize the column.

This arrangement has one real advantage. By using a screw chuck or four-jaw there is not the same tension on the tailstock point, and there will be much less tendency for the spindle to flex and whip as it is turned thin.

Once the profile is finished, wrap three turns of masking tape about a flat (non-tapering) spot on the spindle. Fix the long-work steady to run on the masking tape.

The socket is now drilled out using a saw tooth bit mounted in a Jacobs chuck. When drilling out on a lathe you have to use a saw tooth bit; flat bits are not suitable and augers too brutal. Also remember that if you are producing a socket into which you have to tap a thread (with or without a cross-grain sleeve) you will need to drill to undersize. This usually means drilling to ⅛in (3mm) smaller diameter than the diameter of the tap – with coarse taps the difference needs to be as high as ³⁄₁₆in (4.5mm).

Many spindles will require a cable way

running up the centre. This helps relieve stresses in the wood and reduces the likelihood of later splitting or warp twisting. A long-hole auger is fed through the tailstock quill or a tool post die, and the lathe is turned at the slowest possible speed. Feed the auger in 3 or 4 inches (7 or 10cm) and then withdraw it to clear the swarf. Keep doing this until the full depth is completed. If, as is often the case, the auger bit starts to get very hot, rest for a while and do something else. For jointed long spindles, drill out the spigot socket to get this accurately located before drilling through with the long-hole auger. Saw tooth bits tend to wander if their centre point is not firmly located.

The maximum length of a segment you can produce is probably going to be determined more by the auger length you have available than by the bed length of the lathe. However, as we noted earlier, the drive centre when

117

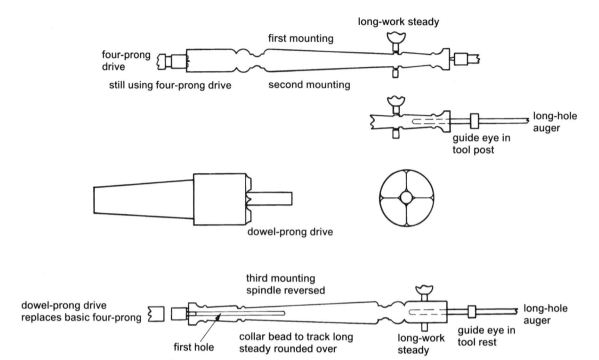

long-work steady

first mounting

four-prong drive

still using four-prong drive   second mounting

long-hole auger

guide eye in tool post

dowel-prong drive

third mounting
spindle reversed

dowel-prong drive
replaces basic four-prong

first hole

collar bead to track long
steady rounded over

long-work
steady

guide eye in
tool rest

long-hole
auger

Double-end long-hole augering.

fitted with a pilot dowel in place of the centre point enables you to remount the piece and auger drill from each end.

Don't forget to finish the segments of the spindle completely before you actually assemble them – you cannot put the whole piece back on to the lathe for sanding and polishing.

Problems with Long Spindles

So we have produced one spindle, a long one such as for a standard lamp. This was probably made from sensible-sized, squared timber – probably of 2 or 3in (5 or 7cm) square.

Across the board, turning really large pieces usually means turning awkward, out-of-balance timber. Probably the only situation where this is not true is the turning of architectural columns from segmented blanks.

If you do have to turn long spindles – even ones 3ft (90cm) long – then there is another problem to deal with. A standard tool rest is likely to be 6–9in (15–23cm) long. To cover

the length of the spindle this means frequent repositioning of the tool post. This is a particular nuisance if you are trying to produce a flowing curve 12in (30cm) or more long. The answer is a long tool rest, so I have one 18in (45cm) long, but even this is not all sweetness and light. There are times when you are working out towards one end wing of the rest and perhaps you lean against it a little too hard. The leverage exerted against the clamp can be sufficient to move the rest, pushing the corner against the rotating cylinder and marking it. This is particularly trying if you are making a table leg with square-to-round elements and the corner of the rest catches a square section. In an instant your legs are redesigned for you!

If you regularly do long spindle work it is worth investing in a spare tool carriage and a long double-post rest. I do not have one – having not yet been able to find one plain carriage for the Wadkin, let alone two!

COPY TURNING

The next aspect of between centres turning must be copying. Here we have two concerns. First, we have to produce genuine copies, not just approximations. There are now regular competitions for turners that require a matched pair of items to be produced. I think the judges use micrometers and work to thous'. This really has to be classed as 'advanced turning'.

Linked with the need to produce close copies there is also the requirement to work efficiently to achieve reasonable quantities. The bread and butter of a spindle turner's life is often turning out hundreds of matched stair banister spindles. Builders merchants will only pay you coppers for production spindles. So large quantities are made using fully automated copy machines, others with manually controlled copy machines. There are still some production spindle turners who work by hand and eye alone. These are the really advanced turners. With a copy turning machine, it's a doddle; without one it can represent the bane of a turner's life.

Willy Stedmond, the brilliant Irish full-time professional, was demonstrating spindle turning at the Dublin seminar of the Irish Guild of Woodturners. He was demonstrating, teaching, stopping to repeat little wrinkles, telling anecdotes, and swapping the gas with fellow professionals; and all the time the pile of pine blanks to his left moved across to the pile of finished spindles to his right in a steady stream. The journey time could be down to under seven minutes if the number of jokes was reduced slightly. There was a marking board, a roughing gouge, one other gouge, and a couple of skews and that was all. Rummage how you might, it was difficult to find any two finished spindles that did not perfectly match each other.

Actually, he frequently did not even bother to pick up the marking board. He had a finished spindle on the back of the lathe bed, lined his pencil up against this and quickly scribed off a few key points.

Automated Copying

Copy lathes are useful for production work, but they have limitations. They give accurate, mirror-image copies, and are quite quick – but not as quick as Willy. The main problems are twofold. Firstly, they work with cutters that are derived from metalworking lathes, and these are effectively a form of tiny scraper. Even with a sharp tip there is a tendency to tear on certain cuts – particularly when cutting across the long grain on pine. Certainly they cannot give you the sweeping smoothness that can be produced with a good skew chisel. Secondly, they follow a finger or tracer which takes its 'instruction' from a template. They read accurately but cannot cope with the finest of detail and particularly with steep-walled V-cuts.

Fully automated copy lathes are fed with bundles of blanks and then left to their own devices. They load, shape, finish and eject. Their output is a clearly mass-produced but adequate commercial product; of course, they cost a bundle and can only be justified on huge regular outputs.

There are then copy lathes costing between £6,000 and £15,000, which have to be hand loaded, and give the operator the opportunity of crisping up the detail with a little hand finishing.

Next down the scale come tools like my £500 Multico 1000, which came with a copy attachment. This is quite adequate for a small run or a job that comes up every so often, though we still have the limitations in terms of crispness of detail. So let's look at hand copying, and the sort of techniques that Willy uses.

Hand Copying

The first requirement is a means of marking off the main features quickly and repetitively. Templates alone are not really quick enough nor adequate for anything but a limited, one-off run.

There are two methods and one of these is

119

half of the total approach. The full method involves a marking-off device and then a template to check the near-finished profiles. The half method does not bother with the template. There are then variations upon the template theme, one of which is a set of fingers.

Actually, even Willy uses templates for one-off or special jobs; it is just that he has made thousands of spindles and could probably make a standard production item blindfold.

The marking board is a strip of wood that has the points of nails or panel pins sticking out at the position of key design details on the spindle to be turned. These are usually set to align with the narrowest parts of the spindle.

The blank is roughed to a round, and then while it is still rotating, the marking board is held against it so that the nail points scratch rings in the surface. A parting tool is then used to groove in to near-finished diameter at these key marks, and a finished spindle is

placed behind the blank now on the lathe. Using a few simple tools – a half-round gouge, a spindle gouge and possibly a couple of skew chisels – the parting grooves are linked with the required design elements using eye alignment of the developing work-piece against the finished spindle at the back of the lathe. And it really is that simple – for Willy at least!

You and I will probably need templates. For a job with only half a dozen legs to turn I generally use only a simple template, cut from thick cardboard with scissors and Stanley knife. If I am planning a longer run, then the template will be cut from 1/8in (3mm) ply with a scroll saw.

The difficulty is that the templates can only be used to check the main length of profile, but not the ends where drive prongs, spigots, or holding bosses will get in the way.

The Craft Supplies' copying attachment is an extremely useful tool for small runs or

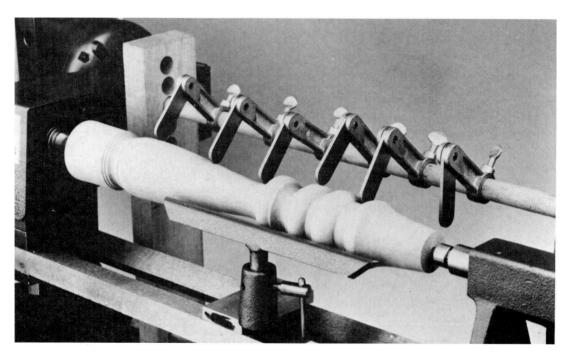

Craft Supplies' copy device. The fingers are set up on a pattern so that they fall in (as the one on the right) the moment the required diameter is achieved.

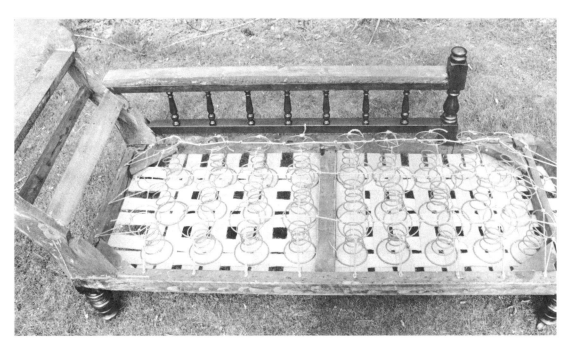

A set of matching small spindles and one larger one are required for this restoration of an 'inferior' chaise. (Inferior chaises were crudely made by the neighbourhood furniture maker.)

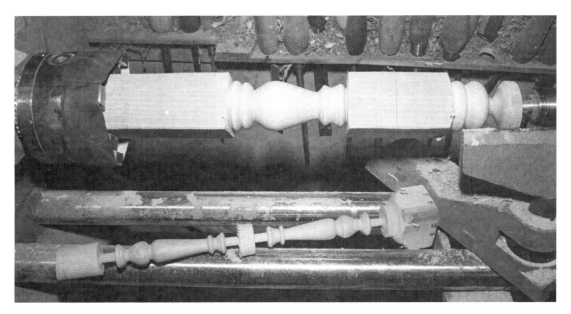

The end pillar and half of the small spindles are replacements for lost items. The frame and bits were bought for £25, but the cost of upholstery materials left little room for profit.

one-off special copy jobs. It consists of a mounting frame that is fixed at the back of the lathe bed, and has a series of fingers to indicate key features on the piece to be turned.

The item to be copied, either an existing element off a piece of furniture, or the sample piece for the production run, is mounted on the lathe. The fingers are clamped on to a retaining bar with small thumb screws. A screw is slacked off, and the finger moved until it corresponds with a feature on the finished piece. This could be a high point, a detail, or a narrow section. The finger is set to rest on the feature and is then adjusted until it just falls through behind the feature on the model piece. At this point it is clamped off. The other fingers are similarly positioned.

The test piece is now removed and a new blank cylinder is clamped up with all the fingers resting on the top surface. The design is then worked and as the finished dimension is reached at each key point or feature the appropriate finger drops through.

While the marking bar is only used to scratch a mark on low points, the finger attachment can be used to indicate high and low (and intermediate) features and can also act as a depth gauge.

A BALL JOB

There are some jobs for which even the most advanced turners still rely on templates. Ray Jones is a time-served turner of bowling balls. Having seen him at work I was tempted to have a go. Hhmmm! It is not a question of applying the bias – all of mine seem to be automatically biased, in one unpredictable way or the other! In other words they may look round, but they are not perfect. With the first one I did, it did not really matter as it was a trophy incorporating a flat-green bowl. Fortunately, being a trophy and intended to be permanently mounted on a plinth, absolute accuracy was not critical.

My next excursion into balls was not a real challenge either. An association that I was connected with wanted a large number of balls for the coconut shy at their annual fête. Again these did not need to be perfect spheres. I must admit also to turning them in willow, which is so light that even with a direct hit, the chances were that the thrower would not knock the coconut off its base! (Well, it was a fund-raising charity organization!)

Then I had a set of croquet balls to make, and here reasonable accuracy was required. The making of balls of this nature well illustrates the use of templates on between centres work.

Key Factors

There are two problems with balls. First is the copy problem we have already discussed; you usually require more than one, and they have to match in size and weight; and the second is that a perfect spherical form is usually required.

There are, of course, also questions concerning the use to which the ball will be put and therefore the material from which it has to be turned. Lignum vitae will knock the coconuts off the pod every time, beech sometimes, and willow never!

Bowling bowls were always turned in ebony or lignum vitae. Now the former is really too expensive for most, so lignum is the general choice. For croquet sets – for which some commissions arise – the highest-quality ones still use lignum for mallet heads and balls. Less high-quality sets use ash for the balls, and I find that a dense, wild-grain olive ash provides both the structural strength and the required weight. Skittle alley bowls can be made from beech or again from ash.

The key to ball turning is really in the templates and their use rather than in the turning techniques and tool manipulation.

Turning Balls

As we said, you are rarely called upon to turn just one ball, but rather pairs or multiples. For this, and for sound practical reasons, balls are often turned in pairs. It is a distinct help to be turning two side by side; not only does it speed up the process but you can constantly cross-check and compare the dimensions and development between the two.

If this is a new size of ball, two templates are made. For a true ball this will provide a perfect circle, for a bowling ball it will be a slight oval. Normally the template is cut from ⅛in (3mm) ply using a scroll saw and is cleaned with a half-round medium or bastard-cut file. The outline is very carefully drawn using a compass and the waste wood is cut away with the scroll saw, tracking a couple of thou' inside the compass mark.

The first template has a complete hemisphere with two straight legs, and will be used for checking the diameter in a vertical plane. The second template has an arc of the circle but is ½in (12mm) short of the centre axis line at both sides. Allowing for holding spigots of 1in (2.5cm) at either end of the ball, this template is used for checking the profile along the lathe's axis. There is a distinct advantage in making two templates. By laying the two one on top of the other and then reversing just one of the pair you can check to see that they match perfectly in every respect. At this you have a true circle (or a perfectly matching wrong oval).

The finishing and fine tuning is achieved by taking the template down to the compass-scribed line using a file, taking care not to lift any of the layers of ply.

The cylinder is now turned, and at this stage is taken down to a fraction over the finished diameter. It is marked off to provide the requisite number of balls, allowing ¼in (6mm) over diameter along the length and then a space of 1½in (3.7cm) between adjacent balls to provide the holding spigots. The

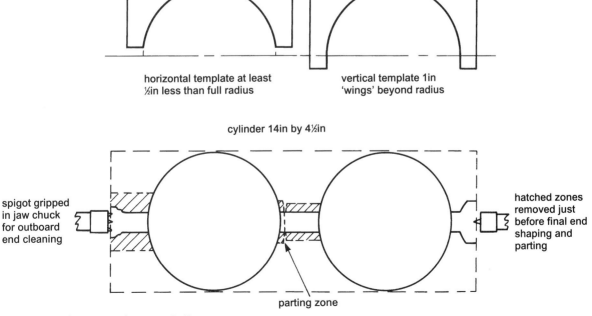

horizontal template at least
½in less than full radius

vertical template 1in
'wings' beyond radius

cylinder 14in by 4½in

spigot gripped
in jaw chuck
for outboard
end cleaning

hatched zones
removed just
before final end
shaping and
parting

parting zone

Layout for a pair of croquet balls.

Turning a ball. (a) Rough rounding over with a gouge. (b) Facing with a skew.

spigots are turned down to 1in (2.5cm) diameter.

Next the centre of each half cylinder is found and a strong line is drawn round the circumference with a soft lead carpenter's pencil. I know that when I have finished shaping the ball this thick line should have been reduced to a thin line, but the line must still be visible. This then allows for a sanding margin to the final finished diameter.

At this stage there is an option. The corners can be taken off and a rough shape achieved using a half-round gouge, or you can continue to work with the skew. I prefer the latter option. Working successively back from the shoulder, cuts are made from the top of the cylinder down towards the axis line by rolling the tool and checking that the cut is kept in the centre of the edge. The short point leads. The tool rest is kept high – a little below the top of the cylinder – which means that the tool must be rolled, and the handle must be lifted as the blade nears the axis. First both outboard ends are worked to near-finished size, and then both inboard ends.

By now I am constantly checking the profile with the templates. If I have got it right, the sphere will be almost complete but a thou or two elongated, or fat, along the centre axis.

The two balls are not parted off, but the spigots are cut through with a pad saw. The cuts are made to provide a boss of about ½in (12mm) at one end and 1in (2.5cm) at the other. The centre of the ½in (12mm) boss is found and imprinted with a punch. The first ball is then remounted, holding the 1in (2.5cm) spigot in a jaw chuck and the tailstock point in the punched end.

The tool rest is now lowered to about half height between the top and the centre axis, and a couple of rolling cuts are made to bring the side walls in to the finished diameter. These cuts go right down into the spigots to start the vertical parting-off cut.

The tool rest is again lowered, this time to axis height, and the skew is used in the vertical plane with the long point to the rest to make vertical parting cuts. At the chuck end the parting cut is kept very shallow – probably only a couple of millimetres deep – but

(c) The ball in a cup chuck. The angled pencil line marks an area not perfectly round. This will be sanded before the nub is parted off. (d) Final checking of the profile with the full template.

is accurately positioned to the finished axial diameter of the ball.

Still checking with the template, the outboard-end spigot is parted off. If, in order to get a good finish, the lathe speed has been fairly high (2,000rpm plus), the speed is now checked back before the final part-through.

The whole ball is now sanded, paying particular attention to the outboard end. It will also be finished and polished (if this is appropriate).

A block of pine – in my case two thicknesses of off-cuts from rafters glued together – is screwed on to the face plate, rounded off and hollowed out. *Before* completing the hollowing a ⅜in (9mm) hole is drilled right through the ply. This is the pusher hole.

The hollowing is slightly deeper than the radius of the ball so that the ball 'drops in' – it is, however, sufficiently tight at the mouth so that the ball has to be pushed in. It bottoms on a ring of sorbo rubber.

(e) The finished ball.

125

The ball is held in this cup chuck for the spigot parting zone to be cleaned off, sanded and polished. The profile can, of course, be checked with the horizontal template. Now you will be glad of the pusher hole. A length of dowel through this will eject the ball.

In fact the whole process is very quick; it takes much less time to make a ball than it does to write about it, and once the templates and the cup chuck have been made you can go into high production. A set of croquet balls in straight-grain ash works out at about ten minutes a ball, including timber-preparation time.

A similar process is used for making the smaller-sized wooden balls used for the cup and captive ball game; but I have to admit to buying marbles for solitaire boards – making balls that size is not my scene!

SPLIT TURNINGS

Split turnings are quite simple and are used as surface decoration. The technique also has wide application in making wall brackets, and particularly turned wall lamps.

Quite simply, 'split turning' is a piece of between centres turning done on two pieces of timber held together to form a single spindle. Once turned the two pieces are parted to give two, mirror-image split turnings. They are not, as the name might imply, a single turning that is then split or sawn apart.

It is sometimes possible merely to plane the inside faces of the two pieces and clamp them together for the turning stage. At other times it may be necessary to join them down their entire length using the glue sandwich approach.

If I am working on a long spindle and I have a little waste wood, I prefer to glue the two elements together somewhere near the centre using hot-melt glue, and then to join the ends with two screws at each end. I find this is preferable to the full glue sandwich for two reasons. First, if the spindle gets at all slender anywhere down its length it is some-times all too easy to split the turning when trying to ease the halves apart if they are glued all the way; with only a little glue at the centre, a hot knife blade is all that is necessary to separate the elements. The other reason is that sometimes the glue sandwich is not strong enough and the tailstock point (which must be bearing into the joint) can cause the elements to start to separate while still turning. For the same reason I like to drive long split turnings using the four-jaw.

When making some wall lamp elements where the split sections are likely to be both short and of greater diameter, the two blocks may be glued at both ends in what will eventually be the waste zone. One end is four-jaw driven, the profile is turned, and the outboard end is parted off. Often the finished piece is given a wrap or two of masking tape to hold the elements together and they are then parted off from the chuck. There is now no separation work to be done at all.

TOTALLY USELESS TURNING

One thing that everybody marvels at – even other turners – are captive rings, and this is the last of the special aspects of spindle turning that we will be looking at here.

Actually the process has been greatly simplified by the production of the ring scraping tool but I would like to take a quick look at the wonderful work that Dave Register does on what he calls his trunnion boxes. Dave produced these as the ultimate challenge to the person who asks 'Yes, but what can it be used for?' to which Dave gleefully answers 'Absolutely nothing – they have no practical use at all.' You may not want to make trunnion boxes, but turned baby rattles are fun and can be a nice little earner.

As Dave himself says, the beauty of his boxes is that they lend themselves to ornamentation and development. He starts with a cylinder of timber, which is chamfered off at one end. The taper he drives direct into the

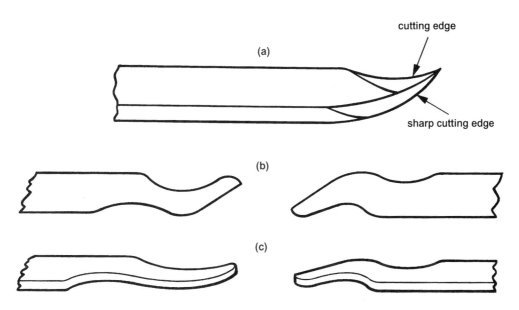

(a)

cutting edge

sharp cutting edge

(b)

(c)

Dave Register's trunnion tools. The pointed, skew-edged cutting tool (a) is ground from a flat chisel and is used to cut captive rings. Round-nosed scrapers (b) and (c) are also ground from flat chisels and are used for hollowing out trunnion boxes.

morse taper on the lathe's headstock, and all working is done from this single fixing.

His special tool kit consists of a standard small square-ended scraper and a spindle gouge. There are then six additional tools, most of which have been ground from single-bevel, plain ½in (12mm) chisels. Two are fine-pointed curved skews with single-sided bevels – one for right-hand cutting and one for left. There are then two round-nosed cranked scrapers and one square-nosed cranked scraper; and finally a pointed, cranked, ring-cutting skew.

First, the outside profile of the lid is developed using a conventional arc-ground oval skew and the top knob is shaped (with the spindle gouge). Next, the small captive ring is formed; this is cut with the ring-cutting skew. The same tool is used to cut down into the space between the top of the lid and the column for about ¼in (6mm). This will eventually form the parting cut to free the lid.

A recess is now cut defining the depth of the lid. This is done with a beading and parting tool and is to provide access for the

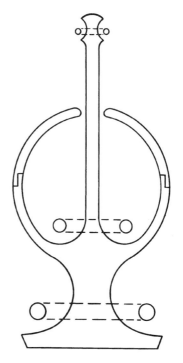

A Dave Register trunnion box. Just what *can* you use it for?

127

A collection of Dave Register's 'trunnion boxes' – the ultimate answer to the question: 'Yes! but what can you use it for?'

cranked scrapers. It is not taken down to the centre spindle as allowance has to be made for the internal captive ring. The first job is to cut the lip inside the lid. Thereafter hollowing proceeds. The main tool to start with is the adapted skew. Once the basic shape has been defined and the lip established, the left-hand bend round-nosed scraper takes over. Throughout this process care is taken to develop the inner profile of the lid to a smooth finish so that by the time the hollowing reaches the top parting cup and the top becomes free, the inside is in a finished condition.

The retaining lip is now cut on the lower section of the box until the lid fits snugly. The lid is held out of the way while the lower box is hollowed – this time using the right-hand bend round-nosed scraper. The internal ring is first formed and then parted from the centre shaft. Then the lower box is hollowed to a

smooth finish, and the shaft is cleaned inside the box. Final finishing is done when shaping of all elements has been completed and everything parted free.

Now the outer profile of the lower box is developed. First, the full depth is established with the beading and parting tool and the box is profiled with the conventional skew chisel. The lower rings are established, shaped (spindle gouge), undercut and parted (ring-cutting skew) and the lower shaft is finished. At this stage the lid is pushed home and the outer profile of the whole piece is lightly sanded and finished.

And there you have it – a totally useless, wonderful piece of nonsense, which is one of the ultimate demonstrations of advanced wood-turning ability. No wonder that Dave gets students flocking to the door of his studio.

9 Face Plate Turning

Despite the case I have just tried to make for more between centres work, I am not naive enough to believe that there will now be a mass exodus from face plate turning. Most of the experimental work, the developments in applied decoration, and the push towards better design is, and is going to continue to be, in the face plate field; although increasingly face plate work is combined with elements of between centres.

There are three areas of face plate turning that the advanced turner is likely to become regularly involved with: very large work, possibly pierced and natural-edged; hollow forms; and thin-walled turnings. Often hollow and thin wall are brought together. There are then the more specialized areas with their own devotees, such as segmented work and the combination of face/spindle turning, appearing frequently as galleried bowls.

LARGE WORK

Let's start with the large stuff. 'Large', in most people's minds, probably starts somewhere near 18in (45cm) in diameter and 6in (15cm) deep. My bigger pieces average 24in (60cm) wide by 12in (30cm) deep or 18in (45cm) wide by 20in (50cm) deep. I have one plane burr waiting that I cannot lift on to the lathe. It is 38in (96cm) in diameter and 17in (43cm) deep.

A massive bowl in burr always looks dramatic, however badly it is executed and often however poor the design is. It is a problem to the detriment of woodturning in general that some turners use sheer size to compensate for poor design and workmanship. Unfortunately, the attitude of the public in general does not help. Size is seductive, and most observers and many potential purchasers are so bedazzled by a large, heavily figured piece, that they too overlook the deficiencies. Big work, even relatively indifferent big work, can command big prices! Quality big work should command even greater prices than it currently does in the UK.

We turners ourselves, even some of the best of our brethren, do not always help. We feel compelled to try to get the maximum out of the block of wood in front of us; and therefore try to create a shape which optimizes wood use. I know that I am guilty of this, and I am conscious that I have this in mind every time I look at the block of plane. The moment that size becomes an objective in itself, consideration of design starts to diminish. So, in any discussion of large work, we must start with a plea. Please, in the name of quality woodturning and good design, don't let size be the only consideration.

The problem with large turning, both between centres and face plate mounted, is the mass, and the irregularities of the blanks most frequently used. We never start with prepared, nicely rounded blanks. This means that at almost any speed of rotation they will set up lathe oscillation. Many of the commercially available lathes – and my large Wadkin is one such – have speeds that only go down to 200rpm, and that really is too high for a 3ft (90cm) diameter irregular, burr bowl blank. Large spindles, of possibly 12in (30cm) in diameter are not too bad; a big bowl, on the other hand, can shake a lathe to pieces.

Most turners who regularly do big work therefore build themselves large face plate lathes with speeds that go down to 50rpm (*see* Chapter 1 for notes on the Ray Key lathe plans).

Using such a massive construction with a

A large burr on the first mounting. It was chain-saw shaped and will make a large natural-top piece.

large foot print, the Ray Key lathe offers considerable stability. Many users increase this by bolting the unit to the floor with large Rawlbolts driven into the concrete.

The need for maximum stability cannot be over-emphasized. If the blank is shaking the machine, there will be a period of vibration which works through the whole lathe including the tool rest. A tool held firmly on the rest will tend to the same vibration pattern, but not always, and not completely. It only takes a moment of out-of-phase vibration and the tool tip can be going forward into the wood as the block is moving out to the tool. A dig-in under these conditions may be OK, but sometimes a broken tool or a broken arm could result, or the block could even be ripped off the mounting, causing a broken head or foot. When roughing out really large items, a hard hat and Toetector boots are the absolute minimum safety requirements.

I will take it for granted that you will not have a band saw of sufficient capacity to accommodate a really large bowl blank. Few of us have access to the very largest industrial units with such a facility. So the usual sawing

to a round is not possible. Instead, a lot can, and has to be done with a chain-saw.

The block is first assessed and a broad design envisaged. At this stage a number of key decisions have to be made: fundamentally our concern is where in the block the top of the vessel will come. We have to take into account whether we are going to work to a natural top; whether we require, or can tolerate holes in the walls; just what overall shape we are aiming for; and, after all that, if the timber where we now appear to wish to mount the face plate is sufficiently sound to bear the load. These critical questions then lead us into a decision on which of two turning approaches will be used.

Mounting

Basically the question is whether to use one mounting or two. With one mounting the face plate will be fixed to what will be the base of the finished item; and the whole job, right through to final sanding and polishing, is then done off this single mounting. With two mountings the first will be to fix the face plate to the top of the vessel, while the base is turned and the outside profile developed; then the workpiece is remounted from the base so that hollowing out can proceed.

Of course, using the single mounting approach can mean that since the face plate will be screwed to the base, the screw holes could remain in the base of the finished piece. They will need filling and smoothing; but there will always be tell-tale signs that the purist will spot.

The main alternative to a finished base with the single mounting is to leave a waste block, which later has to be turned away using reverse chucking. This approach is not used frequently as it is messy, and often quite difficult with large natural-topped items. It is called upon most frequently when the timber on to which the face plate has to be fixed is in poor condition and would require mounting screws that would project well into the inside of the turned vessel.

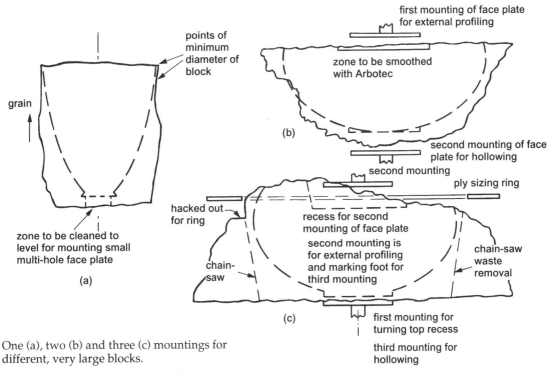

grain

points of minimum diameter of block

zone to be cleaned to level for mounting small multi-hole face plate

(a)

first mounting of face plate for external profiling

zone to be smoothed with Arbotec

(b)

second mounting of face plate for hollowing

second mounting

ply sizing ring

hacked out for ring

recess for second mounting of face plate

second mounting is for external profiling and marking foot for third mounting

chain-saw

chain-saw waste removal

(c)

first mounting for turning top recess

third mounting for hollowing

One (a), two (b) and three (c) mountings for different, very large blocks.

Secure mounting. The face plate was centred and 'tacked' in place with two wood screws. Eight coach bolts of 2in by ¼in (5cm × 6mm) are then driven in. This will provide a sound single mounting for shaping and hollowing, leaving a waste block to be turned away.

A variant on this approach is to use a large-diameter face plate so that the screw holes fall within the zone outside the final foot, which will eventually be turned away using reverse chucking.

If a one-mounting approach is to be used with fixing to what will be the finished base, it is worthwhile smoothing off the base to a finished state before mounting. If a double approach is selected, the place to be pre-worked for the face plate will have to be on the top of the block.

It is necessary to true up the face that will be mounted on to the face plate, particularly if the main mass of the block is off-centre. It is the plane that is established for this first mounting that sets the whole orientation of the piece; and it is the location of the face plate along this plane that basically establishes the format, even the profile of the bowl. It is *never* merely a case of finding the best flat spot.

Frequently the plate that we will be turning off (top- or bottom-fixed) is not mounted to align with the physical centre of the block now in front of us – there may be a major fault down one side that we wish to avoid. The position of the plate has to be fixed for what will be the centre of the finished bowl. This probably means placing the block on the work-bench and wedging it until it sits in the correct orientation for the finished bowl. Two tall try squares are then pushed against the wall of the block to show the narrowest diameter. The distance between the squares is halved and this gives the centre point for the face plate fixing. The marking-off rings described in Chapter 2 may prove useful.

Finding the Centre

I always prefer to do this with the 'bowl' top up on the bench. If I am then going to use only a single fixing, the 'centre' has to be transferred from the top of the block to the bottom, as does the horizontal orientation of the base. This is not always easy.

Once the location and orientation of the face plate has been determined, we need to provide a level base for the plate to sit on. Send in the Arbortec!

The more unruly the block the more firmly it has to be secured to the face plate. There is no hard and fast rule about which screw size to use for which blank diameter because the condition and nature of the timber and the basic grain orientation have a considerable bearing. I range between four 1in × 12s (2.5cm) bright zinc screws, through eight 2in × 12s (5cm) screws, to sixteen ¼in (6mm) coach bolts. If the timber is well spalted or badly shaken, it could require four 1½in × 12s (3.7cm) screws on the outer ring of face plate holes (assuming the standard four holes to a ring) and four 1in × 12s (2.5cm) screws on the inner ring. If into green end grain, it will more likely be four 2in × 12s (5cm) screws and four 1in × 12s (2.5cm) ones.

At this stage the block goes on to the lathe. A chain (or similar) hoist is essential. If you do not have the headroom (and I don't) then mounting the blank *must be* a two-person job. Even if you can manage to lift the block, you will need someone to turn the spindle so that the thread picks up. Trying to do this alone is a very quick route to serious and expensive medical problems. Large and long between centres blocks are usually slightly easier to deal with as these can be blocked up and positioned with a car jack off the lathe bed.

Roughing to a Round

Turning the mounted block by hand will show where there are projecting areas that will cause out-of-balance rotation. Frequently there is a substantial amount of off-balance material and this will require considerable 'adjustment' with a chain-saw. Under less demanding conditions, and as normal practice, I find an Arbortec disc on an angle grinder to be the handiest method for truing a large block to an approximate round. In fact my Arbortec does a lot of my preparation

Using the Arbortec to make a flat area for the mounting of a face plate. Smoothing to a finished state is achieved with a belt sander. This will be a single mounting as the outer face of the burr will be left natural. The screw holes for the face plate will later be filled.

An electric chain-saw is part of the in-workshop preparation equipment.

work in a very cost-effective way. It is high on my list of priority items of kit. It does, however, create a lot of mess, throwing chippings all over the workshop.

Two safety points. Do not attempt to use a petrol-driven chain-saw for this type of work. They are heavy, and best practice dictates that with a chain-saw you should not cut above waist height – here you are at chest height and the bar could kick back into your face. Secondly, you are now inside and both fumes and noise are excessive. So when speaking of using a chain-saw, I am referring to a small electric-powered saw. I find the 16in (40.5cm) bar Black and Decker very satisfactory but use it with caution.

The second safety factor concerns the use of an Arbortec; I believe that it is essential to use an angle grinder with an automatic no-load switch. Some have click on/off switches, which means that if the unit is accidentally jerked out of your hands it continues running, and you may then really appreciate your Toetector footwear.

There is a third point of caution – never

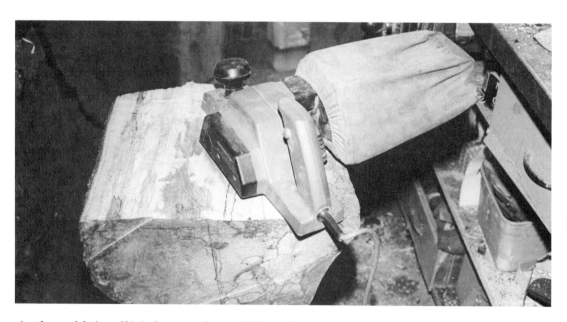

Another useful piece of kit is the power planer, which can often be used to remove larger, balance-throwing bulges before the lathe is started.

lose sight of the profile you are working towards. It is very difficult to stick a bit back on!

Whether the one- or two-mounting approach is being used, it is normal to shape, and even to finish, the outside profile before starting to hollow out.

A large, heavy, bowl gouge is the most effective way of roughing a wild burr. A roughing gouge is too big and can often catch, while scrapers are too uncontrollable when there are still substantial projections and hollows. The very heavy, largest-size bowl gouges now available are fine. It is here that you will really find that the commercially supplied handles are far too short. As noted in Chapter 7, most of my large bowl gouges have handles at least three times the length of the blade when new. I am also slowly moving over to ballasted handles on the larger tools. Roughing large burrs at 200rpm is a bit brutal, and stance and tool holding is important.

I find that the most comfortable position is to have the left foot well forward but a little to the side. This means that I can sweep right round the profile of the bowl, making a single cut without having to change foot position. The foot forward also means that my left side is angled forward. Now the long handle of the tool can be held into the lower tummy and hip, which dampens out a lot of the shock loading. The right hand is well back along the tool handle and a few inches behind the hip. This allows me to keep the arm bent at the elbow, which again absorbs a lot of shock without pounding the elbow joint. The left hand usually grips the blade of the tool from underneath with all the fingers wrapped round the tool. The fleshy part of the lowest phalanx of the index finger is pressed against the tool rest to provide lateral stability.

The tool rest, a robust one, is positioned about an inch below centre line, which means that the cutting tip is working at about axis height. Later, as the worst projections have been removed, the rest is brought closer to

Roughing with a heavy gouge. This block should have been chain-saw trimmed to speed up the roughing process. Note the stance, with the butt of the gouge braced against the hip. Despite a very firm mounting, roughing here is being done left-handed so that the turner is not in the direct line of flight. A hard hat and safety glasses are also worn.

the workpiece and is raised to nearer centre height. Although with the Wadkin I have a long, cranked tool rest, and with the Poolwood there is the cantilevered rest, I now find that I prefer to work the outside of large bowls from the Wadkin free-standing rest. It gives greater flexibility whilst providing complete rigidity.

Once the profile is roughed, then standard bowl gouges (still fitted with long handles) are probably all that is required to finish the outside walls. The final cleaning is with a broad 2in/5cm square-ended scraper.

If you are two-mounting, you now need to make provision for the remounting.

Working at the size we are now talking about I do not feel that any of the dovetail or combination chucks are adequate. There are two alternatives. If the bowl is to have a turned rim, a block of wood can be glued to the base and a face plate screwed to this. This mounting block will later be turned away using reverse chucking. If you are working to a natural-top design then a glued-on wood block may not be capable of standing the initial shocks; so the metal face plate has to be screwed directly to the base using the shortest screws that would still give a safe mounting.

A glue block does need to be of sound timber that will take good-sized screws and hold firmly. The glue could be gap-filling superglue, but for a job this size you could immediately use half a pot. My main alternative is Cascamite for this type of job. Good PVA wood glues can be OK if used in quantity and given ample drying time, but they have failed me on occasions. Hot-melt glues do not give a good enough bonding, as there is difficulty in covering a large area before the glue starts to cool and set.

Before demounting, the new position for the face plate is very carefully marked either on the bowl base or the wood block. This can be done with dividers set to the exact diameter of the plate. If done carefully, the face plate can later be fixed on sufficiently close to centres to be able to remount the block true. Care in getting an accurate position pays off; it is a real bind if you are off-true and have to start the second stage of turning by reshaping the outside profile!

Hollowing Out

The first stage of hollowing out requires the truing of the top face. If it is to be natural top, I prefer to establish the inside of the rim and fix the wall thickness, and to clear the whole inside to a level surface before really starting to hollow out. There are times when a little initial levelling is done with the Arbortec. I have found nothing better than a heavy gauge, diamond-point scraper to take off the main irregularities. A strong normal bowl gouge is the best alternative. A broad-tipped scraper is not suitable. It can cause a series of jarring blows, which will loosen the mount-

ing screws in anything but the soundest timber. Whichever tool is used, the initial levelling off process is done very gently with shallow cuts, working from the centre outwards towards the rim.

Having attained a reasonably smooth top, the next process is almost invariably to take a cone out of the centre of the piece. This for two reasons. First, it usually gives me a blank for a small dish – and this eases my conscience when I see the huge mountains of waste created in hollowing out a large bowl; and secondly I find that taking out a cone is the quickest way of achieving what is otherwise the tedious part of the hollowing process.

The slicer tool of the Stewart system with the tungsten carbide tip is mounted in the arm brace handle. This is perfect for this job. Mine has paid for itself scores of times over in the dish cones that it has rescued. It has certainly saved hours of time. Dangerous as this process appears, it has never yet caused any injury, although I am not entirely happy about the long-term effect of the pounding that it gives elbow and shoulder.

Many think it unsafe, and you do have to take care; but in first testing it I (ab)used it in every way I could think of, locking up the drive on a number of occasions. It caused no problems (*see* Chapter 7 for details on the use of this tool).

Pilot Holes

Once the cone is away, the shaping of the inside profile proceeds. Of course, this can be done in a conventional way using a standard bowl gouge and cutting from the rim of the bowl down and across to the centre. However, this is a fairly slow process on big pieces.

For all bowls it is wise to get into the habit of always drilling a hole in the centre to fix the depth of hollowing – but not until after any cones have been removed. Some turners use a high-speed drill bit (about ⅜in (9mm) diameter) clamped into a suitable handle. A

A largish cone is being taken out with the Stewart slicer. This speeds up the hollowing process but also yields a blank for a nice small dish. The free-standing Wadkin rest is being used with the Poole Wood lathe.

turn of masking tape is wrapped around the bit to give a depth mark. Supporting the bit on the tool rest (set just below centre height), the lathe is switched on to low speed and the drill pushed home to the depth mark. The original Stewart tool kit was supplied with a bit that fitted one of the handles.

Most turners prefer a bigger diameter hole – usually about 1in (2.5cm) – as this gives better access for a bowl gouge to start from. If an auger bit is used for this, mount it in a Jacobs chuck from the tail-stock. I have seen a turner clamp an auger bit in a drill brace and hold the handle of the brace while the lathe was rotating. On one occasion the bit hit an internal check, jerked the brace out of the turner's hands and the handle then came round and smashed his knuckles.

The next requisite is a curved tool rest that can be positioned inside the bowl. The rest should be as large, strong and heavy as possible (*see* Chapter 7 for more detail about bowl rests).

I use an arrangement of pivot pins and a modified bowl gouge – one with the shoulders cut back to provide a top cutting edge. This can be pivoted in towards the centre of the bowl or can cut back uphill pivoting out towards the rim, and gives very rapid waste removal. The depth of cut is controlled by angling the bevel against the timber, and by the amount of leverage load exerted against the pivot.

The final shaping is usually done with a standard bowl gouge. On the other hand, getting that all-essential fair curve down the

Working off pivot pins. Undercutting aggressively by pivoting a reprofiled gouge (above), and cutting outwards on a pivot pin (below).

inside wall without the final touches of a large scraper is not easy.

The case for considering the scraper as a fine finishing tool has already been made; however, we have also identified that when deep inside a large piece, the overhang of the tool on the wing of the tool rest is such that the combined level of flexing can be quite high. The rules of scraping also suggest that the profile of the scraper should be of only slightly sharper radius than that of the wall we are scraping.

Having had so many major dig-ins while trying to clean up the inside bases of large bowls with scrapers, I have learned to make some compromises.

Finishing it off

It has to be said that on some very large pieces in burred or checked woods, scrapers are not very satisfactory. If the tool rest can be positioned such that the gap between rest and wood is less than about an inch, a larger scraper may be used. The problem is that there is usually a much bigger gap, and any imperfections in the wood will cause the tip of the scraper to vibrate, however massive the scraper is. A vibrating tip meets the next imperfection slightly out of phase and there is an immediate bang and a bigger flexing, the tool jumps, and the consequent dig-in can be quite severe. The scraper tips supplied with the full Stewart kit are better. Here the tip is smaller and will only be in contact with a small section of wood, so the possibility of dig-in is quite remote even when working on shaken timber. The tip is also supported on a massive shank so vibration is minimal even with a considerable overhang.

So, what are the compromises? First, make frequent adjustments to the position of the rest. Always try to keep it just above the axis height, and always, always as close as possible to the cutting tip. You cannot make a single sweep from the centre of the base, round, up the walls and on to the rim from a single position of the rest; it is inevitably a multi-cut job.

Next, go for the thickest-section scraper you can find, but ignore the rules on profile. Work with narrower tools, then you can only contact a very small part of the arc you are trying to sweep (the Stewart hooker well meets these criteria). Cut from the base up out towards the rim. Hold the blade firmly on the tool rest but do not tense up on it – you are trying for a whisper-light touch with the tool tip and you cannot achieve this with tightly clenched fists. Above all, keep the tool sharp; this may mean several visits to the grind wheel for one bowl in hard, knotty wood.

So there you have the problem of producing a fair curve with a tight-radius edged tool; the only answer is good tool control, care and *skill*!

I have to admit that on the very largest of pieces I often have to resort to more power sanding to achieve a desired finish. Here

A flexible drive shaft with ball races in the drive head gives easier access to the inside of deeper vessels and removes the drive unit from extremes of dust.

again we run into a problem. It is not always easy to get inside with a sanding pad on a power drill. The answer is a flexible drive.

Sanding

I found that I was getting through the power drills I used for sanding at the rate of one every eight or nine months. Moving up to Proline quality lengthened it to about twelve months. I then tried a Bosch drill, but this has a problem in that the drive freewheels under no load, and the sudden application of a load can cause the gears to snatch as the drive is taken up. Bosch gear trains also went every eight or nine months.

The move up to full professional-quality drills has proved more than cost-effective, my last replacement being over three years ago.

In all fairness to the manufacturers, it has to be said that their machines are not designed for the particular loadings of disc sanding (sideways thrust, continuous running, and dust-laden environment) to the level that many turners undertake.

Then we come on to flexible drives. Again those available in the local hardware shops have bush bearings and light flexible-drive cables. They are only suitable for occasional use. It is essential to get a heavy-duty cable with ball-race bearings and to mount it so that there is the minimum bend between power unit and sanding disc. Ideally the drill should be slung somewhere above the lathe bed.

One immediate advantage of the flexi drive is that it removes the drill from both the sideways loading and the dusty environment that kills off standard power drills; by spending more on the flexible drive you reduce what you have to pay for the drill.

I do have another piece of kit that has been used on some special jobs – the Fordham unit that I use for working decoy ducks. This is a rotary drive module with a very heavy-duty flexible drive, and is designed to be slung above the work zone. It will take standard ¼in (6mm) drive sanding discs (and a range of various-sized rasps and diamond burrs). I do not, however, use it in normal bowl sanding as it is intended for use as a decorating tool, and is a fairly expensive piece of kit.

Just how much sanding do you do? The purists say that with proper tool control a light touch with a piece of hand-held paper is all that should be necessary. This is fine for run-of-the-mill pieces. On a large jarrah burr it may be the only way of achieving a good finish inside.

I am still using the Velcro system discs, with a 3in (7cm) diameter being the standard. If there is substantial finishing to be done, the first disc will be 60 grit but I sand with the lathe stopped. This way I can see where I need to concentrate, and reduce the amount of friction heat generated. I will probably get

down to 180 grit before the lathe is started – always on its slowest speed. Having once worked through 240 and started to get a little polish, the lathe is stopped and a sidelight is shone across the surface to see if there are any blemishes, and particularly whether there are any sanding marks from the 60 grit. If there are, these are sanded away with the lathe stationary.

By now I will also be using sheets of wet or dry applied with the support of a rubber block. I then progress with disc and sheet through to 400, then switch to Danish oil and beeswax-based friction polish.

Once the inside of the bowl is finished, we can do some reverse chucking so that the mounting block can be removed, the foot of the vessel formed, and/or the base cleaned up. Any remaining screw holes are filled with a little sawdust and strong glue or a wax stopping stick.

I have to admit that a clean dovetail recess in the bottom of a bowl does not worry me. It certainly does not offend most customers. In fact some have said that the 'hollowed-out base is preferable to a smooth, flat bottom'. Other turners, and certainly the judges at competitions and adjudicated exhibitions, have very strong views on this subject, and to them any sign of chucking method is anathema. So most better-quality pieces have to be reverse chucked for final base finishing (see Chapter 6).

HOLLOW VESSELS

The greatest challenge to the advanced turner is to produce a hollow vessel with a tiny top aperture and beautiful, evenly thin walls throughout. Universally acclaimed masters such as American David Ellsworth and British Melvyn Firmager make spheres and narrow-neck vases, which, when cut in half (and both have done this to prove it) have walls of ⅛in (3mm) thickness from the top, down the sides and even across the base.

The ability to do this is not something that

is achieved overnight! There is no trick to it, no special tools or techniques – just a lot of practice and many mistakes on the way. It is a skill that is best acquired in stages. In writing about it here we will work through some of those stages.

I once heard a turner giving a talk where he differentiated between 'cutting tools' and 'scraping tools'. Talk to a hollow-vessel expert and they do not recognize this. To many of them scrapers are their mainstay, and are just as much cutting tools as are gouges and chisels. We have already stressed the notion that a properly sharpened scraper, lightly applied, is capable of just as delicate a cut as is any other well-sharpened tool.

The problem starts with the recognition that in hollow-vessel work the more usual cutting tools cannot be presented to the surface of the wood in a manner to give an optimum angle of cut. Anything near proper tool contact breaks down very quickly the narrower the vessel's opening becomes. This has led to three developments. The first has been to make tools that have tips vaguely resembling the profile of a bowl gouge, but then to fix the tip to the end of a long spindle at such an angle of offset that proper edge presentation is possible. The results of this thinking have led to many special tools, including one known as a 'drop-snout hook tool'. From similar thinking came the ring tools. The second

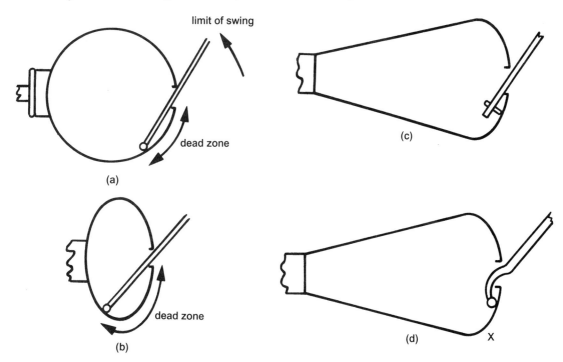

Limits of tools on hollow forms. On a sphere (a), the narrow apertures limit the sweep of straight tools; there is an absolute dead zone. On ellipses (b), the problem is even worse, particularly with end cutting tools such as conventional bowl gouges. The facility to side cut, as with hook and ring tools and modified gouges, for example, gives some improvement. The side-pointing clamped bits (c) and the Stewart hooker can get up under the shoulder eliminating any dead zone. Some forms (d) present a little difficulty; for example, getting at X with the hooker. All hollow forms require either frequent realignment of the clamped bits or several changes of tool between the top and bottom.

development has been to mount scraper tips so that they can work round corners. The third has been to modify conventional bowl gouge tools so that they cut on the edge of the gouge as well as across the tip – the tool we have already talked about in earlier sections.

Edge Presentation

We earlier identified that hook tools feature in the work of Ed Moulthrop. He produces massive pieces. One picture of his work shows a vase with one of his grandchildren standing comfortably inside it, eyes just peeping over the rim. Bengt Gustaffesen and other great Scandinavian turners have followed the long tradition of their part of the world and use only combinations of hook tools and skews. Some of their hooks cut along the top edge like Ed's. Others have a section of bowl gouge on the end of the shaft and cut forward around the U. These are the so-called 'drop-nose gouges'.

Melvyn Firmager, David Ellsworth, Dennis Stewart, and many others primarily use forms of scraper.

While turners have been very innovative in developing tools to overcome the edge-presentation problems, we have not been able to do much about the second difficulty faced in hollow-form work. You cannot get the tool rest inside the vessel so there is no way of avoiding a long overhang between the cutting tip and the supporting rest. Three things can be done to lessen the difficulties. Firstly, and obviously, you can make the tool shaft as large and as rigid as possible; secondly, you can take extra care in keeping the cutting edge sharp. The third, and the one that almost all turners (except Ed) have adopted, is to use tools with smaller cutting tips. The shafts may be 1in (2.5cm) diameter steel, but the tips offer only ¼in (6mm) of cutting edge.

The most important factor, however, is to use appropriate timber. Rough, scrubby, pippy or checked timber, particularly burrs, is only suitable for smaller hollow forms where the length of tool overhang is kept to

the minimum. But even more vital than that is that large, thin-walled, hollow forms can really only be turned from green timber. Green wood cuts much more readily and cleanly. There is less tool bounce and therefore much greater control.

The first stage down the long road to hollow forms is probably the simple undercut rim. This is a scraper job and the common round-nosed side scraper is ideal. Unfortunately, because the tool is being pulled towards you and into the wood it is all too easy to exert too much pressure. In no time at all the rim is undercut but there is considerable fluffy tearing where the rotations have taken you across the end grain. Once you have torn the fibres under an undercut rim it is one awful job to try to clean it up. It is impossible to get in with effective sanding devices. The only answer is to remember the scraper is a cutting tool, not a blunt instrument for beating things into shape. So the first step towards hollow forms is gently to practise lots of undercut rims on dry timber until you get them right every time!

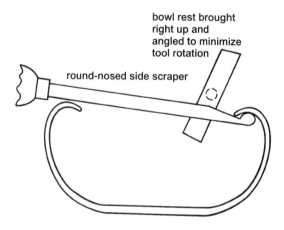

Undercutting a bowl rim with a scraper. It is essential that cuts are very light; the tendency is to pull back too hard.

Even in more open-necked vessels we find that most standard tools cannot be presented to achieve any cut at all; we have to use the specials. We also quickly run into the difficulty of being unable to provide tool-rest support inside the vessel and certainly not anywhere near the cutting tip; therefore we get problems of vibration and tools rolling off the rest. We also get a turning moment trying to twist the tool in our hand.

Basically the situation is this. The force of the rotating wood on the tip of a cutting tool is directly downwards if the cutting tip is in line with the axis of the tool. The support of the tool rest, however far away, neutralizes this. Move the cutting zone away from the tip – that is, along the shoulder of the modified gouge, and there is a turning moment around the axis of the tool. The further out to the side the cutting edge is from the axis of the tool, the greater the turning moment.

The Stewart tool system offers 'the hooker'. This has a cranked shaft so that, in effect, the tip can work around the corner and remain in line with the axis of the shaft, which is held firmly on the tool rest. Because the shaft is ¾in (18mm) diameter soft steel there is minimum vibration and flexing. Using the curved shaft and tiny scraper blades there is virtually no turning moment.

In Chapter 7 we talked about the large tools with small tips that David Ellsworth uses and about the small-tipped tool he sells when demonstrating. Both have tips cutting out to the side and are therefore subject to turning moment. We also saw how Melvyn Firmager has provided a 'bevel' in the shape of a rubbing nub – it does not prevent 'moments', but does give you something to work against.

Now we run into the real problem. A little tool twisting we can cope with quite easily while we can see what is going on; it becomes a major problem when working blind deep inside a hollow vessel.

Here we need all the help we can get, and working with a small-tipped scraper is much more forgiving than would be a modified gouge or many of the hook tools. The new DAHT tool also scores well under these extreme conditions. Firstly, it has a relatively small cutting edge; then the 'lid' prevents dig in, and allows an easy feel of where the cutting edge is; lastly, the robust shaft minimizes vibration.

Spatial Ability

Working blind inside hollow vessels obviously creates a number of difficulties. We have addressed the problem of knowing what the orientation of the cutting tip is in relation to the wood. The second problem is that of knowing whereabouts within the vessel you are cutting, and the third difficulty is that of controlling wall thickness.

Judging where you are cutting is a question of spatial ability (which is not equally well developed in everybody) and practice. David Ellsworth sits on the lathe bed and fixes his eye down the axis of the tool. This enables him to judge fairly accurately where the tip is. Setting his head and neck in this position and holding them under some tension has, however, caused him severe problems with the top vertebrae of his spine. He is not alone in this, and intense concentration with hunched shoulders in a tensed position has given a number of professional turners similar problems.

The curved bowl rest with pivot pins does give some added control over the position of the tool tip within an enclosed vessel.

Tools that cut at the end of or close in to the axis (the DAHT) are easier to align by eye than those that consist of two or three feet of shaft, and then an offset at the tip of an inch or two.

Wall thickness (or thinness) is not quite so difficult to deal with. Some turners (and again David is one) make a lot of use of sound. As the walls get thinner the sound of the cutting does change. If you attune to this it can give a fairly accurate guide to how thin the walls are getting. Some turners have developed their own sets of internal/external callipers as the commercial models will not get into any real depths. Melvyn uses fixed-gap 'callipers' made from bent coat-hangers.

In using any callipers the tip on the outside should be kept in firm contact with the external profile while the calliper is being moved. The inside of the vessel will be somewhat rough and will upset the setting of the calliper. The inside tip is only brought into contact for spot measurements when the gap between the external tip and the outer wall is assessed. And of course these callipers are used with the lathe stopped!

The Stewart hooker has a long curved arm that arcs round the outside of the vessel. At the end of this curving arm is a thin plastic finger. A gap is set between the end of the finger and the cutting tip of the hooker. This gap corresponds to the required wall thickness of the vessel. This device gives a continuous reading while the vessel is turning. The finger is bent down by the friction against the outer wall. Once the wall is down to the finished thickness the plastic finger rides free.

Unfortunately, in normal use, the fingers do not last very long before breaking up. The

Wall thickness. The Stewart hooker is here in use with the wall thickness finger fitted. This arrangement would not normally be used with the open bowl here mounted on the lathe for demonstration.

concept is good and it is worth some innovative individual giving some thought to suitable materials for longer-life fingers.

At the moment I am learning (and still have a long way to go) how to produce hollow vessels of the quality that I require. To date I find the hooker fingers the most reliable measuring device, but even with these I still go through the walls of some grasstree-root hollow forms. Probably one in three of my attempts ends up on the scrap heap, and I am very glad that human fingers cannot be poked inside to test the finish of the inner walls.

Removing Waste

One of the big problems of working with narrow-aperture vessels is that of waste removal. If the bits are not cleaned out frequently enough the build-up can get in the way of tool control.

Removing the vessel from the lathe is OK if it merely means unscrewing a face plate from the drive spindle, inverting the pieces and shaking out the bits. If it means actually opening the jaws of a four-jaw, and then having to reclamp, it is not satisfactory. It is all too easy to remount the vessel on a slightly different line and long, careful repositioning is then necessary.

Specially made spoons and scrapers are used by many hollow formists. Others have taken a side line off their chip or dust collector and use fine nozzles to get down into the vessels. I have an old Aquavac beside the lathe with some small vacuum-cleaner nozzles (it is also useful for the occasional clean-up in difficult nooks and crannies).

My own development in hollow-form turning has travelled through three stages so far, and this still seems a useful route for beginners to follow.

The first faltering steps were taken with grasstree (*Xanthorea*) or blackboy from Australia. This material is very easy to cut and is extremely forgiving. The second stage was turning vases and decanters; and the

Hollow-turning a grasstree root. Before . . .

. . . and after.

third stage advanced into hollow forms with pierced walls. After that I ventured into thin-wall turning, which is a separate section. The next step is yet to come; I intend to go on one of the short courses that Melvyn runs in his workshop.

First Steps: Grasstree Root

Grasstree is an ideal material to start with: it is soft, you can cut it with gouge or scraper with equal facility, it is almost impossible to dig in, and the natural shape of the root lends itself to vases or hollow forms.

A fairly short root can be fixed direct to a face plate (or often clamped in a four-jaw) in such a way that the foot with the screw holes will eventually be turned away.

First the health warning. *Xanthorea* produces a lot of dust and there are suggestions that this is fairly unhealthy to the lungs. So a mask is worn at all times, from first cut to final finish – and after that until the dust settles in the workshop (and I have recently been told that this takes up to three days).

Following the natural contour, a wide top pot is shaped. With a vessel of this size it is quite easy to hollow out through a 1½in (3.7cm) diameter top aperture, and this isn't bad for a first effort.

If possible, drill a depth hole in any hollow vessel and make this as wide as possible. On this first piece a 1½in saw tooth bit is ideal. A wrap of masking tape around the drill shank marks off the full depth you are working to, leaving about ⅜in (9mm) in the base.

The drill bit is mounted in a Jacobs chuck in the tailstock and the lathe is set to the slowest speed, in my case 200rpm. Wind the drill in slowly to about a third of its depth. Now wind it back out to clear the swarf. Drill the second 'third' and again withdraw the drill.

It is essential to clear the swarf at regular intervals. Grasstree is often wet inside and the heat generated by the saw tooth can bind the turnings up to form a real hard shoulder behind the drill head. It once took me almost fifty minutes poking with a long screwdriver to free a bound in a saw tooth head.

145

Typical hollowing-out sequence, using the largest possible saw tooth or auger.

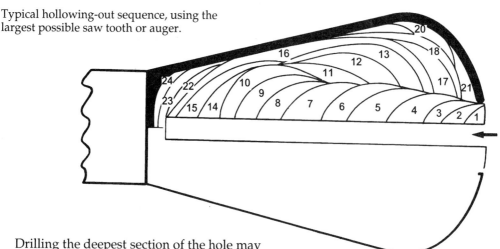

Drilling the deepest section of the hole may well require a repositioning of the tailstock; and, at times, the chuck itself may be inside the hole.

At least half of the hollowing out is going to be done with the profiled gouge, and on an average grasstree head, a ⅜in (9mm) gouge is adequate. Working to this size gives you time to think while making the first few hollow vessels.

Start by widening the hole out somewhere near the centre – again this gives more room to move. From the mid-point come back up towards the mouth still using the shaped gouge.

Hollowing is a gradual process working from the centre outwards. Keep taking a little off the lower parts of the walls and gradually widening out the base; the lower sections should trail well behind the upper walls. This way maximum support is given to the side walls while working out near the top and under the rim.

There comes a point at which the gouge can no longer be presented to give a cutting edge. Now the scraper takes over. At first I used a round-nosed side scraper, and this was quite effective. However, it was at this stage that I first saw the Stewart tool, and having purchased one I found that the scraper tip mounted on the hooker was ideal.

To start with I made full use of the long-radius arm and the plastic fingers to give a

sense of wall thickness, but later found that crude callipers made of bent wire clothes-hangers gave a sufficiently clear indication of how the walls were progressing.

Once the under-rim and upper walls are to the finished thickness, the inside base can be worked out.

By careful control of the scraper a reasonably ridge-free inner surface is possible, but a little sanding is usually necessary. Rotary flap wheels in a small chuck mounted on a flexible drive shaft are very useful for plumbing the depths, but it is advisable to sand out with the lathe stopped. A bouncing flexi-drive inside a spinning vessel could easily jump and shatter the side wall (as mine did on a number of occasions)!

At this stage you might choose to do a little cheating on the first vessel or two.

It is much easier to thin down the walls finely from the outside than from the inside. A couple of cheating cuts down the outer profile can make you look really brilliant!

Finish off the top and the outside walls right down to the holding foot. If you have used the jaw chuck, all that remains is to part off. If not, remove the face plate, and, carefully drawing lines across the diagonally opposite screw holes, find the exact centre-point on the base. This will provide the location point for the tailstock point when the vessel is reverse chucked.

Clamp up a piece of scrap wood in a jaw chuck and turn this down to a spigot to fit snugly into the vessel's top aperture. Softwood is ideal, and I usually have a bag of off-cuts of poplar, pine or willow for this job. (This is the one good use to be made of those free 'trees' from the neighbours.)

Mount the vessel on the spigot with the tailstock point in the centre-mark on the base, but before tightening up test the centre by hand-rotating the piece using the tool-rest gap as an indicator. Once finely centred, tighten up. Do not use much pressure – you don't know quite how thin your walls are and it is awful to see the workpiece crumble like a crushed egg shell. Turn away the foot, sand, oil and polish.

Vases and Decanter Forms

The second phase of development was also based upon grasstree. This time I concentrated on long roots, and used the wide section of the top of the root to provide the wider, lower part of a narrow-neck vase or carafe form. This has subsequently become one of my favourite forms and has scope for many variations based on classical design. It also provides opportunities for various forms of surface texturing.

With a face plate screwed to the base and the tailstock used for outboard end support, the outer profile of the vase is formed. There are two important considerations to be taken into account at this stage.

First, while the top aperture can be fairly small, you cannot have a neck that is very long and narrow, as there is not room to get sufficient sideways swing on most tools when hollowing deep inside. The profiled gouge and the DAHT soon become ineffective. There are also times when you cannot feed the 'bulge' on the Stewart hooker down the neck, so you have to resort to a tool with a straight shaft and a cutting bit that can be angled out to the side. You must therefore design a neck that is workable. It really is worthwhile making a scale drawing of what you are trying to do before you start.

Secondly, when you have completed the profile and removed the tailstock so that you can start to hollow out the top of the neck, there is considerable sideways torque and often some flexing. To overcome this problem, leave a tracking ring around the neck of the vase and hold this firmly in a long-work steady. Turn the tracking ring away only when hollowing out is completed.

It is possible to drill a pilot hole in pieces of this nature using a long-hole auger, and it certainly does help in the initial hollowing out. Keep the auger very sharp, use a locating eye mounted in the tool post, and control the plunge of the auger by hand with the lathe turning at the slowest possible speed.

The new saw-tooth bit kits with long extension drives really come into their own when turning carafe and long vase forms. Although the constant repositioning to keep the hole cleared out is a real pain, it is possible to get a full-depth, full-diameter hole, and again this greatly facilitates the initial hollowing.

A $\frac{3}{8}$in (9mm) shaped shoulder gouge is useful for the inner neck area, but soon it has to be replaced by an alternative tool. From here it is a matter of choice, depending on what you have, and what will feed down the neck.

I find I frequently change from one tool to another as I tackle different parts of the task, but on the narrow-neck vase forms, I basically use the profiled gouge followed by the Ellsworth bit tool, and on bigger items where there is room, the hooker.

The importance of keeping the tools sharp cannot be over-stressed. It matters at any time, but when working inside it becomes vital. Any loss of edge results in tearing and digging in, and a dig-in inside usually means tool bounce and a shattered vessel.

A combination of practice and several broken vessels is the only way to really learn and develop an eye for the position of the cutting tip. I find now that by sitting on the lathe bed,

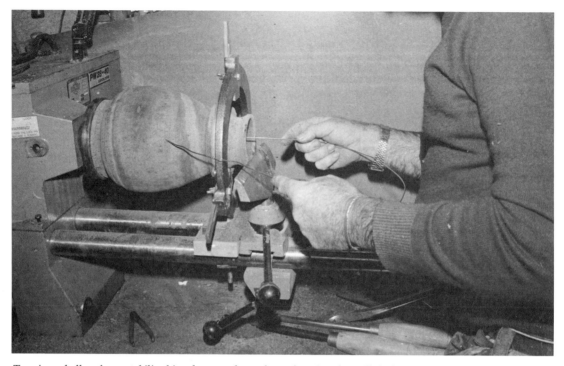

Turning a hollow form, stabilized in a long-work steady, and testing the wall thickness with a bent coat-hanger 'calliper'.

or at least sprawling across it, and looking down the shaft of the tool where it disappears down the neck (like Ellsworth) I can get a fair idea of tool alignment. It is also useful to have a series of depth markers on the tool shaft.

With hollowing complete, a plug is fitted into the open neck and the tailstock brought up for support. The long-work steady is now removed, the running track collar is turned away and the outside of the vessel is sanded and finished.

The final stage is reverse chucking to clean away the base. The drive spigot pushed into the neck is wrapped in a thin layer of polyfoam, and care is again taken not to put too much pressure on the tailstock. Freshly worked grasstree is quite fragile and it is a shame to break open the neck at this stage.

Actually, I find it a good idea not to clean up the base immediately. After two or three liberal coatings of Danish oil have sunk into the porous tree it appears to strengthen up quite considerably.

Pierced-Wall Hollow Forms

Working with burrs presents other difficulties, and by way of illustration I have chosen to make a hollow sphere with pierced walls using a briar root. This actually presents fewer problems with regard to hollowing, but more difficulties in setting up.

The first problem, as with so much burr work, is to orientate the block. Within a briar there is so much burring that the direction of the grain hardly matters. There will be a protuberance that indicates where the 'trunk' left the root, and it would be slightly better if this was where the neck aperture was finally located, but the difference is so slight that I frequently ignore it. The real orientation issue

148

 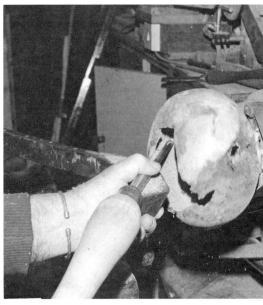

A hollow vessel from a briar root. (a) Shaping the outside from a pin chuck drive.
(b) Hollowing out with a modified profile gouge. (c) The finished piece.

hangs around where you wish to have the wall piercings and where you want a continuous wall to give structural integrity.

Try to aim for a continuous wall immediately above the base and for the first inch or so up the wall. Next, look for a continuous ring somewhere up near the neck; this helps considerably to give rigidity during hollowing out once the walls are fairly thin. Aim to position the centre roughly (but not exactly) mid-way between the two narrowest points. It takes a little more time and judgement to set this up than it did to position the centre of the large, rough block earlier in this chapter.

With the centre and the top aperture point established, drill a hole through the centre of the neck position to accept a pin chuck. On this job use a large pin chuck with a diameter as close as possible to that required for the top aperture; in this example it will be 1½in (3.7cm). We will later drill this hole further to provide a depth-marker hole. Mount the block on the lathe and bring up the tailstock point for outboard-end support.

From my block I can see that I should get a near spherical shape, but I wish to lift the maximum radius just above mid-height to give a little 'lightness' to the appearance of the finished object. I am also allowing for a foot, which will be used for clamping the vessel in a four-jaw chuck for hollowing, but which will eventually be cut away.

The first stage of turning is done not so much to establish the desired profile, but to remove wood until I have a block that, while it still has piercing or holes, has, overall, a sound structure with all the essential bridges required between the holes to provide the ultimate structural integrity.

The finished profile is now developed and the external face is finally smoothed with a light touch with a broad, square-ended scraper and a short spin against abrasive paper.

The scraping has to be done with caution. Scraping is only ever done with light, delicate touches, but when done on pierced walls it has to be especially light. The slightest bounce on the tool tip will cause it to jump inwards and it will then catch hard on the edge of the opening. Shatteration!

Recognizing that it may not be possible to reverse chuck the turned vessel to remove the foot, the piece is, at this stage, fine-finished right down to the foot spigot.

Off with the pin chuck, on with the four-jaw, and clamp up on the spigot. It is essential to mount the vessel accurately, and the tool-rest gap method is normally used to adjust the position finely. Here, however, this is not necessary as, by remounting the Jacobs chuck with the saw tooth bit, the bit will position the block very precisely. The jaw chuck is tightened up. The pin chuck hole is now deepened to full pilot-hole depth with the saw tooth bit.

From here the hollowing out is completed with a profiled gouge and the inside is finally dressed and cleaned up with a small scraper on the hooker. One thing that the pierced wall does is reduce the problem of swarf removal. Merely stop the lathe at intervals, hand rotate the piece and the swarf falls out. Dependent upon the extent and positioning of the piercings, it is often possible to see a broken image of the cutting tool 'through' the wall of the rotating vessel, if an inspection lamp is carefully positioned in the right place. This can be a great boon for developing skills in hollow work.

The vessel is sanded, oiled and polished, and is then cut away from the chuck using a pad or tenon saw. The base is then cleaned up, first on a belt sander, and then by hand.

THIN-WALLED TURNINGS

The next application to think about in face plate turning is that of ultra-thin-walled work. To me, an ⅛in (3mm) thick wall on hollow vessels is ultra thin; to others this is only the starting point. Most ultra (paper) thin turning is open form.

Actually, there is not a lot that is new to

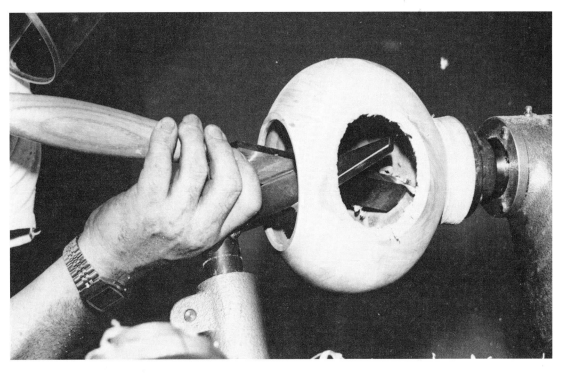

The ideal situation: very green wood, a tool rest that can be positioned inside the vessel, and a large dome-ended scraper. The vessel was turning at 1,800rpm when this demonstration picture was taken.

say about thin turning. It uses exactly the same tools and techniques used for moderate work, but is done with a lot more care.

There is thin and thin. Bert Marsh specializes in small open-form objects, which often have walls a little under 2mm thick. That is 'thin' and is often done in dry wood that will not subsequently move or check.

Ultra-thin turning is usually undertaken in green timber – often very green. The end thickness can be well under a millimetre and sometimes has to be measured in thou'. If spindles are involved they will be worked with skew chisels and beading tools, and detail is often applied with a parting chisel used as a skew. The open form is achieved with a bowl gouge, probably of ¼in (6mm) or even ⅛in (3mm) diameter.

There are four problems with ultra thin

turning. First, as has already been mentioned, it is done using very green timber. As you approach the finished thickness, the frictional heat generated between the bevel and the wood can be sufficient to dry out the wood. At this level of thinness there is immediate and considerable movement, and in a flash the wood can either check severely, or go so out of round that further turning is not practical. For this reason the piece is continuously swabbed with cold water while turning. One thin-form specialist actually turns under running water. I tried it and found I needed a wet suit! The minimum requirement is a rubber apron.

The second problem is that the walls become so flimsy that they will not support the pressure of the cutting edge of even the smallest of tools. It is essential, therefore, to

151

support the wall behind the cutting edge. This is usually achieved with the steadying hand. The thumb rests on the tool blade to steady that and the tool tip is pinched between thumb, timber, and the middle phalanx of the forefinger, which bears on the outer wall of the vessel.

The third problem is that of measuring thickness. We are no longer talking of callipers, rather micrometers. However, you cannot use measuring tools. A calliper applied to the item during turning would immediately tear it apart. If you stop it long enough to measure the thickness then it would, even in that time and well swabbed with cold water, probably move sufficiently to be irrecoverable. When you are getting to ultimate thinness you cannot afford to stop until you have finished.

The most effective way of judging thickness is to have a light on the far side of the object. Once you can see the light percolating through the wall you know it is thin. When the level of light is even throughout the piece you know that you have even thickness throughout. When you can actually read a piece of print through the wall you know you are Dell Stubbs! His demonstration of being able to read print through the wall of one of his goblets at a Loughborough seminar blew all our minds. When he went on to make a thin bowl using only a hand axe as a turning tool the tool manufacturers packed up and went home.

Of course the use of a light to judge thinness does create two difficulties. First, the heat from the light increases the heat level, and thus the rate of drying and the level of movement in the piece. It is also not too safe having a hot, electricity-driven lamp in an area where there is a lot of water splashing around.

The fourth problem is that of finishing. The use of cooling water does tend to lift the grain. If you do nothing then the finish is likely to be fluffy. We therefore have to use very fine wet or dry with liberal swabbings with water. We also have to keep the 'sand-

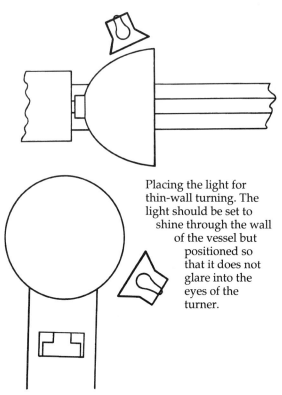

Placing the light for thin-wall turning. The light should be set to shine through the wall of the vessel but positioned so that it does not glare into the eyes of the turner.

ing' to an absolute minimum to prevent heat build-up.

SEGMENTED TURNINGS

The last of the special areas is, I have to admit, not one of my favourites. It is called segmented work or laminar turning.

There are many levels of this technique and some I do find more attractive than others. One thing I do acknowledge is that in its higher forms it is very skilful.

One of the first approaches I tried was to take a plain wood blank (it happened to be 12in (30cm) diameter sycamore) and to drill holes at regularly placed intervals. These were in two sizes, 1in (2.5cm) and 1½in (3.7cm). Dowels were then turned in contrasting wood to make a tight fit in the holes, they were glued and pushed home. From this blank a bowl was turned with the contrasting wood 'dots' appearing in the rim and base.

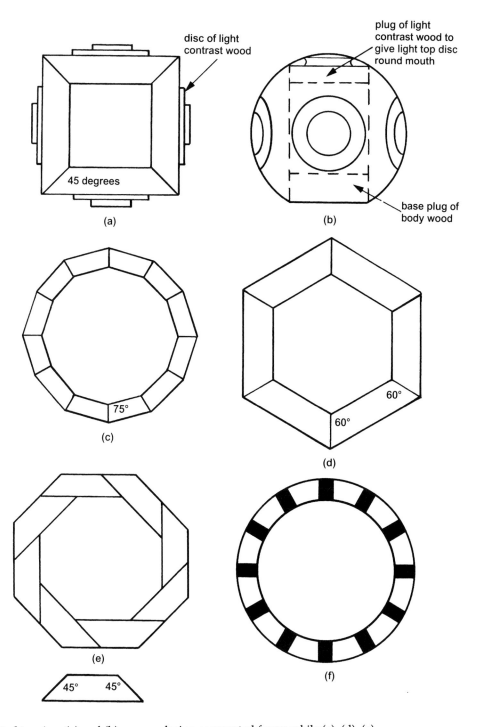

Segmented turning. (a) and (b) are eye design segmented forms while (c), (d), (e) and (f) are various patterns for blocking forms.

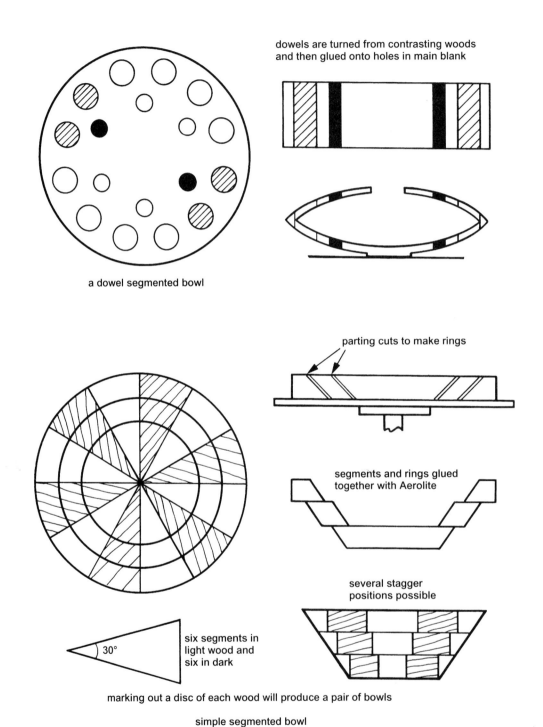

dowels are turned from contrasting woods and then glued onto holes in main blank

a dowel segmented bowl

parting cuts to make rings

segments and rings glued together with Aerolite

several stagger positions possible

30°

six segments in light wood and six in dark

marking out a disc of each wood will produce a pair of bowls

simple segmented bowl

Segmented turning.

Another very simple approach was to cut rings from nine ply, glue the rings together to provide a crude vase shape and then turn it to complete. With careful choice of plys this can look very effective.

From here it is only a short step to making a bowl of rings of contrasting woods, sometimes with a sandwich of a different, contrasting, thick-cut veneer between each of the main wooden rings.

There is now a tool kit that simplifies this process. It is the Marrison system, which enables you to cut all the rings from a single disc blank in such a way that the rings can be stacked one on the other to form a vase or sloping wall blank.

The Marrison used in the normal way tends to produce rings that are reasonably thin and therefore do not give you enough meat to be able to make very exciting shapes. However, it does provide the basis for a more interesting vessel.

By taking two discs of contrasting colours and by using the cutting jig on double spacing, a stack of thicker rings can be built. It is now also possible to mark each ring into segments and carefully saw these apart on the band saw. You can now reassemble the rings alternating the blocks of contrasting wood rather than alternating the rings.

In building the blank some people find it best to use a clamp and assemble the walls without the base. This way the clamp presses the rings together while the glue dries. When the glue is set the clamp is removed and the base stuck on using a heavy weight to get enough pressure. Some turners use good PVA wood glue. I use Aerolite (my favourite permanent glue) or Cascamite – probably because I bought a sale lot of this in large tins!

The construction should be given enough time to ensure that the glue is fully dried and hardened before it is mounted for turning. With Cascamite I would allow two days, with PVA a week. This is probably overdoing it, but I have seen some segmented blanks fly apart.

Decorative Banding

It is not quite in the same field, and it almost comes within the category of applied decoration (our next chapter) but there is one idea that some people have difficulty with. This is inlaying decorative banding into turned work. The beautiful purfling used on guitars and the composite banding inlaid into furniture can lift a relatively ordinary item in a plain wood to a piece of interest and beauty.

The difficulty that people have is that they fit the banding, leave it to dry, and then some time later they find that it has cockled and buckled.

In almost every instance I have found this to be caused by the contraction of the bowl, and is nothing to do with the banding. The solution is to turn the bowl from kiln-dried wood and ensure that it really is down in the 8–10 per cent moisture mark before fitting the band.

Actually applying the inlay is very simple. It is normally positioned somewhere near the greatest diameter – in this area the wall will be virtually vertical. A shallow groove is cut to a depth a fraction greater than that of the banding to be fitted.

The groove is first carefully marked and the edges precisely defined, making vertical cuts with the long point of a sharp skew. These can be slightly deeper than the groove. Next the groove is cleaned out with a narrow square-ended scraper. For narrower banding you may have to use a beading tool or even a parting tool used in the scraper position.

The banding is now cut to slightly oversize and the groove is filled with PVA glue. One end of the band is fitted in position and is held in place with a plastic-jawed cramp fitted just short of the end of the band. The band is then fitted into the groove, working round the piece. Once the clamped end is reached, the band is trimmed off to a perfect fit and is pushed home. A damp sponge is then used to clean off any surplus glue, particularly from the face of the banding.

The final fit and seating of the banding is

checked and then the cramp is removed; the banding is now held firmly in place with two or three full turns of masking tape applied with tension. This holds it in place while the glue dries.

Once the tape is removed, the bowl is remounted on the lathe and by careful use of fine-grit abrasive paper the bowl is fared into the banding – without abrading the band.

This level of caution is only needed on some bands where the colour is only a surface stain. Proper purfling is coloured right through and can be sanded to a perfect merging with the bowl wall.

If the bowl was dry the banding will not lift.

10 Decoration

MAKING PLAIN WOOD INTERESTING

In the past year or two there has been a huge growth in the movement of applying decoration to wood turning. America certainly led the way in this, with interest there burgeoning in the 1980s.

There are a number of factors that have contributed to this movement. The first has to do with the availability of exotic, decorative and highly figured woods. To me the most dramatic of all was the British burr elm – sadly now almost vanished due to Dutch elm disease.

Then there was the huge and ever-growing variety of tropical woods – rich in colour and magnificent in texture. Two factors have affected their use, however. First, there is increasing environmental interest and the huge and wholly justified concern that many of us have over the destruction of the rain forests. Despite what many timber merchants claim, many of the real 'exotics' do not come from sustainable resources. It is interesting that the Brazilian government itself is asking us not to buy native mahogany. I now feel genuine guilt when three-quarters of the wood I buy ends up being burnt as wood shavings.

Then, of course, there is the cost. By the time the wood reaches a retail outlet in the UK the price has risen so high that it is difficult to add working costs and profit margin and yet make the finished item affordable in all but the minuscule gallery market. Would that the natives from whose forests the timber comes got a reasonable percentage of what we pay. Unfortunately most of our money ends up in the pockets of western middlemen.

There is, however, probably even, a deeper reason. There is no doubt that there has recently been a reaction against the 'turn it in exotics and you do not need to worry about the design' brigade.

These, and other factors, pushed many towards a greater interest in pure form in the first instance; and then towards added decoration.

Certainly I have noted this change in my own views. At one time any artificial means of changing the colour of timber, or covering the grain with coatings of colour or varnish, was complete anathema. Oil, and 'natural' polishes (beeswax) were all that I would allow. The change has been gradual but I can now detect some definite influences.

Probably the first dent in my armour was 'seeing the beautiful delicate work of Merryl Saylan with her vegetable-dyed wooden platters. Then, as she moved into spray-applied paints, she took me with her. Another strong influence was seeing slides of the work shown in the American turned objects exhibitions mounted by Al LeCoff. On the other hand I cannot say that I ever had much feeling for the Norwegian painted plates, as it seemed that here the platter form was merely a canvas upon which to display a painting – often of a folky attraction rather than of real artistic merit.

The work of George White took my breath away for its sheer brilliance. Anyone who has ever seen his coffee service on a tray, all of which look like bone china, will probably have been similarly mind-blown. Aesthetically I am still not entirely sure about this, because the very fact that I can, and have to, say 'it looks like bone china', does give me some qualms.

But then I go to a class run by American design genius Giles Gilson, and see his spray-painted items (George was acting as his lab technician) and I know I am being taken further down the road, and shown where one of my next directions lies.

Applied decoration is here to stay and there are now two clearly-defined paths. One is incised decoration, with which we have to lump surface texturing; and then there is applied decoration where the colour of the surface is altered. In this second category we find sub-divisions: changing the colour of the wood itself by chemical means – bleaching, fuming, and oxidizing (burning); changing the colour by staining – with wood stains and coloured dyes; and covering the wood by applying a film of paint. In this chapter we will consider carved or incised decoration and texturing. In the next we will look at changing or enhancing the wood colour with bleaches, stains and dyes.

TEXTURED DECORATION

Until recently, incised decoration was largely the prerogative of the skilled carver; this is no longer the case. Tools have now been developed that greatly simplify several of the processes.

There are probably four areas of incised decoration to take account of; however, one of these – that of ornamental turning – is highly specialized and is really outside the scope of this volume. The other three are surface texturing, which can range from random to regular patterns; representational carvings – such as a rose carved in relief in the face of a platter; and carved or routed patterns, such as fluting on a bowl wall or pot lid, or along a spindle.

Surface Texturing

Surface texturing is probably the first form of ornamentation that the developing turner tries. This is understandable because it requires fewer skills than actual carving, and can often involve no special tooling.

Some texturing approaches use the rotation of the lathe, and probably the simplest of all is applying ridges or grooves to the outside walls of a vessel using the tip of a gouge or chisel – the point of a vertically presented skew, or of a diamond scraper. Texturing applied in this way can look very effective on timbers such as oak burr, and may completely cover the outside wall or just occupy the upper or lower halves. The size of the scraper and the depth of penetration are naturally geared to the size of the vessel. What is particularly effective is to set up a contrast between a zone of roughened wood, and an oiled and polished area.

To create a reasonably strong effect, first use a diamond-pointed scraper ground to a point of about 60 degrees. Follow this with a vertically held skew and incise the troughs of each of the scraper grooves to crisp up the detail. Finally, turn the workpiece against a stout wire brush to take off any splinters or snags.

Wire-brush texturing is also very effective if applied in the direction of the grain in an area of soft or rotten wood.

A similar effect to the wire brush can be achieved using a sand blaster; this can produce one of my favourite effects, where the annular growth rings are naturally contoured as the softer wood is etched away. The trouble is that it takes quite a bit of kit. Small, self-contained sand-blasting cabinets can be picked up at some garage sales for a few hundred pounds; but you still need a compressor. The alternative is to make up a cabinet within which you can operate a spray gun-type blaster. The sand-blasting guns can be obtained for about £50 but they require something like 8cu ft (2cu m) of free air per minute and this is beyond the capacity of the average DIY car-spraying compressor.

What sand blasting does is to allow you to explore the different textures of the wood as defined by faults and growth rings. The basic figure of wood can be etched to emphasize the natural patterns; and wild grain, such as on elm, looks particularly interesting. Pine

A 20in (50cm) diameter bowl in oak burr. The rim shows considerable post-turning movement. The outer wall is skew-point textured with the rotted area heavily wire brushed.

sand blasts well but oak (and other hard timbers) is not amenable.

A simple texturing can be achieved with the ball head of a small hammer, and again this is an effect that can be applied all over or in selected zones. The best results are achieved on greener woods and is applied before the hollowing out processes begin; this way you have a mass to hammer against. First completely finish the exterior, including sanding and oiling, then belt the hell out of it with the ball face of the hammer. Only when you have achieved the surface finish you require do you start the hollowing-out process. Finally, carry out a light sanding of the exterior with 400 grit wet or dry to remove any snags, followed by oiling and polishing. A small zone of polished smooth wood above or below the hammered zone gives a contrast and an emphasis to the tex-

turing, and a quirk between the zones emphasizes the contrast.

Tooled Finishes

From here we start to move into tooled finishes using chisels, gouges, punches and others. A randomly applied broad-blade, shallow-curve gouge can give a most attractive adze-like finish. I have tried to wield a mini adze but the effect was too uncontrolled. Vessels finished in this way look very 'antique', and if a little patinating wax is applied the selling price climbs appreciably. It is, however, a tedious job and you have to be clear from the start as to whether you are aiming for a clearly random pattern, or for some sort of organized arrangement.

A number of devices have appeared recently that are based on a cutting blade mounted on a pivot arm. The simplest of these is a micro gouge (up to ⅛in (3mm) size) mounted on an arm, which in turn is pivoted off the tool post. This was developed by Maurice Mullins, who works in the Lake District, and it is now sold through Craft Supplies. With these, the arm swings the tip back and forth over the static surface. A regular pattern can be produced using an indexing head but a random effect is very pleasing. The limitation of this as a decorating tool is that it only operates on a fixed arc, governed by the distance from the pivot point. The longer the arc and the more shallow the curve of the surface being decorated, the longer will be the decorations. It is therefore best for use on the lids of smaller-sized boxes.

A tool with a similar problem of only being able to work on fixed arcs is the 'Power Gouge', developed in Australia and available through the Arbortec organization. This really is a brutal device and takes a lot of practice before its potential can be fully exploited. The basis of the Power Gouge is that it has a 12in (30cm) long drive shaft, which screws directly on to the drive boss of an angle grinder. On the other end of the shaft a standard Arbortec saw disc is fixed. The shaft is held in a sliding, fully gimballed head, which is clamped firmly into the tool post. The Power Gouge is used with the lathe turned on and creates swirling groove patterns on the wall of the vessel. In fact the tool looks much more vicious than it is because the gimballed head stops the blade from flying about. The problem I found with this device under test was that it took huge shock loadings – due only in part to my ineptitude.

Mike Mullin's cutting tool pivoting off a post mounted in the tool carriage. The shavings show how finely this cuts with sharp tips.

The Power Gouge. This is an Australian-made tool for use with the Arbortec, pivoting off a fully gimballed head. (a) Shaping the outside of a grasstree. (b) Power hollowing a burr bowl. The process takes about three minutes!

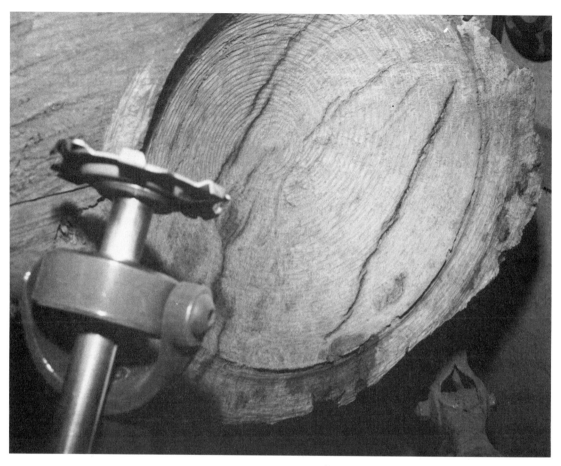

(c) The textured finish. The tool only works on hard, dense woods.

Unfortunately, the loading increases with softer wood, which tears rather than cuts, and grinder burn-out occurred.

However, the idea of pivoted cutters mounted off the tool post is one to pursue. Mike Scott has developed the use of a small chain-saw mounted on the tool rest, and he uses this for shaping, texturing and piercing through. The use of a Black and Decker Powerfile was developed by Jules Clare and he has used this in a particularly striking way for producing effects on grasstree vases.

Chattering

It is a little difficult to place chatter decora-
tion – not that it matters, for the categories that we are looking at are purely arbitrary and chosen only for the convenience of discussion.

Basically, 'chatter' is a means of applying incised patterning that is little more than semi-organized, vibration-induced texturing. It is achieved by making use of the flexing properties of thin strips of tool steel. The strip of steel that forms the cutter is given a pointed or rounded cutting profile and is clamped into a stout shaft and handle with about 2in (5cm) projecting. The shaft is placed on the tool rest and is offered up at right angles to the rotating wood. The tip cuts but is pushed down by the rotation. Once it has bent far enough it flies back upwards, creating a ridged cut on the surface. As the tool is moved sideways the ridges form a spiral pattern.

The nature and depth of the pattern and the swirl of the profile are influenced by a number of factors. First, the period of vibration is affected by the length of exposed tool tip – the shorter the overhang, the higher the frequency of vibration. The distance between adjacent spirals is affected by the vibration period, but it is also influenced by the speed of rotation of the lathe. Clearly the profile of the cutting tip will also affect the pattern, as will the speed of travel of the sideways sweep.

The main limitations of chattering are the nature and grain orientation of the wood. The clearest patterns are achieved when applying the tool to end grain of dense hardwood. Some turners can achieve a moderate chatter work across the grain of hardwoods, but I only seem to get tearing. Bonny Klien has found that solid acrylic, vegetable ivory and bone all chatter very well – but then everything that Bonny ever does is done very well.

The Stewart tool system has a series of chatter cutters available, but it is an easy job to make your own cutters and to mount these on to a shaft. Bits of cabinet scraper steel or strips off the arm of a set square have given excellent results.

Representational Carving

Representational carving on turned items has not really been developed in this country and it is worth considering. In the main it has been expressed in carved design inside and across the face of platters; carved patterns on the flanges of broad-rimmed bowls; or carved flowers, heraldic devices and patterns on the outside walls of bowls.

Obviously this pattern of decoration will have a strong influence upon the type of wood used, and oak is a favourite. An incised Tudor rose in the bottom of a stained and patinated oak platter can look very attractive.

Carving Approaches

Probably the mainstream of activity in terms of carved decoration on turning has now focused upon carved and routed fluting; and both hand- and machine-applied carving approaches are widely used. So let's look at these in detail. We find carving applied both to face plate items – bowls and platters – and to between centres work – chair, table and bed legs.

Although there is a whole array of carving approaches available to us, there are a number of separate, identifiable techniques. It is, however, a continuum as one slips into the next often with some shared elements.

At the start of the range we have pure hand working. For representational carving the design is usually traced on. For fluting patterns, such as on the side of bowls, it may be measured, or assisted by the use of a marking disc. It is really simplified with an indexing head. Depending on your skills with carving chisels the results may look anything from 'obviously hand done', to 'quite effective'!

Tooled texture, and several aspects of applied carving, are greatly facilitated by the use of so-called powered chisels. Units have been available for some time, and have been widely used by American decoy duck carvers. Some turners started to use them in the late 80s and now the use is spreading.

The early units were fine for duck carving and delicate work on small vessels; however, many were too lightweight for continuous use on bigger pieces. This has now changed with the introduction of heavy-duty units based on stone masons' and sculptors' tools.

The mechanism of some of the very lightest power chisels is a head into which fine blades are clipped; the reciprocating motion of the blade is achieved through vibro-magnetic induction. These are not suitable for decorating anything bigger than micro turning. Avoid them! The more robust machines take the rotary motion of a motor and then use this to drive a cam, which hammers

163

directly on to the back of a punch, chisel or gouge.

So the second approach along the line uses marking discs or indexing heads and the carving employs a power chisel. This usually improves the finish, giving better shape to the grooves and flutes. Representational carving, however, can be equally good with hand or power chisels.

The third level uses the indexing head and a machine cutter. This is very quick and gives a very well-organized, attractive and crisp effect.

We next have to include the various copy carvers. These basically use a small-powered router held in a carriage at the end of a pantograph. The operator traces the profile of the piece to be copied with the pantograph's stylus and the router accurately carves the design on to the workpiece. Some copy carvers are very good and will reproduce three-dimensional work of considerable detail. The problem is that you have first to carve your template!

At the far end of the spectrum we have various totally automatic machines. Trend now produce a special jig that will produce barley-twist carved legs.

The advanced turner, as distinct from the pure production turner, will probably be more interested in the hand approaches, and in simple machine aids.

Carving a Bowl

In looking at the detailed methods of applying carving to turned items, we will first concentrate on bowl carving, and particularly on decoration applied to the outer wall.

The first stage in the total hand approach is to determine the frequency and spacing of the pattern to be carved on the bowl and then to mark this off.

Measure the diameter of the bowl at both the top and the bottom of the area to be carved. If you are going to do a lot of this type of work it is worth making a simple wide-jaw calliper (or a marking disc as

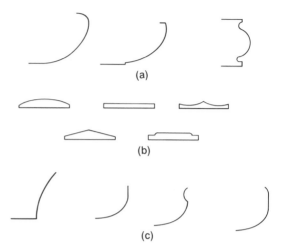

Profiles for power fluting: those in row (a) are poor profiles, the lid profiles in row (b) are suitable and the flat and slightly concave surfaces in (c) provide a good basis for power fluting.

described later). Multiply the diameter by pi (3.142) and divide by the number of incisions required. Set a pair of dividers to the exact spacing and mark off the top and bottom of each groove.

Here is an example. A bowl has a maximum diameter of 12in (30cm) that occurs about a third of the way down from the rim. We are going to carve broad vertical flutes from about 1in (2.5cm) above the maximum diameter on down to about 2in (5cm) below. Let us call the upper limit A and the lower one B.

We measure the diameter at A and B. It shows 11.5in (29cm) at A and 10in (25cm) at B. Using the formula, circumference = pi × diameter (C = πd); this gives us 36.133in (91.118cm) at A and 31.42in (78.55cm) at B.

We have decided that we will be making 48 flutes, so the spacing of the top of the flutes on ring A is 0.753in (1.898cm) (36.133/91.118 ÷ 48), and at B is 0.654in (1.636cm). Dividers set to 0.753in (1.898cm) are used to make 48 marks around ring A. They are then reset to 0.654in (1.636cm) and the same is done round ring B.

Alternatively it may be worth making a

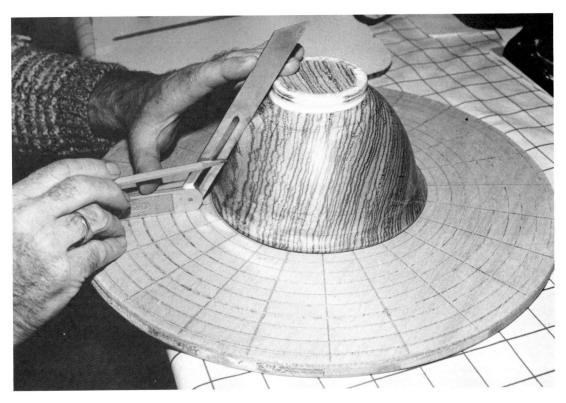

A marking disc. The bowl is centred on the rings and alignment is made with a square or bevel gauge. Marking is normally done with a Chinagraph pencil.

Once the spacing has been determined, spiral and curved patterns are sketched on by hand. For more complex shapes a card stencil can be used.

165

'Hand' carving. (a) Spiral carving a bowl. It is held in a specially made clamp. (b) A pot in beli with alternating types of groove. Carving only occurs when light pressure is applied to the heel of the handle.

marking disc. This is a ply disc turned and marked on the lathe. Mine is 18in (45cm) in diameter and has a series of concentric circles with rings marked off at ¼in (6mm) intervals. The rings are incised with the point of a skew and then darkened with ballpoint pen. With regard to the above example, the exact diameter of the outer ring is measured, and again using the pi × diameter formula with a divisor of 48, the ring is carefully marked with dividers. Lines are drawn from the outer mark to the centre of the disc. The full 48 lines are only taken in as far as the 10in (25cm) diameter mark. At this point only every second ring is marked to give 24 lines into the centre.

If you are considering a regular need for marking off, then it is also worth making a second, similar disc with 60 radials. Why 48 and 60? It is because these allow a wide number of variations of spacings. With 48 you can have an equally spaced set of marks with 1 spacing (48 marks); 2 spacing (24 marks); 3 spacing (16); 4 spacing (12); 6 spacing (8) and 8 spacing (6 marks) and so on. A 60 ring disc gives 60, 30, 15, 12, 10, 6 and so on.

To use a marking disc the bowl is placed upon it rim down and is centred on the closest ring marking. Two or three nubs of Bluetac will hold it in place.

A sliding-bevel angle square is now used to locate the cutting line on the bowl wall, and as the bowl is probably already oil finished, a china graph pencil is used.

It is very much a matter of personal preference whether the carving is done with the bowl in the horizontal position laid rim down on the work bench, or whether it is clamped so that the carving plane is more vertical. Whichever is adopted, it is essential that the bowl is held firmly. Working horizontally a series of bench stops can be sufficient. To facilitate vertical carving I have a clamp that can be held in the bench vice.

There are now two critical points. First, as always, the carving tools must be very sharp. This will not be achieved on a grind wheel only (*see* notes in Chapter 7 on tool sharpening). Secondly, the direction of cutting has to be carefully chosen.

If you are carving vertical, or even angled fluting on the side wall of a bowl, remember that you are cutting across the grain. With really sharp tools the actual cutting should be no problem; but as you come to the end of the cut you will be working into unsupported

An early group of free-hand carved bowls.

The consequence of cutting into unsupported grain!

cross-grain and break-out is not uncommon. Often the result is not torn fibres under the cut itself, but the breaking away of the shoulders between two adjacent flutes.

Machine Aids

The first variation on this carving approach is the use of a power chisel carver. There are professional devotees of both hand and power chisel methods. The same two schools are evenly divided between free form and clearly-designed, organized patterning.

Having started with hand carving, I have now gone totally over to power methods for both organized (regular) patterning and random texturing.

The unit that I use is the Bourdet, a French-made machine with a 1hp motor. This will drive a ½in (12mm) chisel deep into a block of wood. When used with a broad gouge it will 'adze finish' a 12in (30cm) diameter bowl in under ten minutes. It is rated to run continuously (all day). The 'gun' housing the cam and the chisel stem fits comfortably in the palm of the hand and the chisel only reciprocates when under load. There is, however, a high-frequency vibration (6–10,000 cycles a minute) applied to the hand and wrist, and this may contribute to the medical syndrome known as RSI (repetitive strain injury); long periods of use should be avoided.

Even with a marking disc, the spacing between marks can wander a little; the only real answer is an indexing head. Some lathes have indexing rings built in, but there are now universal bolt-on models available. The inveterate DIYer can easily make his own.

*Power chisel and sander drive units. The
Fordham directly drives rotary burrs and discs
through a heavy-duty flexible shaft. The
stonemason-quality Bourdet gears up the motor
speed through a flexible rotary drive, which is
then converted to a reciprocating motion to drive
a power chisel.*

My Poole Wood lathe has a basic 24-hole
indexer on the outboard end of the main
spindle. This is OK for simple jobs, but does
not really provide sufficient spacings and can
jump out in use. A good indexing head
allows the chuck to be hand rotated and then
locked in position with great precision.

One of the best I have found is a simple
unit designed by Tony Bunce and supplied
by Middlesex Woodturning Centre. This consists of an alloy ring that can be clamped on
the back of jaw and combination chucks. It is
predrilled to forty-eight holes and is space
numbered. It comes with a post and set pin,
which clamps to the lathe bed.

From here, marking off with up to 48
points is easy. The tool rest is brought along
the side of the bowl wall and is set so that the
point of the pencil or marking tool is exactly
on the centre line, and away you go with
whatever spacing frequency you require (1, 2,
3, 6, 8 and so on).

Hand rotating the piece against a pencil or

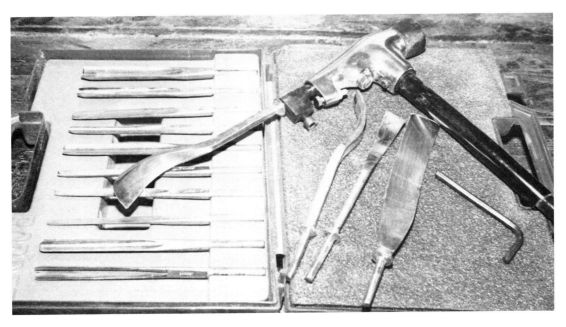

*Bourdet power chisel and bits. A cam in the handle turns the rotary drive into a
reciprocating motion. Chisel bits in the box are by Bourdet. The larger bits are DIY-
modified Ashley Isles carving tools – equal quality, half the price!*

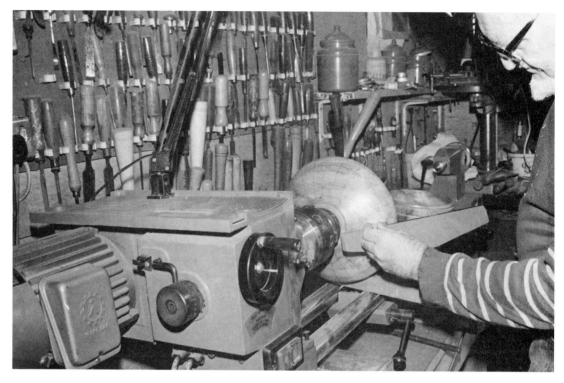

Poole Wood simple index ring. This offers only 24 positions, and slips out too easily.

chinagraph can mark off the top and bottom of the zone to be carved, as all traces can be easily removed in final finishing.

While it is difficult to get the spacing really tight and even, it is even harder to get each incision of exactly the same shape and depth. They invariably look 'hand done', and while this is fine if that is the impression you wish to convey (as in a pseudo-antique oak bowl), it is at variance with the concepts of formal design on fine woods.

It was a little galling when, having invested in the Bourdet and started to build up the skills to produce cleaner decoration, a device was launched on the market that brought superb, clean, precise incised decoration within the capabilities of novice turners.

It was another of Tony Bunce's brain-children and is again available from the Middlesex Centre. The fluter carver provides the answer to many a prayer.

This approach uses the indexing head to position the workpiece and a simple cradle to house a standard power router. By using a bed board, pivot arms, and proforma guides, a huge variety of patterns can be cut; often it takes only a few minutes to finish a bowl.

The router power unit is mounted in a frame, which acts as a slider block. The router is clamped in the horizontal position and can be set to any desired height. An MDF board is clamped to the lathe bed for the router block to slide on. The slide is controlled in one of two ways. First there is a pivot arm from a pivot pin to the slide block. By moving the pin position around, altering the effective arc by lengthening and shortening the arm, and positioning the pivot in front or behind the block, arcs of almost any required radius can be produced. By pivoting from in front or behind the router you can work to both con-cave and convex forms.

The Middlesex fluting tool. The tool carriage is designed for a standard small router. Here a Bosch die grinder is used. In the pictures the unit is being guided by shaped profiles clamped to the bed board. The 48-hole index ring system in shown.

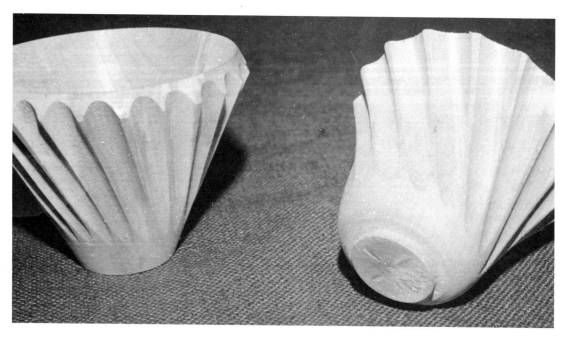

Highly organized, regular patterning produced with the Middlesex fluting tool.

More examples of the Middlesex fluting tool's ability.

If the MDF board is flat and the router head is set to the axis height of the lathe, evenly spaced vertical flute cuts can be quickly incised on the outer walls of bowls and boxes.

By raising and blocking up the outboard end of the board the pattern produced is spiral form. It may also be from or across the centre height.

The possible permutations are considerable. Experimentation with the rise and angle of the board and the arc of cut will give almost endless possibilities on both bowl walls and platter faces.

But it does not end there. Instead of using the pivot arm to control the line of cut, an alternative is to cut a curved former (something like a French curve) in a piece of MDF

and clamp this to the main board on the lathe bed. The profile can itself provide complex patterns rather than simple curves, allowing the decoration of a multi-plane workpiece.

Fluted Table Legs

To the spindle turner this tool can be the best thing since sliced bread, as the saying goes. It could even be used (heaven forbid!) in the place of turning tools to cut tricky coves and beading; it is absolutely superb for reeding or grooving table legs. The leg is turned, the MDF board is fixed in place, a long straight MDF former is clamped on, the router head is set to centre height and a pointed round engraving cutter (A11/50 Axminster) is locked in, and you are away. It takes longer to set up than to finish a leg, and about a tenth of the total time that it used to take setting up and grooving with a scratch stock.

On a 2in (5cm) diameter leg I would index sixteen marks on three hole spacings for power routing, and twenty marks at 0.312in (0.792cm) spacing for scratch stock grooving.

One thing you will find is that carving reeding with a router will test the accuracy of the taper on the leg and the straight edge of the former against which the router runs. Unless both are completely true the reeding will not be even.

There are some traditionalists around who do not like machines.

Reeding a leg without a router requires the construction of a trough or cradle into which the leg is placed. The circumference of the leg is marked off to provide a regular spacing between the reeds, and the leg is then positioned in the cradle.

Scratch stocks are simple wooden blocks into which cutting blades are clamped. Most stocks employed for reeding and producing beading along the edges of tables and the like are home-made and use sections of machine hack-saw blades as cutters. The blade is shaped to the required profile on a grind wheel and clamped in such a way that the block fixes the depth of cut.

Not long ago I had to make a drop-leaf gateleg table from three extension leaves off an old mahogany table. The two router cutters (Ovolo and Radius) required for the male and female parts of the rule joint between the leaves, and the beading around the table edge, would have cost almost £100. Two bits of machine hack-saw blade in a couple of scratch stock blocks did the job in thirty-five minutes.

Barley Twist Legs

There comes a point at which the element of carving exceeds the element of turning, and barley sugar twist legs must come within this category.

There are lathes specially made to turn twist legs, but they are very expensive when found. One or two people have made hand-turned 'lathes' where the hand rotation of the workpiece also drives the tool carriage at a geared rate. A router is fixed to the carriage to achieve the actual cut.

Most craftsmen who regularly make twist legs will tell you that they always carve the twists by hand and that they can do it as fast as most machines by the time you have taken into account machine set-up times and preparation. Twenty minutes a leg seems to be the professional norm!

The classic barley twist table leg of up to 2in (5cm) in diameter has two flutes, and they make one complete twist over a length that equates with the diameter. Hence on a leg of 2in (5cm) diameter the twists will make one complete turn over a length of 2in (5cm). Once the diameter exceeds 2in (5cm) a longer-pitch twist is often used, so a 3in (7cm) diameter leg may well have a 4in (10cm) pitch twist.

The most important part of cutting twists is the marking out. Let's work with a basic 2in (5cm) diameter leg to describe the process.

First the cylinder is turned. This should be complete with all detail: square ends, beads and coves and so on should all be finished. The remaining cylinder will be the twist part, although there will be a cove at each end to define the twist section. Again for symmetry it is best to make the twist section length an exact multiple of the diameter. Hence on our 2in (5cm) diameter leg we may have an 18in (45cm) length of twist, which will give us nine full turns.

Most makers like both to mark out and carve the twist with the leg mounted on the lathe. This enables them to work the gouge with the right hand while locking and turning the leg with the left.

Working from the start of the cylinder, mark off a series of rings spaced at diameter intervals – in our case at 2in (5cm) spaces up the cylinder to be carved. Now, mark a horizontal line along the cylinder at the quadrant

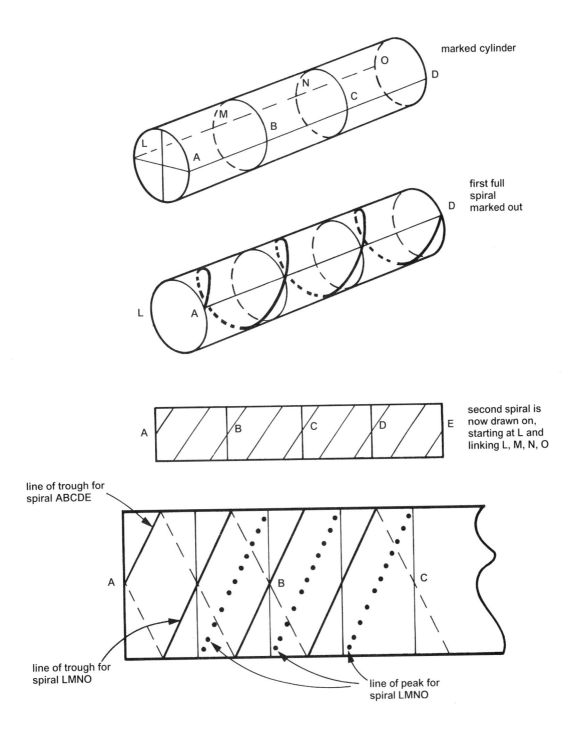

Marking off for barley twist carving.

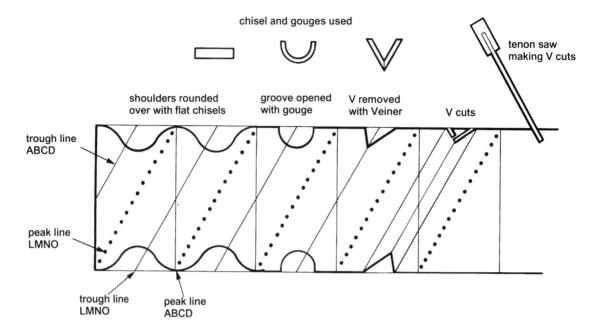

Carving the barley twist.

points. This is again facilitated by using an indexing head; with a forty-eight hole head mark off at 12, 24, 36, and 0/48.

Using any one of the quadrant marks as the base line, mark this off at each point where a ring intersects the quadrant line. Point A will be the first intersection, while B, C, D and so on lie up the length.

You now need a strip of thin card or paper, about an inch (2.5cm) wide, which is roughly one and a half times the length of the section to be carved.

Start by holding the strip on point A (a tag of masking tape will hold it in place) and wind the strip around the cylinder so that it neatly touches points B, C, D and so on. Now with a soft-lead but fine-point pencil, trace off along the edge of the paper the spiral linking points A, B, C, D, E and so on. This line will mark the bottom of the trough of the first spiral.

Instead of using a strip of paper some workers use a strip of masking tape to mark off the spiral.

Next rotate the cylinder through 180 degrees, and repeat the marking-off process

to provide the line L, M, N, O, P and so on; this is the trough of the second spiral.

Some workers use only the two marks now in place. Others also sketch in the peaks of the spiral waves. If this is done it is better to use a contrasting marker. The troughs can be traced with a broad felt-tipped marker knowing that this will be cut away. A fine pencil line for the peaks will easily sand out.

Start by chasing a marking groove the full length of the flutes to be carved. With a small tenon or pad saw, and rotating the workpiece by hand, cut a line along each of the trough marks.

Next, inclining the saw first on one side, and then the other, cut the first saw mark out to form V-grooves. Repeat the process for the second trough.

These two grooves provide the gouging lines. Depending upon the diameter of the spindle, choose a ⅜in (9mm) or ½in (12mm) gouge and hollow out the Vs along the length of the spiral. For a 2in (5cm) spindle a ½in (12mm) gouge is ideal. The use of very sharp cutting tools obviates the need for the use of a

Carving a barley twist. (a) The sawing line is marked with a run of narrow masking tape and the trough is sawn to near full depth with the saw held vertically.

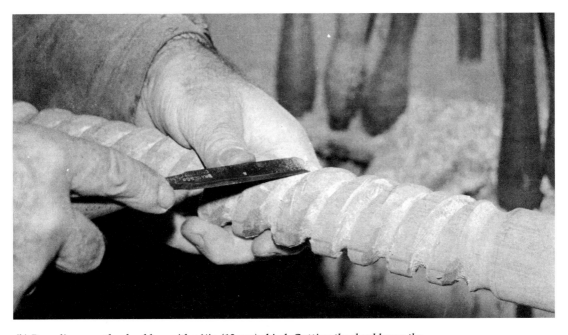

(b) Rounding over the shoulders with a ½in (12mm) chisel. Cutting the shoulder on the other side has to be done by reversing the chisel and working towards you across

(c) The near-finished pair. Smoothing is done first with a round file with the lathe static, and then by running a roll of abrasive paper up the groove with the lathe at slowest speed.

mallet – it should be possible to do all hand carving on turned work using only hand pressure.

It will probably take two or three passes to cut each groove to a full depth. Unevennesses in the groove can be taken out with a round Surform file.

Next, using a ½in (12mm) carpenter's chisel, round off the shoulders of the grooves to a finished profile. The apex of the spiral will be defined by the fine pencil line and this should not be cut away. To round over, always cut from the peak down into the trough, angling the blade of the chisel to cut the top off supported grain.

Once you have achieved a satisfactory profile, take a piece of abrasive paper and roll it up. The roll will be used to sand out the grooves in the spiral. It is unlikely that the first few spirals will be gouged to a reason-

able finish, so the abrasive paper may start as coarse as 60 grit, working down to 320 for a fine finish.

The final stage of sanding may be done with the lathe turning, particularly if speeds of under 200rpm are available. Hold the roll of abrasive in the start of the groove at the headstock end and allow the twist to take your hand up to the tailstock with the abrasive staying in the same groove. The motion is a quick sweep.

The ultimate stage of twist turning is the perforated twist. Here the spirals are independent of each other with a central space between each. This is achieved by further hand carving. First the two- or three-spiral form is marked out and the grooves are rough carved as above.

Next, using a drill of about ¼in (6mm) diameter, a series of holes are drilled through from one trough to the opposite one. Now the gouging is deeper, following the line of holes until the spiral is pierced right through. The final shaping is again done with a flat chisel.

This time the sanding process is made a lot easier with the use of strips of abrasive cloth pulled through the inside spirals.

With larger-diameter legs, and to achieve particular effects, both the number of grooves around the diameter and the ratio of wave length to diameter can be varied.

HAND SKILLS V. TOOLS

There is probably one force more than all others that is the drive behind the increase in carved and coloured decoration. Let's face it, with the very minimum of basic instruction, and often even without that, anybody can produce a turned item. With very little application and a moderate eye for form they can make things of some beauty. The actual real skills can be quite minimal. For this reason

Using the Middlesex fluting tool to produce reeding on table legs is simplicity itself. The trueness of your straight edge profile guide and your ability to turn a regular taper on the spindle is severely tested!

there are 10–20,000 people up and down the country who get great satisfaction from the odd hour or two a week that they spend on their lathes. There are also hundreds who sell some of their work at craft fairs and shows. About a score actually make a living on the craft-fair circuit. Many who do sell offer run of the mill work that many a school kid could produce. I am not saying that all turning is simple stuff requiring little skill, but a lot is.

To many this does not matter ; it *is* very satisfying to make anything with your own hands, and something that looks as good as a simple turning, and receives so many accolades from family and friends, justifiably gives the turner great pleasure.

But there comes a time when producing items that require only basic skills is not enough. It is at this stage that the transition from hobbyist to craftsman is begun. It is at this stage that you start working on delicate and difficult hollow forms, multi-element composite and segmented work, or decorated pieces. These all require special skills – skills that cannot be picked up overnight. So a successful carved piece is to me infinitely more satisfying than a plain turning.

However, with each piece I make I am brought face to face with the realization that I have more to learn about carving than I do about turning – and I still have a lot to learn about that! Looked at critically, I find more to fault in my carved work than I do in many of my turned pieces.

Something else has also become clear. The more I have to rely on my own skills, the greater the satisfaction gained, even with less than perfect results. I always thought I was a person driven by the belief that any means could be justified by the ends. I find little difference in skill requirements and ultimate satisfaction between hand chisels and my Bourdet. In fact the Bourdet does require some particular skills and overcomes the problem of holding chisels in an aged (four-jaw chuck, and natural-edged bowl rim), battered, arthritic left hand.

On the other hand, the fluter carver is a production tool. It gives perfect results every time. It requires ingenuity in setting up, rather than in technical operation; for that you need really very little skill. Customers like the results and the appreciative comments are pleasing; but *I* know! So it is a good means to the end of making sales, but a poor way to generate satisfaction in the gut!

11 Colouring Wood

THE CHANGING FACE OF TURNING

There are people who are just as against coating wood with stain, varnish or paint as I was. I think in my last book I dismissed polyurethane as being 'for boats' (but ideal for that purpose).

In the last chapter I said that one of the factors that had influenced my conversion was seeing the platters produced by Merryl Saylan. Merryl uses food and vegetable dyes that do not hide the nature of the grain, rather they produce delicate, grain-enhancing tinting. But that was not the only factor.

The move into furniture was probably the biggest influence. Until very recently the tradition was that all mahogany furniture was stained. My first work with furniture was mainly concerned with antique repairs, and later I started turning matching pieces to make up sets or replace broken elements such as legs and filials: I had to get into staining.

It was not long before the challenge of matching a particular colour and finish became a fascinating pursuit in its own right.

The interest in period furniture took me to many old houses where something else took my eye. It was Haddon House in Derbyshire with its beautiful long gallery in limed oak that made the greatest impression. Other, often less significant examples, soon convinced me that there is also a place for bleaching.

Then there came a job for Jacobean oak. However dark the stain I used it did not have the necessary body. So I tried fuming the piece of oak that I was using. I then had to make up and use a number of different stains (in combination) in order to get the required effect. It was finally wax polished, and looked wonderful!

Recently I was asked for a set of platters and coasters to match a given sample. The figure looked a little like oak as the colour seemed to be grime- and polish-impregnated brown oak – but not quite. To cut a long story short it turned out to be stained chestnut. So staining and polish had to be augmented by distressing and patinating.

Finally I even came to terms with polyurethane! It took one coffee table and one dining table that the clients kept marking and staining, that convinced me that for normal family use french polish, or oil and wax are not robust enough. Satin polyurethane carefully applied and flatted can look quite good.

A distressing commission. The sample platter that turned out to be chestnut, and a set of precut blanks. A plank was obtained for the second set! The customer did not require the shot-gun pellet holes to be replicated.

Part of the finished set of platters and coasters. The treatment included boning with a wood block, a home-brewed, water-based stain, a spirit stain, patinating wax, and 'dirty' beeswax polish.

The problem with the beauty of bleaching and staining is that it is often only skin-deep! It therefore has to be done on the finished piece, and can sometimes cause deformation. Bleaching is the worst in this respect, because it usually involves periods of immersion in aqueous liquids.

Most bleaching processes are based upon the use of chlorine. The immersion bath either has a free chlorine element in it in solution, or it is a liquid which, with the adding of an agent, releases free chlorine, both into the liquid and into the air (which is not very good on the lungs!). Fuming uses lethal concentrated ammonia; and caustic stripping in soda will attack the hands like a shoal of piranha fish. Some paints are toxic, some extremely so. Some solvents are addictive

(through the fumes). So changing the colour of wood can be fraught with dangers, even though the results can be very pleasing. What we have to put up with for our art! Stout rubber gloves are essential and a rubber apron and rubber boots are a good idea for all bleaching. We will deal with the different fume problems as we look more closely at each application.

BLEACHING

Let's start with the bleaching processes. Wood may be bleached for one of three reasons. First, the effect of bleaching a strongly figured wood is very attractive – a burr elm looks particularly interesting with the base wood turned to an ash grey. The second is that it is sometimes necessary to take away the aged colour before staining to match another piece. Lastly, pine looks more antique if it is bleached; so bleaching is often the first step in an 'antiquing process'.

First select your wood! The denser tropical woods do not bleach very readily; but then it is difficult to see why anybody would wish to bleach exotics. Several native timbers respond well – oak, chestnut, walnut and elm can be turned to an ashen off-white, even beech and ash show a distinct colour change. Mahogany also bleaches if required. The fruit woods, on the other hand, do not respond well.

To test the suitability of wood for bleaching, you can do a lot worse than use neat domestic bleach on a small sample. This will create localized patches but does give an indication of what you might expect with full bleaching.

Three 'production' methods are normally available. The oldest approach is to used slaked lime; however, this is slow and has now been replaced by using lime with an accelerator. The oak panelling at Haddon House would probably have been done, centuries ago, by rubbing a paste of freshly slaked lime (locally burnt or quicklime with a little water added) into the grain of the wood and then burnishing off the surplus; the wood would then be polished by rubbing it with a block of smooth, dry oak.

Today a solution of chloride of lime is used. This is made up by dissolving 8oz (225g) of lime in 1¼ gallons (5 litres) of water. Usually the solution is made by using half the water, stirring and allowing to stand. The liquid is filtered off from the sediment and then the second half of the water is added to the chloride. It is again shaken and allowed to stand before filtering and then the two lots of liquid are added together. Meanwhile a second solution is made by dissolving 14oz (400g) of soda crystals in a gallon (4.5 litres) of water.

The two solutions are mixed together,

releasing chlorine into the liquid; the mixture may be used hot or cold, but hot bleach works much more quickly. It is probably the fastest and most effective method of bleaching. On mixing, the solutions will turn green and there is a strong smell of chlorine. With this mix the fumes are not excessive, but are unpleasant, so the process is better carried out in a cool, well-ventilated outhouse.

The wood is immersed in the solution and left for a period. Constant monitoring is maintained until the required colour has been achieved.

The bleached object is now thoroughly washed off in running water and then wiped down with a diluted acetic acid (white vinegar is ideal). This will stabilize the change process and help to prepare the surface for later finishing.

After this the pieces should be positioned so that they dry fairly quickly. You need to apply a finish when they are thoroughly dry, and to get this finish on within two or three days of bleaching, otherwise oxidization and darkening of the wood will start.

The second method is the one most widely used by furniture makers before staining and french polishing.

Here a pound (450g) of oxalic acid crystals are dissolved in a gallon (4.5 litres) of hot water, and the solution is brushed on as hot as possible. When the required colour has been achieved the wood is thoroughly washed in cold water, and then is again wiped over with acetic acid. Here the idea is that the mild acid wipe-down will reduce any residual acidity in the surface and make finishing that much easier. For wood treated in this way precatalysed lacquers are good, the catalyst itself being an acid.

When brushing on any bleach or stain you should work with a soft brush and always run along the grain. Any variations in density of colour will then look totally natural.

The third method is effective but does have a major problem. It uses two solutions, and one of these is based on 880 ammonia, the fumes of which will choke you, stop you breathing, cause a black-out and can be terminal. This is the same concentrated ammonia that is used in fuming – and there it is the only suitable agent – so we have to learn to cope with it.

It is unlikely that you will have a fume cabinet; I certainly do not. Hence any work with 880 ammonia is done outside and on a day when there is a significant wind. I position myself upwind of the working area and wear my Racal airstream helmet. The helmet does not prevent the fumes from passing to me, but by drawing my breathing air from behind my head, it further reduces the possibility of a draught of ammonia fumes being carried up to my nose by an air eddy. I also immediately put any open vessel with ammonia into a large, heavy-duty polythene bag and fold over the neck.

The bleaching use of ammonia involves making a solution of 2 pints (1.2 litres) of 880 ammonia to ½ pint (0.3 litres) of water, and a second solution of 2 pints (1.2 litres) of water to ½ pint (0.3 litres) of 100 vol hydrogen peroxide.

Standing outside on a windy day in rubber gloves and airstream helmet (and usually also in a souwester as probably it will be raining!), you can then brush the ammonia solution on to the wood. The wood will probably darken and the higher tannin woods, such as oak and chestnut, will darken appreciably. The wood is given two or three coats and is then left for about ten minutes for the solution to penetrate.

The peroxide solution is now brushed on and bleaching begins. By now there is less danger from the ammonia fumes.

Once the required level of bleaching has been achieved, the surface is wiped down with a cloth soaked in methylated spirits. On drying, this process can cause the formation of a white powder on the surface. This is no problem, as the powder will quickly disappear with a light sanding.

Again you require the drying process to be quick so that finishing can be undertaken within two or three days.

FUMING

The fuming process involves the use of 880 ammonia, and darkening is a result of the action of the fumes on the tannic acid or tannin in the wood. It produces a colour, which, once dry and sealed, has a high degree of stability. Prior to sealing, however, there is a rapid reversion to the original colour upon exposure to air and light. Other than the problems of handling, ammonia is a quite simple and inexpensive agent to use.

Some woods are tannin-rich, and oak is by far the most suitable, with chestnut a reasonable second. Most 'fuming' done on other woods is artificial in that the tannin is manually applied, usually with other agents.

The process works best on green wood, which is fine for the turner but not so good for the makers of reproduction furniture.

The object to be fumed is placed in a large polythene bag (or a polythene tent) together with one or more saucers of 880 ammonia. The bag or tent is then sealed and is left for a period of anything between a few hours and a few days. The process is affected by the ambient temperature and the moisture content of the wood; summer temperatures and green wood are the best combination, and here a lot of change can be seen in half a day. With air-dried wood in winter temperatures, it can take up to a week to get the desired effect. It is also better if the work, in its fuming bag, is covered over with a black polythene sheet to keep off the sunlight.

While naturally fumed oak is most attractive as turned work, I find the colour is not deep enough for Jacobean oak furniture. So if the darker, deeper colour is required, make up a solution of tannic acid and warm water (4oz/113g of acid crystals to a gallon/4.5 litres of water). This is brushed on and allowed to soak in. The wood is then heavily fumed (allow a larger number of saucers and leave to fume for a full period of time) and the colour is fixed with a water-based solution of bichromate of potash made up at the same concentration.

After this, some pieces of furniture will be treated with a stain before polishing and patinating. More of this in a minute.

None of the chemicals used are difficult to obtain. Some can be purchased from the local dispensing chemist, although chemists often have to order them in the quantities required. Most of the manufacturers of wood-finishing products will supply them direct, and Mylands have a delivery service. Obviously buying from these sources is much cheaper than going through the local dispensary.

However, before venturing out into the High Street, it is interesting to experiment with what the house and garden shed can offer. The iron salts in moss killer will nicely darken some woods and mention has already been made of domestic bleach.

STAINING

You have to go to Mylands or other manufacturer/wholesaler for some of the materials required when you move into staining. Today's DIY stores do not provide the powder paints and chemicals that were at one time available through ironmongers and drysalters.

We have all stained or dyed wood – usually shelves if not whole pieces of furniture – and been very disappointed with the results.

Once the turner becomes involved with furniture making and restoration, he very quickly finds he has to stain woods, and will immediately encounter two problems. The first is matching an existing colour; and the second is keeping the matched colour permanent. It is not easy to make one chair-leg colour match the other three, but you eventually manage to get it right. The customer then becomes very irate if after a year or two the leg you made ends up a substantially different shade.

There are three types of stain normally available in the local hardware shop. One is of little interest to the turner and that is the combined stain and varnish. For their purpose (usually floors and skirting boards)

these are very good, giving a good finish and high colour permanence. The stains that most turners use are either wood dyes, which are water-based, or wood stains, which are spirit- or oil-based. The water-based dyes give much greater colour permanence, but of course lift the grain on application; the spirit stains fade in the light. Some colours are particularly bad, especially those with red in them. 'Red mahogany' becomes yellow-brown mahogany within a couple of years in even modest levels of daylight.

Unfortunately, the majority of stockists have large quantities of the spirit-based stains while you have to seek out a specialist dealer to find the water-based ranges.

It is usually possible to achieve a desired shade by mixing the proprietary colours, and I find that a lot of my work ends up with a mix, the base of which is Libron Georgian mahogany, with a red mahogany and dark oak added to get the tint right. Sometimes the water-based Georgian mahogany is allowed to dry, and this is then followed by a light coat of spirit-based mix to give additional depth to the effect.

I also do some of my own colour making and the palette has a base of:

Bichromate of potash	
Permanganate of potash	
Black	
Mahogany red	
Green	Dry powdered
Methylene blue	aniline dyes
Walnut	
Vandyke brown	

The green and the blue are used to produce a malachite (green copper) finish.

As a starting point for dark mahogany, try dissolving in a gallon (4.5 litres) of water:

1¼oz (35.5g) bichromate of potash
2 drams (7.75g) of the black dye
1 dram (3.87g) of the mahogany red dye

This is then adjusted, usually by increasing

the red, according to the job I am trying to match.

Dyes are applied to the workpiece after it has been sanded down but before any sanding sealer or grain filler has been applied.

To get a good depth of colour it is usual to apply three or so coats and allow the piece to dry between each application. It is always brushed on using a soft brush with the strokes going along the grain. Have a small sample of the same wood ready and stain this at the same time as the main piece. You can use this sample to test the darkening effect of oil or polish.

After the penultimate coat the piece is lightly sanded with 400 grit wet or dry as there will be some raised grain. After the final drying it is again lightly sanded. There are times when a little spirit stain may be used at this point, but only if a dark brown/black is required. It is also at this stage that sanding sealer may be applied, but this only with open-pored woods.

In fact, I like to see the grain rather than a glass-smooth finish. If the surface is too smooth, it begins to look like plastic or imitation wood.

There is one 'staining' process where the aim is to produce a totally wood-like effect but of a wood that does not look like a real wood! This is what is known as 'ebonizing' and the aim is to produce a finish that looks like highly polished ebony. Of course you do not see any grain or figure on the highest-quality ebony, just an even, intense, deep black.

It is the depth of colour that is the problem. First the piece has to be perfectly finished and all flaws and imperfections removed. The stain used is water-based and consists of extract of logwood and a very small quantity of potassium chromate. Occasionally a trace of washing blue is added to increase the depth. It is applied as a hot solution and is brushed on liberally before being worked well into the grain. Then the very lightest of sanding and checking to ensure there are no 'thin' patches is followed by a coat of shellac.

FINISHING

After a number of years I have found that for general turning, there is nothing to beat the basic finishes that most turners use, although as I said at the beginning of this chapter I have now added satin polyurethane for domestic tables and some table wear. For ultimate waterproofing there seems to be nothing to rival the two-part polyurethane finishes.

The moment you apply any of the finishes you are given yet another strong reason for not using the spirit-based stains – all finishes pick up some of the colour, and oil can 'wipe off' a lot of the body colour.

My favourite finish is Danish oil, followed by wax. I did make my own beeswax, carnauba and turpentine mix, but must admit to relying heavily now upon Briwax. The workpiece is given one or more coats of Danish oil, depending on porosity.

When each coat of oil is applied, the wood is given a moment or two to absorb it and is then burnished to generate a fairly high friction heat. It is then allowed to stand for a few hours. The oiling is complete when it burnishes to a shine. At this stage the piece is done if it is to be used for foodstuffs such as wet salads. Otherwise it is then waxed.

A liberal coat of wax is applied all over and the wood is then allowed a few minutes for the solvents to start to evaporate. It is then burnished with a cloth pressed hard against the surface as the lathe turns at medium speed. You can actually see the wax melt and then harden into a smooth film. The wax-caked cloth is now replaced with a clean soft cloth and the timber is burnished again to a mirror finish.

The finish next in line is precatalysed, or friction lacquer. A minimum of two coats is used, with a couple of hours between them to allow the first to harden chemically before the second is applied. Again, after a pause the surface of some items is finally waxed.

I used to recommend medicinal liquid paraffin for woodware to be used at the table.

Since that time Rustins have shown that their Danish oil is non-toxic and suitable for tableware; and it has subsequently been demonstrated that there could be some problems with the liquid paraffin. It must be noted that some Danish oils are very crude, and often contain quantities of linseed oil. While these are perfectly satisfactory for finishing wood not destined for the dining table, they are best avoided for salad bowls and the like.

Of course, in the production of furniture elements you will also fall back on the more traditional furniture finishes of french polish and button polish, neither of which are difficult to apply if you use a little patience. There are times when all you use is oil – furniture oil, teak oil or Danish oil. Oak will provide a beautiful finish if it is first burnished with a block of dry oak, and then oiled.

AGEING

Achieving an 'aged' look is either great fun or very distressing according to your feelings. There are three characteristics of ageing that you have to work towards. First, an old piece of woodwork will have had many blows and knocks during its life and there will be blemishes on the surface. Secondly, there will be parts that have been worn very smooth. Thirdly, there will be colour variations, with a build-up of darkened old polish and grime in the corners and recesses.

Producing the surface blemishes is the easy part. Beating the object with a piece of old chain or a sock filled with old, large nuts and bolts is all that is required. Remember, however, that some parts of an object will always get more knocks than others in real life, so work mainly on the corners, the feet and forward faces.

Achieving the polished look requires a lot of hard rubbing with a wood block to burnish the surface.

Patination is the hardest part. Libron now make a patinating wax that appears to be lampblack in a wax polish. It is good but

looks a little too evenly grey/black. Working it into the corners and cracks does provide a good base, but you then need to build up a layer of 'old' brown polish. A traditional beeswax polish with a little Vandyke brown colour added can do the trick. Finally, one of the coloured Briwaxes is liberally applied – sometimes with a little more sock distressing between applications.

BURNING

Again we need to go back to the object as it comes off the lathe for the next of our finishes – 'carbonizing' (or burning)!

You would think it easy to burn wood; well, it isn't, not in a controlled way, at any rate.

Obviously the first of our problems is that unless the wood is very dry – probably under 10 per cent moisture – the burning process can cause differential contraction and splitting. The second difficulty lies in preventing the process from going too far and producing charcoal.

The burning is done with a clean, high-temperature flame, and this really means a propane gas torch. The heat has to be sufficient to carbonize (turn nearly to charcoal) not only the surface but a millimeter or so in below. It has to achieve this, however, without actually igniting the wood and turning the charcoal to ash.

To minimize movement, start inside the bowl at the base. Move the torch slowly but continuously along. There will be a yellow flame of burning right under the flame, but if the burning continues after the flame has passed, remove the torch and blow the flame out on the burning zone.

Work round the bowl bringing each ring up towards the rim. Once the inside is completed, start immediately on the outside, again working round from the base up to the rim. Go back and pick up any brown patches where burning was not complete.

Now with a piece of 0000 grade wire wool,

Interesting effects can be achieved by burning the wood with a high-temperature brazing torch. Working from the centre outwards and moving round in a spiral minimizes movement and splitting.

remove the loose charcoal, taking care not to break through to the unburnt wood.

You will find the piece very thirsty when you brush on the Danish oil, so you need three or four very liberal coats to fix the surface charcoal. I apply the first coat of oil with the pad of wire wool used for removing the dust.

You may wish to add further effects. Jim Partridge, who was one of the first to burn his bowls, dusts french chalk into the surface, brushing away the surplus and then colouring the ingrained chalk with blue ink.

COLOURED WORK

Fundamentally, this is probably the simplest of all forms of decoration to handle; at the same time, it is also the most difficult of all to get right. Some basic materials are readily available, and are easy and totally safe to handle. They are inks, food dyes, clothes dyes, and now the special wood dyes produced by companies such as Libron.

They are used to change the colour but not the texture of the wood. Ideally they should enhance any natural features, such as grain,

188

Liberal applications of Danish oil on a pad of 0000 grade wire wool remove any loose charcoal and bind the surface together.

rather than hide them. The first secret of successful use is restraint and delicacy, and the second is enhancement not superimposition.

In the main, you would not normally think of colouring a dramatically figured piece of wood, nor would you apply yet more colour to a richly coloured exotic. I say 'normally', because subtle colour washed into a piece of bleached elm burr can be breathtaking.

The starting point, then, is likely to be a piece of light-coloured wood, possibly with a hint of figuring; the object will be designed to present planes for the colour to sit on, and it may be worked to give an interesting but not strident texturing.

A coloured piece is usually intended to be pure decoration. It will most frequently be displayed rather than put in a position where it might be used. Even a bowl form is more likely to be positioned at eye-level rather than placed upon a coffee table where it would be looked down into (and probably loaded up with fruit or knick-knacks). If it is a platter

form, and many are, it will more likely be displayed up on a rack, or hung on a wall.

The piece may be coloured with just a single shade if the figure or texture are sufficient to provide interest. If not, the effect is likely to be achieved by the use of two or more colours. The really successful pieces do not go for multiple colours, but often have large zones of complementary or contrasting colours merging into, or offsetting, each other. In order not to swamp, the colour is applied as washes or stains and not as 'coats'.

Hard edges are not usually possible because stains or dyes will always run into each other; we therefore tend to go to the other extreme so that there is no appearance of the running of colours looking like an accident. In application the edges of colours are not overlapped but are allowed to merge.

Application can be by soft brush, but most of the masters use air brushes – miniature-sized compressed-air-driven paint sprays. The kits can cost anything between £150 and

£500 but only a graphics artist would go to the top end of this bracket.

It is not, however, necessary to buy a kit until you are sure you have to. A reloadable scent spray with a rubber-bulb 'drive' is quite effective and some of my early experiments were done with a very simple mouth-blown spray. It was a fixative spray (for pastel and charcoal drawings) obtainable at most technical drawing and artists' supplies shops.

Colour-stained pieces also have to have a surface finish applied in order to protect the colour. Again, as the colour was water-based there may have been some grain raising, so a very light sanding is first needed. Whatever finish you use you have some basic requirements. First, it should be colourless and wholly transparent. Second, it must be waterproof so that it can be wiped down. Third, it must not build up to a glossy cover. Two thin coats of aero-modellers' Clear dope is very effective, as is pastel fixative. There is also a very good 'varnish' used with acrylic artists' paints, called a 'matt varnish'. The dope is a mouth-blown spray, and the acrylic varnish is brushed on.

If, heaven forfend, the platter is to be used, then you have to use precatalysed lacquer (or worse).

As we noted earlier, covering the wood with paint brings us into another whole technology which warrants a book on that subject alone: this is the world of spray painting the wood so as to hide completely the nature of the base material. The answer to the question 'Why do it?' is that wood allows you to use some colours that would not stand the firing processes involved with pottery.

Once you embark upon this trail you need forced ventilation, air extraction, a compressor and spray guns. Various colours and media are used – cellulose paint and fast-drying acrylics. Very quickly we are in a situation where the fact that the item being coloured was originally made of wood seems totally irrelevant. Not that I wish to decry it – often the turning involved is of a very high order and the colouring uses a high level of artistry. Certainly it is an exciting field to move on into, and it will be one of my next!

Index